Boarding School Blues

Indigenous Education

SERIES EDITORS:

Margaret Connell Szasz
University of New Mexico
Brenda J. Child
University of Minnesota
Karen Gayton Swisher
Haskell Indian Nations University
John W. Tippeconnic III
The Pennsylvania State University

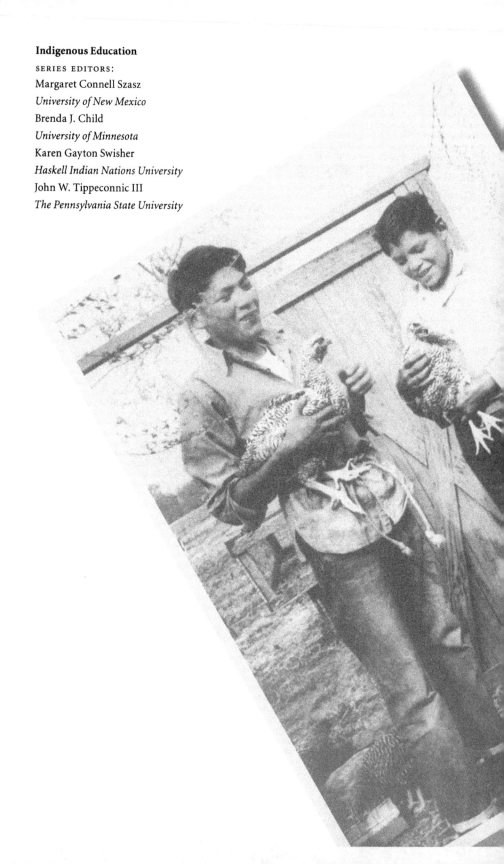

Boarding School Blues

Revisiting American Indian Educational Experiences

Edited and with an
introduction by Clifford E. Trafzer,
Jean A. Keller, and Lorene Sisquoc

University of Nebraska Press   •   Lincoln and London

Library of Congress
Cataloging-in-Publication Data
Boarding school blues : revisiting
American Indian educational
experiences / edited and with
an introduction by Clifford E.
Trafzer, Jean A. Keller, and Lorene
Sisquoc.
p. cm. (Indigenous education)
Includes bibliographical
references and index.
ISBN-13: 978-0-8032-4446-7
(cloth : alk. paper)
ISBN-13: 978-8032-9463-9
(pbk. : alk. paper)
ISBN-10: 0-8032-4446-0
(cloth : alk. paper)
ISBN-10: 0-8032-9463-8
(pbk. : alk. paper)
1. Off-reservation boarding
schools —History. 2. Indian
children—Relocation—United
States—History. 3. Indian
children—Education. 4. Indians
of North America—Government
relations. 5. United States—Social
policy. 6. United States—Race
relations. I. Trafzer, Clifford E. II.
Keller, Jean A., 1953– III. Sisquoc,
Lorene.
E97.B754 2006
371.829'97—dc22
2006004484

Set in Minion by Kim Essman.
Designed by R. W. Boeche.

The editors respectfully dedicate this book to past and present students of American Indian boarding schools and First Nations residential students. Through this publication, we honor the students who died at the schools and never returned home to their families and communities. The authors have pledged the royalties they earn from Boarding School Blues to the programs of the Sherman Indian Museum.

The Soboba Band of Luiseño Indians, the Pechanga Band of Luiseño Indians, the James Ramos family of the San Manuel Band of Mission Indians, the Department of History and Center for Ideas and Society of the University of California, Riverside, through the Cloning Grant of the Ford Foundation, and the University of California's Humanities Research Institute provided grants to support the presentation of these essays through the symposium "Boarding School Blues: Revisiting the American Indian Boarding School Experience."

Contents

Illustrations

Following page 154

Preface

The American Indian boarding school experience left an indelible mark on the history of the United States and Canada, and only recently have we tried to understand the significance of the schools in the lives of students, teachers, administrators, and Indian communities. Perhaps we have waited so long for this scholarly examination because of the difficulties involved in addressing the dramatic impact of the boarding schools on the lives of so many people. For some American Indian students, the pain they suffered inhibits our intrusion into their lives. For other students, their boarding school days were filled with fond memories, sometimes mixed with melancholy, sometimes with humor. Understanding the many and varied levels of the boarding school experience is a complex business. No single interpretation of this experience exists today or ever will. Native American students and their parents viewed the schools in many different ways. Oral and written accounts by Indian students and non-Indians involved at the schools are extremely diverse. Historian Tsianina Lomawaima recently wrote to the editors that "part of that message, importantly, has been that the schools were not monolithically destructive or successful in their assimilative goals, but the harsh reality is—for some people, they were."

The editors of this volume agree with Lomawaima's assessment, and we have tried to offer essays that address the multiple aspects of the boarding school experience in the United States. Because of the layered meanings of these experiences and the many "gray" areas existing within memories, the question of whether the schools proved a positive or negative experience for students, parents, and Indian communities cannot be answered. Lomawaima reminded the editors that "the central message of b.s. [boarding school] experiences is how varied—but almost always deeply affecting—they have been across individuals, schools, time and space." Students, parents, and American Indian communities felt the boarding school experiences deeply, and they continue to consider and reconsider the meaning of the experiences in their lives and the lives of other Indian people.

The editors have used the motif of a traditional Native American monster story as a metaphor in analyzing the boarding school experience. We would like you to think in this way when reading the essays. Traditional Indian stories are the first body of historical literature we have within the Native universe. These are the famous creation stories shared orally for thousands of years, texts that portray imperfect worlds where positive and negative exist side by side, counterimages that balance each other. Often storytellers refer to these negative forces as monsters, and tribal elders can name these negative beings. For the students, the boarding schools, the English language, a foreign curriculum, and white officials represented monsters. Within many traditional stories, heroes also exist, offering themselves up to fight the monsters. Within the stories, the heroes combat the monsters for the benefit of their people, not to enhance their own ego. Most often the heroes survive their struggles with the monsters and use their newly acquired powers to do additional good for their people. Sometimes the heroes die during their struggles with the monsters, but someone always arises in the stories to carry on the good fight on behalf of the people. Indian students at the boarding schools became heroes of their people, and their contributions resonate throughout Indian country today.

Some students chose to enter school, while others were forced to attend by parents, relatives, and government agents. In either case, students took a hero's journey into the unknown, wrestling with many monsters, from loneliness to hunger and punishments. Too many children died fighting the monsters. Administrators sent some students home in coffins to be buried in the heart of their homelands, but they buried other children in cemeteries located on school property. Their families and friends have not forgotten these children. They are symbols of the casualties suffered by Indians at the schools, but they are not the only symbols that exist. Some of the positive elements of the schools remain, living within American Indian communities through the children, grandchildren, and great-grandchildren of boarding school students. Tribal leaders from many corners of Indian country remember their boarding schools days or those of their relatives. The stories have shaped their lives and made them more informed about an important component of American Indian history.

We hope that the essays presented in this volume will continue and extend American Indian boarding school stories. We believe that the circle of stories found here will form a whirlwind that will enlarge the circle of stories, creating more conversation, understanding, and analysis. This was the intent of the editors when we joined hands to coordinate a symposium at Sherman Indian High School in November 2002 to assess some of the recent scholarship focused on the American Indian boarding school experience. We named the symposium "Boarding School Blues: Revisiting the American Indian Boarding School Experience." The Humanities Research Institute of the University of California, the Department of History of the University of California, Riverside, Sherman Indian High School and Museum, the Soboba Band of Luiseño Indians, the Pechanga Band of Luiseño Indians, and the family of James Ramos of the San Manuel Band co-sponsored the symposium. The editors gratefully extend our thanks to the sponsors and participants who shared with us their boarding school experiences. The essays included in this volume are all original, researched and written specifically for the symposium held at Sherman.

We thank the many institutions that helped us create this book, including the National Archives, Sherman Indian School Museum and Archives, Rivera Library of the University of California, Riverside, Smiley Library, and Cumberland County Historical Museum. We thank the students, administration, and staff of Sherman Indian High School for making their facilities available to us and for the student participation in the symposium. In particular, we thank the Sherman students who spoke at the conference and the Apache Dancers of Sherman, who shared their unique form of dance. We express our sincere appreciation to the University of Nebraska Press, particularly Gary Dunham, who took an interest in our work. We thank our families for the time they gave to us to read, edit, and write. The editors wish to remember and recognize the heroes of this story, the current and former students of federal Indian boarding schools. They turned the power and have made the schools into Indian institutions today, educational institutions that help secure a place for Indian people in contemporary society and often encourage the preservation of Native American cultures and languages.

Introduction

Origin and Development of the
American Indian Boarding School System

Clifford E. Trafzer, Jean A. Keller, and Lorene Sisquoc

Among North American Indians, the boarding school system was a successful failure. The practice of removing Native American children from their
homes, families, and communities and forcing them into an educational
system designed to assimilate them into American and Canadian societies
both succeeded and failed. The governments succeeded in providing some
measure of academic, domestic, agricultural, and vocational education to
First Nations children, but they failed to assimilate completely Indian children or entirely destroy the essence of their being Native peoples. Ironically, the American boarding school and Canadian residential school experience for many Native American children provided new skills in language,
literature, mathematics, and history that strengthened their identities as Native Americans. Many children attending boarding schools returned home
or moved to urban areas where they embraced their American Indian heritage in a heightened manner, communicating their strength in being the
First Americans in ways that preserved Indian identity. Thus the very system that non-Indians had established to "Kill the Indian in him and save the
man"[1] provided Indian students with the experience and expertise to "turn
the power."[2] Students used the potentially negative experience to produce
a positive result—the preservation of Indian identity, cultures, communities, languages, and peoples. For many Native Americans, the initial expo-
sure to boarding schools gave them the blues, and the illness and death of
so many children left their mark on the hearts and minds of Indian people
from the outset. Still, the American Indian boarding school experience also

resulted in many students living dynamic lives that forever changed American history and Native American cultures.

In the first years of the twenty-first century, interpreting the American Indian boarding school experience is both difficult and dangerous. It is difficult because of the diverse views Indian people have about the schools and the various elements of their school experiences. The experience of one boarding school student is different from the experience of other students. As we learn more, we sometimes generalize with "some students believed" or "most students acted" in certain ways. We try to be precise in our examples and provide our best historical analysis. Interpreting the boarding school experience can be dangerous because we are representing several students, their lives, a different time, and a variety of diverse experiences. We provide our best analysis based on written and oral documents as well as our personal experiences visiting and working at Indian boarding schools. We offer our stories based on a close reading of the sources and our examination of historical sites, material culture, and the experiences of former students. We feel that the most insightful stories of the American Indian boarding school experience lie with former students who are heroes to us. They lived the stories we are trying to present, represent, and understand.

The motifs of traditional Native American stories about heroes and monsters are woven into stories about the modern boarding school experience. Some students set out to engage the adventure by willingly attending boarding school, or embracing the "monster." Lakota student Ota Kte (Plenty Kill), better known as Luther Standing Bear, decided to go to Carlisle Indian School in 1879 to fulfill a warrior's journey. "I was thinking of my father," Luther wrote years later, and the number of times his father had told him that men earned greater honor by dying young for the people than by dying "old and sick." As a result, "it occurred to me that this chance to go East would prove that I was brave."[3] Standing Bear believed that if he died at Carlisle, his passing would have meaning and benefit to Lakota people and bring honor to himself, his family, and his people. Many more Indian children were thrust into the boarding school experience without their consent and had to engage the "monster."

Regardless of how they came to be a part of the boarding school system, students had to cope with new places, new people, and policies designed to

destroy their cultural identities. Originally, the United States created boarding schools as a sphere of governmental power, not of Native power. Non-
Indian policy makers and administrators designed the institutions to swal-
low up American Indian people and transform them into "civilized" human
beings. As Richard Henry Pratt, the creator of the modern American Indian boarding school system, put it, white Americans should feed "the Indians to our civilization."⁴ Students fought the monster, struggled with it,
and many survived the experience. Indian children who lived through their
boarding school days were transformed. Many learned to speak, read, and
write English, and they shared this and other knowledge with people back
home. Students learned new subjects and trades, further developing themselves in new ways. But most Indians did not turn their back on First Nations people or discard their cultural identities as Indians.

Like the heroes of the most ancient American stories, students survived
their confrontation with the monster. Through their engagement with the
monster they killed the concept of assimilation, which eventually gave way
to cultural preservation through the use of some skills learned at boarding
schools. American Indian students who fought the monster often emerged
stronger, wiser, and better prepared to help their own people. In a very real
sense, they turned the power to their advantage and that of their people.
They became stronger. In an old Maidu Indian story from California, a
young man had grown stronger and stronger as a result of venturing forth
from his home. The farther he traveled and the more he accomplished, the
stronger he became. When Lizard Monster sought out the young man for a
fight, the boy destroyed the ogre and returned to his family to serve his people in a loftier manner. He became Thunder Man, the one still heard above
the mountains, valleys, and foothills of northern California.⁵

We still hear the echoes of children who attended boarding schools. We
are still learning from these voices and those of contemporary Indian children who attend off-reservation boarding schools. More and more, we are
learning about their boarding school days through public programs, films,
and publications. The students and their voices are, for us, more than survivors. They are like the old-time heroes who returned to Indian country to
benefit other Indian people. They held onto their Native American identities
in the face of an attempted cultural genocide, and they used lessons learned

at the boarding schools to contribute to the well-being of their families, communities, and tribes. The manner in which students put their boarding school education to work for themselves and their people is best seen in the writings of former students. During the twentieth century, American Indians used the English language to compose books and essays conveying their own analysis of the boarding school experience. Until recently we had not known a great deal about the American Indian boarding school experience in Canada or the United States. Autobiographical accounts by Luther Standing Bear, Don Talayesva, Polingaysi Qoyawayma, Pauline Murillo, Frank Mitchell, Charles Eastman, Francis La Flesche, Minnie Braithwaite Jenkins, Hubert Honanie, Basil Johnston, Viola Martinez, Helen Sekaquaptewa, Jim Whitewolf, and others allow us into their world and provide views on the boarding school experience.[6] Recent scholarship has added a great deal to our knowledge and understanding of the boarding school experience. Michael C. Coleman, for example, has brought together a number of first-person accounts in *American Indian Children at School, 1850–1930*.[7]

The boarding school system had its origins in the colonial period of American history.[8] The Spanish created the first Indian boarding school in Havana, Cuba, in 1568. Like people of other European nations, Spanish officials viewed Indians as "savages." Based on "facts" provided by Father Pedro de Cordoba, one Spanish soldier reported that Indian people were "stupid and silly" and had "no respect for truth." He stereotyped Indians, saying, "They have no knowledge of what foresight means" and were "incapable of learning." This Spanish soldier remarked that Indians "exercise none of the humane arts or industries." Finally, he stated categorically that Indians were "more stupid than asses" and that they "refuse to improve in anything."[9] This view of European superiority and Native American inferiority set the stage for the first Spanish boarding school for Indians and others that would follow. Europeans assumed incorrectly that Indians had no systems of education, no forms of governments, no religions, no valuing of wisdom, no methods of advancing knowledge, and no way to teach their children. In her brilliant essay "Systems of Knowledge," Clare Sue Kidwell details that American Indians educated their young people in a variety of ways and that they had been doing so for thousands of years prior to the European invasion of America.[10] Tsianina Lomawaima addresses this issue in "The Un-Natural History of American Indian Education," found in a provocative book by Karen Swisher and John Tippeconic, *Next Steps*. These Native American authors demonstrate that Indian people had their own forms of education long before Europeans arrived.[11]

Traditional Native Education

Indian people argue that education, schooling, and the pursuit of knowledge have always been part of their lives and cultures. Tribal elders, grandparents, parents, aunts, uncles, singers, and storytellers imparted knowledge through the oral tradition and practical instruction. Elder teachers taught children about a host of subjects, including literature, religion, biology, botany, pharmaceuticals, geology, geography, cartography, dance, art, architecture, astronomy, agriculture, music, material culture, mathematics, marine biology, and hydrology.[12] Indian people throughout the Native universe listened to and learned from others. They learned the languages of their neighbors, pottery techniques, agricultural advancements, artistic designs, watercraft manufacturing, and technological advances. Indian people absorbed knowledge, just as peoples around the world had incorporated new learning into their lives since the beginning of time. Native Americans had never existed in an archaic time warp. Time and travel, interaction with other people, and a willingness to learn encouraged First Nations peoples to grow, adapt, adopt, and expand their ways of knowing. American Indians shared ideas with each other and with those outside their families, clans, and tribes. Knowledge was never static, since most people enjoyed a pragmatic approach to their world. Their knowledge, experiences, and educations worked for them, and for hundreds of years Indian people lived and survived without the intervention of non-Indian newcomers. Yet, when they met the new people, Native Americans learned from African, Spanish, French, Portuguese, English, Russian, and others—sometimes to their betterment, sometimes to their detriment.[13]

In order to survive, each group of First Nations people developed a body of sacred and practical knowledge that formed the foundation of its culture. In oral traditions, children learned about creation of their people, the laws by which they would live, and the governance of families, clans, moieties, and tribes. They learned the essentials of being sovereign people. Most often, families and clans provided the first teachers of Native children. Fathers, grandfathers, and uncles taught boys to track, hunt, and clean deer,

elk, bighorn sheep, buffalo, antelope, rabbits, squirrels, and many other animals. Mothers, grandmothers, and aunts taught girls to till the soil and raise
a host of nutritious and unique American foods, including varieties of po-
tatoes, beans, squash, tomatoes, corn, avocados, and peanuts. Elders taught
children to gather medicinal and food plants, including tobacco, acorns,
creosote, camas, kouse, cactus, sage, and maple syrup. Adults taught young
people how to prepare plants and animals for food and medicine, how to
build appropriate houses from natural materials, and how to pray, sing, and
dance. They taught children the mysteries of the stars and the solar system,
creating calendars and special days and times for ceremony, ritual, and
thanksgiving. For thousands of years, American Indian people taught a variety of subjects significant to their specific needs and wishes.[14]

In 1980, Palouse Indian elder and spiritual leader Andrew George from
Washington state explained that in his youth during the early twentieth century his parents and grandparents gathered the children together to learn.
In the cold winter months when winds blew snow and freezing weather, the
children gathered their blankets around a fire and prepared to listen and
learn. Andrew remembered the elders giving their lessons until at some
point, after repeating the story many times, the elder asked a particular
child to repeat that story. Teachers expected students to retell the story exactly, and if a child got the story wrong, elders corrected the story and had
the child try again. Through the oral tradition, children learned their lessons. In this manner, Wyandot elder Eleonore Sioui learned her lessons, as
did millions of American Indian children over many generations, gaining
knowledge and practical experiences that informed their lives and people.
Native American education occurred on many levels and in many ways, including some formal "schools" located in villages and urban centers. But
most Indians learned through the oral traditions in their own homes and
communities until the arrival of non-Native educational institutions that
rapidly and widely influenced Indian education.[15]

Colonial and Revolutionary Periods

After 1492, the educational institutions brought to the Americas by newcomers, including the boarding school system, significantly changed Native
American education. Until the mid-nineteenth century these institutions
only influenced small pockets of North America. Most Europeans brought

a superior view of themselves and their ways of knowing, ridiculing Native peoples and labeling them "savages." Spanish conquistadores ravaged the land and the people for economic gain until after 1512, when a series of laws from the Spanish crown and the Council of the Indies set in motion the mission system. In the sixteenth century, Roman Catholic orders established missions to convert Native neophytes, often separating children physically and geographically from their parents in order to Christianize and "civilize" them. Mission fathers attempted to create a space where they could assimilate American Indian children into the Roman Catholic Church and Spanish society. The priests established schools within the missions where they indoctrinated young neophytes into new ways of thinking, believing, and acting. After the French established Quebec in 1608, Jesuit priests followed the same pattern of assimilating First Nations children into the Catholic faith and French society. This became a well-established pattern during the colonial period, one pursued by the Russian Orthodox Church in the eighteenth century among Aleuts, Tlingits, and other Native Alaskans. Some Christians among English settlers also followed this pattern, including Dr. Eleazer Wheelock, headmaster of the Moors Charity School—an institution that became Dartmouth College. Wheelock removed American Indian children from their families and homes and boarded them in schools and Anglo-American homes where the newcomers could isolate, assimilate, and civilize "heathen" children.[16]

Although the English had declared their intent to Christianize Indians, both Anglicans in Virginia and Calvinists in New England lagged in their missionary obligations. Their charters spoke glowingly of Christianization as a major goal, but they initially focused far more on the resettlement of Indian land and the economic development of Native resources than they did on Christian education of Native American children. Puritan missionary John Eliot proved a notable exception. Eliot learned a dialect of Algonquian and preached sermons in the Native language. Some American Indian parents wanted their children to be educated in the ways of white people, and to this end Eliot created "praying towns" of Indian people. Eliot and other missionaries created day schools for Indian children, a development that proved successful.[17] He and Wheelock as well as some governmental officials of the General Court shared the goal of assimilating, civilizing, and Christianizing Native American children, even though their techniques sometimes differed. Some colonists sent Indian boys to be educated in Europe or to Harvard, William and Mary, or Dartmouth. Indian education during the colonial era did not focus primarily on academics but on the principal objective "that the Christian faith may be propagated amongst the Western Indians."[18] Still, the marriage of Christian and secular objectives emerged out of the colonial educational experience, and this union formed the foundation of Indian education within the United States and Canada. Although Christian denominations led the educational endeavors among Native Americans during the colonial era, the state provided encouragement and limited funding. Margaret Connell Szasz deals with some of these issues in *Indian Education in the American Colonies, 1607–1783*.[19]

During the early years of the American Revolution, the First Continental Congress created the Committee on Indian Affairs, authorizing it to employ "a minister of the gospel, to reside among the Delaware Indians, and instruct them in the Christian religion; a schoolmaster to teach their youth reading, writing, and arithmetic."[20] The Congress also authorized the government to hire a blacksmith to teach Indians one of the industrial arts, thereby establishing the foundation of the government's emphasis on trade school education among Native Americans. Indeed, after the United States separated from Great Britain, American education focused strongly on Christian values and vocational education so that Indian people could be "useful" to the dominant society and at the same time achieve a measure of "civilization." In addition, the government could help indirectly Christianize Indians using government policy, power, and funds. Christianization and civilization through education became the foundation of Indian education as conceived by non-Indian policy makers in the United States and Canada. Not long afterward, the Continental Congress voted to pay five hundred dollars to educate eight or nine Indian males at Dartmouth College. This act by the national government provided the first financial aid to Indian students, but Congress authorized the funds as a military strategy, not to force assimilation. This appropriation did not signal a blossoming interest on the part of the government to fund Indian education. But Presidents George Washington and Thomas Jefferson both expressed great confidence that American Indian people could "improve" their lot through formal education and that Indians had the capacity of learning and adopting white culture. In other words, Washington and Jefferson believed Indians could be "civilized" and that full assimilation into white society was feasible, if not inevitable. Furthermore, both men recommended that whites provide a minimal education for Indian people through vocational education. They shared a view with many non-Indians that Native Americans could be "useful" if they learned low-level training in American agriculture, mechanics, and domestic skills. In this way, Indian people could work within white society in the lowest positions, assimilate into the white world, and become civilized.[21] These are themes often developed in the writings of Francis Paul Prucha and James Axtell.[22]

Early Nineteenth Century

During the late eighteenth and early nineteenth centuries, the Cherokees, Choctaws, Chickasaws, Muskogees, and Seminoles developed their own schools, providing public education to their Native students. And after Sequoya conceived the Cherokee syllabary, Cherokee schoolchildren learned to read and write in their own language at their own schools. The five southern tribes controlled their own schools and curricula. They used their institutions to strengthen their political and economic sovereignty and became the precursor of tribally owned and operated schools of the twentieth century. These tribes continued their Indian schools even after the federal government forced most of the southern tribes to remove to Indian Territory during the 1830s and 1840s. Devon A. Mihesuah has explored elements of the Cherokee educational system in a remarkable study, *Cultivating the Rosebuds: The Education of Women at the Cherokee Female Seminary, 1851–1909*, pointing out that by 1852 eleven hundred students were enrolled in twenty-one common schools in the Indian Territory and received an academic education.[23] Indian children at these schools studied Greek, Latin, astronomy, botany, algebra, and music.[24] In the early nineteenth century, Cherokees and other southern tribes had started their own tribal schools, but by 1818 some government officials wanted to control Indian education. Reformers within the House Committee on Indian Affairs urged their fellow lawmakers to "put into the hands of their [Indians'] children the primer and the hoe, and they will naturally, in time, take hold of the plough; and, as their minds become enlightened and expand, the Bible will be their book, and they will grow up in habits of morality and industry, leave the chase to those whose minds are less cultivated, and become useful members of society."[25] Indeed, in the following year the reformers encouraged Congress to pass the first significant legislation supporting Native American education.

On March 3, 1819, Congress passed the Indian Civilization Act. The bill continued the thread that missionaries and governments had established during the colonial era. Lawmakers designed the act to civilize Indians and, indirectly, to Christianize them. Under the terms of the act, the president could employ "persons of good moral character" to instruct Indians "in the mode of agriculture suited to their situation, and for teaching their children in reading, writing, and arithmetic."[26] Commissioner of Indian Affairs Thomas L. McKenny selected missionaries as the "persons of good moral character," and he authorized them to teach Indian people agricultural techniques and the three R's. Christian missionaries received support for their work among the tribes through the Indian Civilization Act and through annuities (annual payment of funds) Congress provided tribes as a result of treaty negotiations and in compensation to tribes for lands and resources (water, timber, minerals, game, farms, etc.) that the United States withdrew from the Native American estate. In 1820 the government began designating specific annuities to Indian tribes for education, and in 1824 the secretary of war reported the existence of twenty-one Indian boarding and day schools with an enrollment of approximately eight hundred students.[27] Most of these schools were operated by Christian missionaries, not federal employees.[28]

Mission schools provided most Indian students with formal education before the late nineteenth century. These schools established the philosophy of using the curriculum to Christianize and civilize Native American children, the hallmark of Indian education throughout the nineteenth century and part of the twentieth. Many mission schools operated near Native communities and served as day schools for those communities. Christians also established off-reservation boarding schools during the eighteenth and nineteenth century, and the governments of the United States and Canada looked to these Christian schools to solve the "Indian problem." After the U.S. government removed many tribes to the trans-Mississippi West, the Methodist Episcopal Society established the first Indian boarding schools dedicated to manual labor or vocational education. The Methodists built a large boarding school in Fort Leavenworth, Kansas, to serve many scattered tribes from the area and those the government had removed. The Methodist school and those that followed offered students "letters, labor and mechanic arts, and morals, and Christianity."[29]

Post–Civil War Reform Era

Such denominational schools prevailed in Indian country until the 1850s, when reformers began to question the school system offered by the United States. Some reformers recommended the uniform administration of the schools, better oversight and management, and stronger instruction.[30] Before the Civil War, reformers wanted greater direct federal participation in Indian education to improve the path of Indian people from "savagery" to civilization. This theme is developed by Michael C. Coleman, but it is countered by the work of Devon Mihesuah, who convincingly demonstrates that Native Americans could launch their own education institutional that effectively addressed education in a far more sophisticated way than that proposed by non-Indians.[31] The Cherokees may have been the exception rather than the rule, although Choctaws and Chickasaws also established their own educational institutions. During the Civil War, the federal government paid little attention to Indian education, but after the conflict the nation developed the Peace Policy, an approach that gave schools a renewed prominence. The carnage of the war encouraged reformers to find new ways to deal with Native nations other than warfare. American Indian successes against the U.S. Army on the Great Plains, in the Northwest, and in the Southwest also encouraged federal policy makers to find new ways to cut costs and make peace with the tribes. Indian education became a central component of the new peace policy, and as government agents framed new treaties they included provisions for schools and formal education. Although some policy makers fully intended to provide Native American children with quality education, Congress did not provide sufficient funding for schools, administrators, and teachers. Still, the treaties framed in the 1860s and 1870s generated renewed discussions about the place of Indian education and schools within the national agenda.[32]

In 1870 Congress allocated $100,000 as the first annual appropriation for Indian education. Policy makers earmarked the funds to support industrial schools already operating in Indian country. Indian students boarded at some of these industrial schools, and the government intended to continue funding them. However, in 1873 federal officials began aggressively establishing and staffing day schools on reservations. The government became more directly involved with Indian education, following the recommendations set down in the 1850s. Indian agents, often drawn from Christian denominations, established these day schools on the reservations once they could secure a minimum student population of twenty children. Like schools in many parts of the American West, the Indian schools were one-room affairs that often included housing for a teacher and a small garden plot for the teacher and students. Government officials encouraged a curriculum of academic and vocational subjects, and sometimes the Office of Indian Affairs paid a reservation carpenter, farmer, or blacksmith to offer courses. Vocational and agricultural education played an important role at the schools and in future endeavors by the federal government. Many Indian children passed through the doors of these small schools, receiving some knowledge of English and a cursory introduction to the Euro-American educational system. Many American Indian parents preferred the day schools to on- or off-reservation boarding schools, although some adults saw the advantage of boarding schools where children received some measure of housing, food, and health care. However, policy makers rarely concerned themselves with the views of Indian people or followed paths they considered to be in the best interest of Native children.

In the same year that the Office of Indian Affairs raced to establish one-room schoolhouses on reservations, Commissioner of Indian Affairs Edward P. Smith submitted his annual report favoring boarding schools over day schools. It was "well-nigh impossible," wrote Smith, "to teach Indian children the English language when they spend twenty hours out of the twenty-four in the wigwam, using only their native tongue." Voicing the opinion of many non-Indians, Smith stated that the use of English and the elimination of Native languages was the key to assimilation and civilization. Smith believed that a boarding school "takes the youth under constant care, has him always at hand, and surrounds him by an English-speaking community."[33] Other policy makers considered boarding schools too expensive, but over time the concept of large, off-reservation boarding schools for Indians took shape. Commissioner of Education John Eaton Jr. proposed that Indian boarding schools focus on agricultural and vocational training as well as basic academics.[34] Eaton did not advocate the far-reaching academic curriculum found in Indian Territory, where Cherokees, Choctaws, and others offered a strong academic emphasis, but he proposed to use academics to augment and strengthen vocational education. Unlike many Americans who believed Indians to be too inferior in intelligence to learn and advance academically, Eaton believed that Native American children had the capacity to grasp intellectual ideas. He also believed that when Indian children returned to the reservations, they would share their knowledge—both academic and technical—with tribal elders.[35]

Captain Pratt's Educational Philosophy

Captain Richard Henry Pratt further developed Eaton's idea that Indians could learn through formal education and put it into practice at the first federal off-reservation American Indian boarding school. Pratt convinced the federal government to fund the first school at the old army barracks at Carlisle, Pennsylvania. Drawing on the beliefs of past reformers, including Eaton, Pratt developed his own theory about Indian education while he directed the lives of American Indian prisoners of war at Fort Marion, Florida. Kiowas and Cheyennes under his control became the subjects of the captain's grand experiment. "It is a great mistake," Pratt wrote, "to think that the Indian is born an inevitable savage. He is born a blank, like the rest of us. Left in the surroundings of savagery, he grows to possess a savage language, superstition, and life."[36] Thus, like Washington and Jefferson, Pratt believed in environmental determinism. It was the "primitive" and "uncivilized" environment of Indian people that created their "savagery," not their race.

Pratt and other reformers believed that Indian people had the ability to learn and grow intellectually, but in order to bring this about, Pratt wanted to segregate Indian children from their parents and cultures, gradually integrating them into the white world in a controlled fashion. Only in this way, he believed, could Indians become assimilated and contribute to the dominant society. This idea formed the basis of Pratt's experiment at Fort Marion and, later, at Carlisle Indian School and became the fundamental basis of the off-reservation American Indian boarding school system. In an isolated institutional setting, Pratt planned to destroy what he termed "savage languages," "primitive superstitions," and "uncivilized cultures," replacing them with work ethics, Christian values, and the white man's civilization. In sum, Pratt created Carlisle as a space to take "the savage-born infant to the surroundings of civilization." Like the reservation system, the off-reservation boarding schools became a purgatory, the space between heaven and hell—civilization and savagery—where Indians would suffer a transformation from "primitive" to "civilized." Indians could be redeemed through the process and become civilized human beings. In this way, Pratt would solve the "Indian problem" by allowing Indian children to "grow to possess a civilized language and habit."[37] Or, as Pratt wrote in his book, *Battlefield and Classroom*, and used in the masthead of Carlisle's publications: "To civilize the Indian, get him into civilization. To keep him civilized, let him stay."[38]

Pratt wanted to destroy the cultural foundations of Native Americans so that they could enjoy full citizenship. In order to do this, he established the off-reservation boarding school, where he would "feed" Indians to the American way of life. "We make our greatest mistake in feeding our civilization to the Indians instead of feeding the Indians to our civilization."[39] He likened his educational experiment to a child learning to swim: "The boy learns to swim by going into the water; the Indian will become civilized by mixing with civilization." To effectuate the swimming lesson, Pratt generally stood against on-reservation schools where school officials told Native Americans: "You are Indians, and must remain Indians. You are not of the nation [United States], and cannot become of the nation. We do not want you to become of the nation."[40] The captain believed that Indians should not be isolated completely from white Americans. Pratt thought Samuel Chapman Armstrong isolated African Americans at the Hampton Institute in Virginia, and the captain reportedly opposed segregation of African Americans and American Indians from whites.[41]

Pratt established an educational system to isolate Indian children from their families, cultures, and languages where white teachers could indoctrinate them into nineteenth-century American society and the English language. At the same time, white people could teach Christianity and the value of the dollars to Indians by allowing them into their homes and businesses through the "outing" program, a version of the modern work-study program. This extension of the educational system provided by whites offered Indian children an opportunity to learn the value of hard work and money. At the same time, Indian students learned a trade, agricultural techniques, and the "domestic sciences," a euphemistic name for a field of study that taught girls to be good wives, housekeepers, and maids. At the Fort

Marion prison, Pratt had Indian prisoners make bean necklaces, pick oranges, milk cows, handle baggage, clear land, and tend horses.[42] This experience spawned the outing program at Carlisle, which opened the world of practical labor to boys and girls who worked at hotels, restaurants, ranches, farms, and businesses. Eventually, all off-reservation boarding schools adopted an outing program as part of the government's goals of assimilation and making Indians useful.

Pratt introduced other measures to assimilate Indians, and future school administrators followed his lead. Pratt determined that Indians needed "civilized" names in order to function in the white man's world, so he and other administrators forced children to change their names from their Indian languages to English, often allowing them to select from among several Judeo-Christian names for males and females. As a result, several Indian girls received the names Mary, Esther, and Ruth. Boys received such names as David, Joseph, and James. Ota Kte (Plenty Kill) became one of the first Lakota children to attend Carlisle, where white administrators forced him to change his name. In a cultural ritual created by Pratt, the young man and other Indian students at Carlisle selected names.[43] In this way, Ota Kte became Luther Standing Bear. In his remarkable book, *My People, the Sioux*, Standing Bear reported that Pratt "conceived the idea of placing these Indians in a school to see if they could learn."[44] In order for these students to fit easily into the dominant society, Pratt decided to changes their names. In doing so he followed the action of several Indian agents on reservations who did the same thing through tribal consensus. School superintendents and reservation agents change Native names for convenience in tracking members of a family and to facilitate assimilation.

Children within Boarding Schools

Like many Indian people, Luther Standing Bear respected Pratt, but he eventually opposed most of the ways white people attempted to solve the so-called Indian problem. In the early twentieth century the United States shifted its emphasis from Pratt's belief that all people were created equal and had the mental capacity to grow and develop intellectually. Instead, many government officials, including leaders of the Office of Indian Affairs, developed a racial and racist position that Indians were too inferior to benefit greatly from formal education. Government officials established a new goal for Indian education: to force Indian students into domestic sciences, trades, and agriculture, fields that whites believed would make Indian students "useful."[45] Meanwhile, in Indian country, many people resented the government for having taken their children to boarding schools located far from their reservations. And after children began dying of diseases at the boarding schools, Native American parents sometimes resisted the government's attempt to send their children away. When children saw their parents again, they often provided lengthy negative reports about various aspects of their boarding school days. Many children suffered separation anxiety when they boarded trains headed to boarding schools and when they landed at the bleak institutions far from home. They missed their parents, families, and friends. They missed their homelands, playmates, and foods. They missed their languages, which white people and Native interpreters told them not to speak. Not all American Indian children or their parents disliked the boarding school system, but most children missed their homes and families.

However, other students grew to love the boarding schools, and in their letters and books they refer to the schools as their homes. Sometimes students grew up unconnected to their families, tribal cultures, and languages. When these children went home, some Indians met them with anger, disgust, and disdain. According to some student accounts, tribal members made fun of them for their lack of language skills, dress, ideas, deportment, religious beliefs, and outspoken behavior. This cultural divide sometimes made students more closely aligned with the schools. In some cases, students criticized their Native relatives for not having furniture, more varied foods, or basic measures of sanitation to prevent the spread of tuberculosis, trachoma, and other common diseases. As Viola Martinez has pointed out, when she arrived at Sherman Institute she noticed that the sun did not enter her room the way it had back in her Paiute home. This small distinction spoke volumes to the girl: she recognized that her life would be changed forever, even in the most basic of ways. Margaret L. Archuleta, Brenda J. Child, and K. Tsianina Lomawaima develop a similar them in their graphic portrayal of the boarding school experience. They provide a window of understanding about the loneliness suffered by children through their graphic interpretive and documentary study of some of these experiences in their fine book, *Away from Home: American Indian*

Boarding School Experiences, 1879–2000.[46] The authors point out the difficulty in generalizing about boarding school experiences, because students, teachers, and administrators contextualize the experience in many varied ways. Anishinaabe scholar Brenda Child has shown us this clearly in *Boarding School Seasons*, sharing the rich correspondence between parents and children as well as between Indian people and school administrators. Layers of experience and reaction to those experiences existed and continue to exist in Indian country. Native Americans, past and present, assess the boarding school experience differently, but many themes emerge that offer an introduction into the student's world in transition from reservation life to institutionalization at boarding schools.

Without a doubt, the boarding school experience changed the lives of thousands of American Indian children. As soon as the children left their families, non-Indians began their work of transforming them from "savages" to "civilized" humans, and when the children reached the school they faced an institution designed to assimilate Indian children. School superintendents, teachers, matrons, and disciplinarians often stripped the children and took their clothing, blankets, ornaments, and jewelry. School officials bathed the children and cut their hair "to kill the bugs."[47] If this did not work, school officials used pesticides to kill lice. This began the process of taking away the child's outward appearance as an Indian person, a sad and humiliating process for many children who took pride in their unique clothing, material objects, and long hair—connections to their home communities. School officials attempted to peel away layers of Indian identity, working from the outside into the hearts and minds of Native American children. The outward transformation occurred immediately as Indian children lost their clothing and hair, but the inner deconstruction of Indian identity proved a much more complicated task, often impossible. School officials issued children military-style uniforms, which at Carlisle were smart and stylish but at other institutions often shabby and mediocre. Administrators took before-and-after photographs of children, graphically depicting the outward transformation of Native American children from "savage" to "civilized."

Dressed in their military uniforms, Indian children quickly learned to live a strict life and to respond to bells, clocks, and whistles. Non-Indians conceived of American Indian parents and communities as unstructured, permissive, and negligent. For these reasons, administrators were determined to put discipline, order, and precision into the lives of every Native pupil, regardless of age or personal problems such as poor eyesight, lack of hearing, or physical deficiencies. Many non-Indians conceived of Indians as wild, untrained, and spoiled. As a result, school officials endeavored to train the students like drill sergeants break new recruits. In the late 1930s, Serrano elder Francis Morongo de los Reyes attended Sherman Institute. "We had to wear uniforms," she recalled, "and we marched everywhere, everywhere we went, and we had to salute that man [Superintendent Frank Conser] whenever we saw him." Francis hated being treated like a little cadet, When she became ill, school officials placed her in the hospital, and from her hospital bed, "I could see my home [from the rock formation of an arrowhead cut into the south side of the San Bernardino Mountains]; I could see the foothills and the reservation. This made me feel good to see my home, but I was homesick." Under cover of darkness, Francis "deserted," escaping the Sherman hospital and walking more than twenty miles home to the San Manuel Indian Reservation.[48]

Like so many other American Indian children at the various boarding schools, Francis used her feet to express her dissatisfaction. As an elder, she used her words. Another student at Sherman, Cahuilla Robert Levi, remembers leaving the institute for short durations to meet other boys in the orange groves, where they ate fruit, sang songs, spoke their language, and smoked. Robert did not run away to his home, but he left campus and became a truant to defy the rules and "have some fun." In this way he enjoyed some "Indian time."[49] Boarding school officials used military terminology for people like Francis and Robert, calling them deserters who were absent without leave. Many children reported being homesick, and they yearned for companionship with fellow students and relatives who shared their thoughts and feelings, who spoke words in their own languages. In *They Called It Prairie Light*, K. Tsianina Lomawaima provides many oral histories by former boarding school students about their boarding school experiences, including stories of homesickness among the children at Chilocco Indian School in Oklahoma. Her depictions offer a window into the lives of lonely children who missed their families and their homes while attending school.[50] And Brenda Child shares many letters from children and their parents regarding the reasons for "deserting" the boarding schools in her moving portrayal, *Boarding School Seasons: American Indian Families, 1900–1940*. Her book presents unique written documents that allow readers into the thought processes of children who fled schools, of parents who worried about their truant children, and of school administrators who dealt with the runaways. Child points out that some children ran away because they missed their families, but they also ran away from whippings, jailings, psychological pressures, lack of food, poor instruction, and unhealthy conditions.[51]

Boarding school environments differed dramatically from the Native American communities children had known before their arrival. Students sometimes had to adjust to prisonlike environments run in a strict, military manner. Most of the schools had high fences, sometimes surrounded by barbed wire, and each school had strict rules regarding the children's personal freedom. Students had to adjust to daily schedules set by bells that signaled the day's events: waking up, toilet breaks, lining up for meals, classroom attendance, work periods, and bedtime. Children marched to cafeterias to eat their meals when they heard the bells ring, and they ended their meals and went back to class at the ringing of the bells. Jim Whitewolf recalled learning table manners between the bells: "When we got to a certain table he [another boy] told me to just stand there. There was a lady there in charge who had a little bell, and when she hit it, everybody sat down." Whitewolf "watched the others and what they did. After we sat down they rang the bell again and everybody had his head bowed" for a prayer. When the woman rang the bell again, "we started eating."[52] The children ate new foods at the boarding schools, oftentimes food very different from what they had known at home. Hopi student Don Talayesva remembered eating salty bacon, sloppy oatmeal, hash, prunes, rice, and tea—a far cry from the diet of corn, squash, and game that he had known before boarding school.[53] And Hopi Helen Sekaquaptewa remembered being hungry all the time, a chronic problem at most of the boarding schools because of the lack of farm-fresh foods and adequate budgets. Even if the students had been given healthy diets and abundant foods, their bodies were built biologically to absorb nutrients from traditional Native foods, not the high-carbohydrate diet found at most boarding schools.[54]

Health of American Indian Children

Indian students and their parents often objected to the foods served at the boarding schools, a theme developed nicely by Brenda Child in *Boarding School Seasons*. Parents well understood that diet contributed to good health in many ways, including a nutritional preventative to disease and death. When nutrition declined at the schools, children became more susceptible to tuberculosis, pneumonia, influenza, diphtheria, typhoid, colds, and a host of other infectious diseases. Poor nutrition did not cause diseases. Bacteria and viruses usually caused the illnesses, but poor nutrition led to weaker bodies that could not fight infection actively.[55] As a result, children became ill at the boarding schools and spread their diseases by sleeping together in bed, sharing eating utensils, drinking from the same cup, and spending hours with contagious and infectious people, including students, teachers, and matrons. At Sherman Institute students taking music classes even shared the same instruments, sucking on reeds to prepare them before playing clarinets and placing their lips on the mouthpieces of musical instruments used by other students without first sanitizing them.[56]

Most children survived their illnesses, but individuals died at the schools as well. In her moving book, *Viola Martinez, California Paiute: Living in Two Worlds* (by Diana Meyers Bahr), Paiute student Viola Martinez recalled that there was "a lot of illness" at Sherman Institute and "it seemed to me there were always real sick children in the hospital." Many children at the Indian schools contracted tuberculosis, the foremost infectious disease among American Indian children during the first half of the twentieth century. "Tuberculosis was very common," Viola recalled, and before she "went to Sherman, I used to hear them [Indian people] say that a lot of the children from Sherman came back dead." The only time Viola went home from Sherman was to escort "my cousin in a casket to the reservation."[57] School officials often shipped home the bodies of fallen children, but when this became too embarrassing they sent terminally ill children home to die. Some of these children inadvertently infected their family and friends, spreading pathogens that then spread on the reservations. Jean Keller has provided the most comprehensive study of Indian health at a boarding school in her pathbreaking book *Empty Beds: Indian Student Health at Sherman Institute, 1902–1922*. She points out that some sick children at Sherman never made it home and that they lie in cemeteries far from their homelands. Each off-reservation boarding school has its own cemetery where children and school officials buried the students. These cemeteries still exist, reminders of the high price some children and their families paid in the campaign to civilize, assimilate, and acculturate American Indians.[58]

Rules and Punishments

School officials pushed Indian children to obey their instructions both inside and outside the classroom. When students spoke their own languages, lied, used obscene language, fought, stole, destroyed property, acted stubbornly, or misbehaved, teachers, disciplinarians, matrons, and superintendents could inflict corporal punishment or imprison the child. School officials withheld food, restricted student privileges, or forced children to march, mop floors, paint walls, clean filthy bathrooms, and perform other distasteful jobs. Teachers slapped the palms of students' hands, made students stand in the corner, lie on the floor in front of classmates, wear dunce hats, stand on one foot, and clean the mortar between bricks with a toothbrush. Teachers and administrators sometimes ordered older students to perform the punishment of their classmates. This included whipping the backs, buttocks, and thighs of boys and girls. Hopi student Helen Sekaquaptewa reported that "whipping with a harness strap was administered in an upstairs room" as one person "held the culprit while another administered the strap."[59] A student from Fort Sill, Oklahoma, recalled: "Generally the officers in charge of the companies gave the whippings. They either used a board or a belt. They had what they called a 'belt-line'; everybody took off their belts and they ran the student right down through the company."[60] Company officers and others also confined children to stockades, jails, or guardhouses—often hidden from plain view of curious visitors to the schools.

Still, in spite of harsh punishments, Pratt believed Indians to be rational, people of reason who could become human beings equal to white Americans. He represented the Jeffersonian ideal of equality and established the boarding school curriculum to reflect both academics and trades. However, after 1900 this philosophy gave way to a racist view held by many whites, including those managing Indian affairs, according to which Indians were not equal to whites but were lower beings who should be trained at boarding schools to be subservient, obedient, and "useful." They felt that Indians did not have the ability to perform on an equal footing with whites and did not have the mental capabilities to master academics, so some officials of the Bureau of Indian Affairs encouraged trades and domestic sciences at the expense of academics.[61]

Resistance

Just or not, most students took their punishments, but they did not comply with every whim of teachers, administrators, or matrons. They resisted many aspects of the boarding school environment and often defied school officials, finding innovative ways to deal with arrogant administrators, abusive rules, and severe punishments. When children first arrived at the school, many cried themselves to sleep and continued to cry for days, weeks, or even months. To comfort themselves and others, some children sang in their Native languages. They sang at night before going to sleep, and they sang when they sequestered themselves away from others who might tell on them. In similar fashion, some children ran off to riverbeds, nearby woods, or orchards where they comforted one another, danced, drummed, sang, and told stories—all in their own languages. Noted historian Clyde Ellis provides details of a children's circus performed by students near the Rainy Mountain Boarding School in southwestern Oklahoma in his insightful book *To Change Them Forever*. Sometimes children hid away from the school in order to build fires, smoke tobacco, cook foods, and share in their cultural traditions, thereby preserving their identities as Indian people. Viola Martinez remembered climbing the palm trees at Sherman Institute where Paiute children spoke their language so they would not forget it. Viola and other students tried to hide from authority figures and ignore school rules intended to destroy Native culture.[62] Sometimes children hid Native foods that they had gathered, brought from home, or secured from visitors. At other times, children stole food from the cafeteria, often because they were hungry and did not mind breaking the rules. When children disliked a particular employee at the institution, they gave the person an Indian nickname that would belittle the person. At one institution located on the Navajo reservation, students called a non-Native administrator Maíí (Coyote), the trickster figure who could not be trusted.[63]

Students resisted the boarding school system and authority figures in many ways. They cut classes or feigned sickness. They pretended to be ignorant, unable to understand what administrators asked them to do. Sometimes children agreed to do certain tasks but purposely did them incorrectly to frustrate the teachers or encourage teachers never to ask them to do that task again. Students broke fences, furnaces, doors, plumbing, toilets, and vehicles. They played pranks on school officials, practical jokes and more serious offenses intended to hurt teachers, matrons, or administrators. At one school, officials refused to provide boys with toilet facilities during the evening when the school locked the dormitories. The boys rebelled by urinating and defecating on the floors, which got the attention of school officials. At some schools, officials suspended such unruly children, thinking they would punish them by sending them home, but soon too many children resisted in like manner with the hope of being sent home. School officials caught on to this technique and simply punished the children at school.[64]

Many children who attended boarding schools tell stories of defiance and resistance. Martha Manuel Chacon, a Serrano Indian from southern California, attended St. Boniface Indian School in Banning, California, where nuns assigned her to the laundry and forced her to wash only underwear. As an act of resistance, Martha washed a load of Levis. When the nuns realized what she had done, they corrected Martha, telling her to wash only the underwear. When Martha refused and continued with her work, a nun slapped Martha in the face. Martha slapped her back. The nun told Martha she was going to go to hell for such an act of defiance, so Martha responded that if she was going to hell for slapping the nun, the nun would be there too because she had slapped Martha. In frustration, the nun ran off to find a priest who took Martha aside and whipped her with a leather belt. When Martha visited her home on the San Manuel Reservation, she told her parents she would not return to the Catholic boarding school, and she never did.[65]

Perhaps the best-known act of resistance resulted from students running away from the schools. In spite of high fences, barbed wire, guards, locked doors, and bolted gates, many students ran away. School officials caught some of these children and forced them to return to school, but others got away. Children oftentimes returned to their homes, but at other times they fled to cities or farms to work and hide out from school officials. Brenda Child points out that Indian parents expressed their concern for these children and often asked the school officials to explain the circumstances that had forced their child to bolt.[66] Students also resisted the schools by setting fires, trying their best to burn down a building. Many schools reported such arson, and school authorities tried their utmost to discover who was responsible. Often older children set fires as their means of defiance, but smaller children demonstrated their displeasure and loneliness by drawing and painting pictures of familiar scenes from their homes. Smaller children made dolls, homes, wagons, horses, and dogs—entire villages—to resemble the world they had known before going to boarding school. In this way, they created material culture and art that linked them to their Indian heritage, a grounding they never wanted to forget. Such art served these young people as acts of resistance.[67]

Boarding School Classes

After days, months, or years at the schools, some children grew to like the institutions and many aspects of the curriculum. Some had a love-hate relationship with their schools, as examined in Sally J. McBeth's *Ethnic Identity and Boarding School Experience of the West-Central Oklahoma American Indians*.[68] Other students may have been forced into the schools, but they adapted and grew to value their boarding school days. This is a significant theme found in *To Change Them Forever* that Clyde Ellis shares in many segments of his groundbreaking book.[69] A wealth of oral histories can also be found in Sally Hyer's *One House, One Voice, One Heart: Native American Education at the Santa Fe Indian School*.[70] Former students have reported enjoying the academic and vocational curriculum. Some students took pleasure in learning how to read and write in English, understanding the power of the written word. Some students became voracious readers of many different literary and historical genres, while others actively sought advanced knowledge about metal working, carpentry, cooking, sewing, lace making, printing, masonry, agriculture, animal husbandry, art, wagon making, mechanics, tin production, and many others. In part, students grew to appreciate their educations because of the care and dedication of some superintendents and teachers. Robert A. Trennert focuses on this topic in his pathbreaking book *The Phoenix Indian School: Forced Assimilation in Arizona, 1891–1935*.[71]

Not all students enjoyed their boarding school days. Ojibwa author and teacher Basil H. Johnston offers a relatively negative view of his time in boarding school, but his book is far more than a statement against Canadian residential schools. Johnston offers detailed information on everyday life he experienced at the boarding school. He points out in *Indian School Days* that students spent half their day doing academic work and half their day learning trades and working for the benefit of the school.[72] Canadian scholar Jim Miller deals with the work program in the residential schools in his comprehensive and classic book *Shingwauk's Vision: A History of Native Residential Schools*.[73] He points out that at most of the boarding schools in Canada and the United States, American Indian students generally spent half their day in class and the other half at work, doing odd jobs to raise food, milk cows, repair buildings, cook, or launder clothes. However, whether the children worked inside or outside the classroom, school officials forbade them from speaking their heritage languages.

Administrators forced Native American children to speak English in their everyday lives, and they expected Indian children to speak only English all of the time. Otherwise, administrators would punish children. As a result, school officials created more distance between themselves and the students. The language barrier between Native American speakers and English speakers proved difficult for both students and teachers. Ellis examines this issue in detail using the students at Rainy Mountain Boarding School and Methvin Institute of southwestern Oklahoma.[74] But students did their best and learned some English, sometimes mastering the difficult language to such an extent that former students like Luther Standing Bear, Basil Johnston, Charles Eastman, and others wrote books about their experiences. In addition to language issues, cultural divides separated the students from each other and from the teachers. Many Native American students did not enjoy the competitiveness fostered by teachers, choosing not to embarrass other students by speaking up and sharing answers. Some Indian students did not embrace the individualism encouraged by teachers but chose to remain loyal to their classmates.

In the classroom, students learned in English about geography, mathematics, literature, biology, and astronomy. Not all children thrived on the curriculum, but some of them did and they hungered to know more. Many Indian children failed to do well in classes because they simply did not understand English and the many meanings of words and phrases. Sometimes the curriculum conflicted with traditional educations they had brought with them to the schools, particularly the spiritual nature of plants, places, and animals, sites of Native learning that had no standing in the boarding school classes. Perhaps no discipline was more trying for Indian students than American history, which was filled with the Whiggish glorification of European settlement, conquest of the "wilderness," westward expansion, and the founding fathers. Before 1924, American Indians in the United States were not citizens, and the push toward patriotism of the Stars and Stripes held little credibility among many Native American students. However, even before federal citizenship, other American Indian students and parents championed the United States and stood strong in their patriotic zeal for the country, the land that held the bones of their ancestors.

Many American Indian students had grown up during the era of the Indian wars of the late nineteenth century, and many of them had little loyalty to the United States or Canada. Some students had a difficult time celebrating the Declaration of Independence, the Constitution, George Washington's birthday, or other events that ran contrary to their own people's experiences. Some of them had a more difficult time accepting the American and Canadian interpretation of westward expansion and the blatant depictions of First Nations peoples as savage barbarians in the way of enlightened civilization and progress. This was the way textbooks cast Indians within the narratives well into the twentieth century, and writers and teachers moved slowly to present history as an invasion of Native American peoples. Non-Indian writers chose to ignore the deeds of land-hungry and materialistic pioneers who resettled Indian lands. Historians chose to cast a kind light on the theft of Indian lands through treaty making and by right of war. Scholars writing texts for children failed to explain the displacement of Indian populations and the greed of miners, cattlemen, and farmers who exploited natural resources that First Nations had once owned and enjoyed. As First Nations people gained greater control of their children's educations during the self-determination movement of the 1970s, this interpretation of Indian-white relations shifted. Nevertheless, much more work is needed in presenting the history of Native Americans for school-age children.

Music and Sports

The boarding and residential schools used many subjects to "civilize" Indian children. Most schools taught them to play instruments such as flutes, clarinets, trumpets, tubas, and other wind and brass instruments. Most schools boasted bands that played at sporting events, including football and baseball games. School bands marched proudly in parades, providing outward symbols and expressions of the civilization process occurring at the Indian boarding schools. Most schools also had choirs where boys and girls learned to sing songs in English and perform them for school audiences as well as white visitors to the schools. Members of the school choir enjoyed field trips to towns where they performed patriotic and Christian songs at non-Indian schools or for civic groups. In similar fashion, some schools offered students the opportunity to join drama clubs, which performed plays on and off the campuses. Historian William Medina is expanding this topic into a book-length study about the way Indian schools marketed or sold Indians attending their schools through music, drama, and sports.

All of the schools encouraged boys to play sports, and at one time the Indian schools had some of the best college teams in the nation. Indian boarding school teams competed against Harvard, Yale, the University of Pennsylvania, Dartmouth, and the University of Southern California. Carlisle football became legendary with the famous Jim Thorpe, Alexander Arcasa, Gus Welsh, and Tansil Powell. In 1902, when Sherman Institute opened its doors in Riverside, California, the football team began its annual rout of the University of Southern California team. Indian males played a number of sports against worthy opponents, and over the years, Indian females did the same, gaining great notoriety for their athletic prowess. In recent years, John Bloom and David Adams have examined sports as an important theme at the boarding schools, and their works will lead to new research. This is also true of the social events held at boarding schools. After many sporting events, for example, the schools encouraged young people to attend dances where they could learn to dance in a "civilized" manner dressed in formal European-style clothing. The social events mirrored those offered by non-Indians of the period, and these social events became part of the assimilation process offered at the Indian schools.[75]

Blues

The American Indian boarding school experience is layered with deep meaning that cannot be understood simply by framing the schools, administrators, and teachers as good or evil. Teachers, administrators, matrons, and disciplinarians were all individuals, and they did their jobs in their own ways. Some students liked the superintendents and teachers, and others hated them. Some American Indians liked their boarding school days, and others loathed that time of their lives. For some students, remembering their days in school brings on the blues. Chemehuevi elder Joe Mike Benitez cannot speak about his time at the St. Boniface Indian Boarding School without changing his facial expression, frowning and widening his eyes, remembering the regimented life, bad food, loneliness, and forced Christianization. The priests and nuns tried to steal his language. More than sixty years after he attended St. Boniface, mere mention of the school brings on a melancholy that transforms the former boarding school student. Many students had difficulty adjusting to the boarding school system, but others thrived on learning how to read, write, and speak English. Some students enjoyed learning a trade, playing sports, marching in the band, or giving dramatic readings. In some cases, students turned the power, making the school experience benefit themselves and, by extension, their people. Students learned to be dual citizens of the United States or Canada as well as their Native nation. Some students left the schools hating and resenting the experience, while others became very loyal to their alma mater, sending friends, relatives, and their own children to the Indian boarding schools.[76] Many students took a position somewhere in between the two poles, and their experiences and memories are layered and complex. The boarding schools have a multitude of meanings, but regardless of students' feelings about the schools, the institutions became an integral part of the Native American experience, and one we are only recently beginning to unravel, discuss, and interpret.[77]

In a very real sense, we are unpacking the American Indian boarding school experience just as students unpacked their belongings at the schools, their minds swirling about the unknown and complex situation they faced. The contributors to this volume have analyzed various components of their baggage a little at a time, trying to make sense of a significant historical institution and its many complex influences on Indian children, parents, and peoples. These essays continue the conversation opened by Indians and non-Indians alike in past books, articles, exhibits, and discussions. Some of them are written by established scholars who have been working on the meanings of the Indian boarding schools for years, while others are written by emerging scholars. Together, they offer new perspectives on boarding schools and the students who attended them. All of the essays are original contributions for this volume, and the topics addressed in these works were first offered at a symposium sponsored by the University of California, Riverside, and the Sherman Indian School Museum entitled "Boarding School Blues: Revisiting the American Indian Boarding School Experience," held at Sherman Indian High School on November 22–23, 2002—the one hundredth anniversary of the opening of Sherman Institute.[78] These essays address various aspects of the American Indian boarding school experience, allowing readers to enter the lives of students and to learn more about this little-known period of American history when many Native American children entered a new world that transformed them and in turn transformed the dominant system that brought them into the schools. In a real sense, the federal boarding school system was a successful failure that changed the lives of thousands of Indian children who used their knowledge to benefit their own people. For too many children, their days at school were filled with the blues, but most persevered and grew as a result of their experiences. Like heroes of old Native American stories, the children who attended boarding schools were forever changed, but they also emerged victorious, champions of their cultures, languages, and peoples.

Notes

1. The quote is from Richard H. Pratt, "The Advantages of Mingling Indians with Whites," *Proceedings of the National Conference of Charities and Corrections, 1892*, 46. Also see Pratt, *Proceedings and Addresses of the National Education Association, 1895*, 761–62, and the discussion in David Wallace Adams, *Education for Extinction: American Indians and the Boarding School Experience, 1875–1928* (Lawrence: University Press of Kansas, 1995), 52; for insights into Pratt, consult his *Battlefield and Classroom: Four Decades with the American Indian, 1867–1904*, ed. Robert M. Utley (New Haven: Yale University Press, 1964).
2. "Turning the power" is a Native American phrase meaning to send negative power back to its source, using the same power to effectuate a positive outcome for Indian people. In this case, over time, American Indian students, parents, and community leaders learned from the boarding school experience and used their knowledge to the benefit of their people.
3. Luther Standing Bear, *My People, the Sioux* (Lincoln: University of Nebraska Press, 1975), 124.
4. Pratt's statement is quoted in D. W. Adams, *Education for Extinction*, 53.
5. Dalbert Castro, interview by Clifford E. Trafzer, spring 1988, Auburn Rancheria, California.
6. David Adams uses most of these accounts in *Education for Extinction*, but for Hubert Honanie's story see Marjorie Thayer and Elizabeth Emanuel, *Climbing*

the Sun: The Story of a Hopi Indian Boy (New York: Dodd, Mead, 1980). For Pauline Murillo's story and that of her mother, Martha Manuel Chacon, see Pauline Ormego Murillo, *Living in Two Worlds* (Highland CA: Dimples Press, 2002).

7. Michael C. Coleman, *American Indian Children at School, 1850–1930* (Jackson: University Press of Mississippi, 1993).

8. Karen Swisher, "Education," in *The Native North American Almanac*, ed. Duane Champagne (Detroit: Gale Research, 1994), 855.

9. Clifford E. Trafzer, *As Long as the Grass Shall Grow and Rivers Flow: A History of Native Americans* (Fort Worth: Harcourt, 2000), 24.

10. Clara Sue Kidwell, "Systems of Knowledge," in *America in 1492: The World of Indian Peoples before the Arrival of Columbus*, ed. Alvin Josephy Jr. (New York: Vintage Books, 1991), 369–403.

11. Tsianina Lomawaima, "The Unnatural History of American Indian Education," in *Next Steps: Research and Practice to Advance Indian Education*, ed. Karen Swisher and John Tippeconic (Charleston WV: Eric Clearinghouse on Rural Education and Small Schools, 1999), 1–33.

12. Kidwell, "Systems of Knowledge," 374, 377, 379, 383, 387, 390, 392, 396, 402.

13. Don McCaskill, "Canadian Native Education," in Champagne, *The Native North American Almanac*, 879–80.

14. McCaskill, "Canadian Native Education," 879–80.

15. Andrew George, interview by Clifford E. Trafzer and Richard Scheuerman, November 15, 1980, Yakama Indian Reservation, Washington; Eleonore Sioui, interview by Clifford E. Trafzer, May 2000, Wendake Reserve, Quebec.

16. Swisher, "Education," 856.

17. Swisher, "Education," 856; Francis Jennings, *The Invasion of America* (New York: Norton, 1975), 230–37, 248–53; Neal Salisbury, *Manitou and Providence* (New York: Oxford University Press, 1982), 178–88, 206; James Axtell, *The Invasion Within* (New York: Oxford University Press, 1985), 220–31; J. R. Miller, *Shingwauk's Vision: A History of Native Residential Schools* (Toronto: University of Toronto Press, 1996), 39–60.

18. Alice C. Fletcher, *Indian Education and Civilization* (Washington DC: Bureau of Education and Government Printing Office, 1888), 34.

19. Margaret Connell Szasz, *Indian Education in the American Colonies, 1607–1783* (Albuquerque: University of New Mexico Press, 1988).

20. *Journals of the Continental Congress*, cited in Theodore Fischbacher, "A Study of the Role of the Federal Government in the Education of the American Indian" (Ph.D. diss., Arizona State University, Tempe, 1967), 32.

21. Leleua Loupe of the University of California, Riverside, is presently engaged in researching the issue of "usefulness" as a theme within the boarding schools, specifically Sherman Institute.

22. Two sources most helpful are Francis Paul Prucha, *The Great Father: The United States Government and the American Indian*, 2 vols. (Lincoln: University of Nebraska Press, 1984); and Axtell, *The Invasion Within*.

23. For the finest scholarly work on the Cherokee seminary see Devon A. Mihesuah,

Cultivating the Rosebuds: The Education of Women at the Cherokee Female Seminary, 1851–1909 (Urbana: University of Illinois, 1993).

24. D. W. Adams, *Education for Extinction*, 39–40.

25. Fletcher, *Indian Education and Civilization*, 162–63.

26. Samuel Lyman Tyler, *A History of Indian Policy* (Washington DC: Bureau of Indian Affairs, 1973), 45.

27. For two important works on the subject, see Robert F. Berkhofer Jr., *Salvation and the Savage* (New York: Atheneum Press, 1976); and Henry W. Bowden, *American Indians and Christian Missions* (Chicago: University of Chicago Press, 1981). Also see Evelyn C. Adams, *American Indian Education: Government Schools and Economic Progress* (New York: Arno Press, 1971), 32.

28. Cary Michael Carney, *Native American Higher Education in the United States* (New Brunswick NJ: Transaction, 1999), 48.

29. D. W. Adams, *Education for Extinction*, 36.

30. Swisher, "Education," 857.

31. See Coleman, *American Indian Children at School*; Mihesuah, *Cultivating the Rosebuds*.

32. Trafzer, *As Long as the Grass Shall Grow*, 230–55.

33. *Annual Report of the Commissioner of Indian Affairs, 1873*, 8.

34. E. C. Adams, *American Indian Education*, 51.

35. E. C. Adams, *American Indian Education*, 51.

36. Pratt, "The Advantages of Mingling Indians with Whites," quoted in D. W. Adams, *Education for Extinction*, 52.

37. Pratt, "The Advantages of Mingling Indians with Whites," quoted in D. W. Adams, *Education for Extinction*, 52.

38. On March 10, 2004, Barbara Landis informed Clifford E. Trafzer in an e-mail message that this masthead attributed to Pratt appears in all the publications generated at the Carlisle Indian School, including *Indian Helper, Red Man,* and *Carlisle Arrow.* Also see Pratt, *Battlefield and Classroom*, 283.

39. *Annual Report of the Commissioner of Indian Affairs, 1873*, 8.

40. Pratt, "The Advantages of Mingling Indians with Whites," quoted in D. W. Adams, *Education for Extinction*, 53.

41. Pratt, *Battlefield and Classroom*, 213–14. The most comprehensive study of Native Americans at Hampton Institute is Donald F. Lindsey, *Indians at Hampton Institute, 1877–1923* (Urbana: University of Illinois Press, 1995).

42. D. W. Adams, *Education for Extinction*, 41.

43. D. W. Adams, *Education for Extinction*, 108.

44. Standing Bear, *My People the Sioux*, 134.

45. Frederick Hoxie, *A Final Promise: The Campaign to Assimilate the Indians, 1880–1920* (Lincoln: University of Nebraska Press, 1984), 194–207.

46. Margaret L. Archuleta, Brenda J. Child, and K. Tsianina Lomawaima, eds., *Away from Home: American Indian Boarding School Experiences, 1879–2000* (Phoenix: Heard Museum, 2000), 19–20. One of the editors, Tsianina Lomawaima, acknowledged that "the germ of this book" was "an exemplary piece of scholarship" by

Rayna Green and John Troutman. *Away from Home* was an outgrowth of Green and Troutman's scholarship.

47. Frank Mitchell, *Navajo Blessingway Singer* (Tucson: University of Arizona Press, 1978), 57–61. Charlotte J. Frisbie and David McAllester edited this classic and insightful autobiography.

48. Francis Morongo de los Reyes, interview by Clifford E. Trafzer, Pauline Murillo, and Leleua Loupe, October 9, 2001, San Manuel Indian Reservation, California.

49. Robert Levi, interview by Clifford E. Trafzer, fall 1992, Medicine Ways Conference, University of California, Riverside.

50. K. Tsianina Lomawaima, *They Called It Prairie Light: The Story of the Chilocco Indian School* (Lincoln: University of Nebraska Press, 1994).

51. Brenda J. Child, *Boarding School Seasons: American Indian Families, 1900–1940* (Lincoln: University of Nebraska Press, 1998), 87–95.

52. Jim Whitewolf, *The Life of a Kiowa Apache Indian*, ed. Charles S. Brant (New York: Dover, 1969), 84.

53. D. W. Adams, *Education for Extinction*, 115.

54. Clifford Trafzer develops the significance of food in Native American communities in *Death Stalks the Yakama: Epidemiological Transitions and Mortality on the Yakama Indian Reservation, 1888–1964* (East Lansing: Michigan State University Press, 2001), 4–5, 71, 88, 94, 100, 132–33, 140, 198–99, 202–5.

55. Trafzer, *Death Stalks the Yakama*, 73–75, 189.

56. Jean A. Keller, *Empty Beds: Indian Student Health at Sherman Institute, 1902–1922* (East Lansing: Michigan State University Press, 2002), 69.

57. Diana Meyers Bahr, *Viola Martinez, California Paiute: Living in Two Worlds* (Norman: University of Oklahoma Press, 2003), 53.

58. Keller, *Empty Beds*, 132–33, 143–46, 160.

59. Helen Sekaquaptewa, *Me and Mine* (Tucson: University of Arizona Press, 1969), 136–37.

60. Sally J. McBeth, *Ethnic Identity and the Boarding School Experience of the West-Central Oklahoma American Indians* (Washington DC: University Press of America, 1983), 106.

61. Clyde Ellis, *To Change Them Forever: Indian Education at the Rainy Mountain Boarding School, 1893–1920* (Norman: University of Oklahoma Press, 1996), 126–27.

62. Bahr, *Viola Martinez*, 58.

63. In the mid-1970s, Navajo students, staff, and faculty at Navajo Community College (present-day Diné College) called a non-Indian administrator "Maíí" (Coyote) to convey their contempt for the untrustworthy administrator who, in their estimation, had done them and their school harm. He left the college in 1977.

64. D. W. Adams, *Education for Extinction*, 51–55; Edmund Nequatewa, *Born a Chief: The Nineteenth Century Hopi Boyhood of Edmund Nequatewa*, as told to Alfred F. Whiting (Tucson: University of Arizona Press, 1993), 91–92.

65. Clifford E. Trafzer, *The People of San Manuel* (Highland CA: San Manuel Band of Mission Indians, 2002), 124–25.

66. Child, *Boarding School Seasons*, 88–91.

67. A photograph taken at the Crow Agency depicts a miniature Indian village at a school, complete with wagons and tipis that young girls attending school erected. See Archuleta, Child, and Lomawaima, *Away from Home*, 28.

68. McBeth provides numerous examples in *Ethnic Identity*.

69. Ellis, *To Change Them Forever*, 91–130.

70. Sally Hyer, *One House, One Voice, One Heart: Native American Education at the Santa Fe Indian School* (Santa Fe: Museum of New Mexico, 1990).

71. Robert A. Trennert, *The Phoenix Indian School: Forced Assimilation in Arizona, 1891–1935* (Norman: University of Arizona Press, 1983).

72. Basil H. Johnston, *Indian School Days* (Norman: University of Oklahoma Press, 1988), 28–47.

73. See Miller's masterpiece on the Canadian residential school, *Shingwauk's Vision*, 251–68.

74. Ellis, *To Change Them Forever*, 117–18.

75. Archuleta, Child, and Lomawaima, *Away from Home*, 98–114.

76. Ellis, *To Change Them Forever*, 196–97.

77. The complexity of responses and meanings is a prominent theme in recent works on the boarding schools. In addition to the studies by D. W. Adams, Child, Coleman, Lomawaima, and Ellis cited above, see Scott Riney's remarkable volume, *The Rapid City Indian School, 1898–1933* (Norman: University of Oklahoma Press, 1999).

78. The Humanities Research Institute of the University of California, the Soboba Band of Luiseño Indians, the Pechanga Band of Luiseño Indians, Sherman Indian High School, the James Ramos family, and the Department of History of the University of California, Riverside, sponsored the three-day symposium.

I. Beyond Bleakness

The Brighter Side of Indian Boarding Schools, 1870–1940

David Wallace Adams

David Wallace Adams is a distinguished professor of education at Cleveland State University, where he teaches the history of American Indian education. Although Adams has published widely, he is best known for his pathbreaking book *Education for Extinction: American Indians and the Boarding School Experience, 1875–1928*. He states in this essay that federal policy makers intended boarding schools to assimilate American Indian children by removing them from their homes, cultures, and languages. School officials sought to destroy Native American identity and to replace it with new values that reflected the dominant society. Adams understands that in spite of the fact that Indian students suffered loneliness, harsh punishments, isolation, dangerous diseases, and a continual assault on their traditional cultures, many students found ways to cope with and to enjoy their boarding school days. Native parents and tribal elders often implored their children to work hard and learn as much as they could so that the students could better serve their communities. Many students felt obligated to make the best of their schooling, while others openly embraced their educational experience.

Many students enjoyed making money through the "outing" (work) programs, and they sent money home and bought things they had long wanted. Students enjoyed learning a number of trades, including harness making, carpentry, masonry, and sewing. They often enjoyed participating in the school band, choir, or drama clubs. Some students traveled to other communities, including big cities, to share their talents. They had an opportunity to see new and exciting places. Athletes at the Indian schools also enjoyed traveling to new places and felt privileged to have the opportunity of representing their schools in football, baseball, and track. Indian students sometimes fell in love at the boarding schools, and many children came home with rich stories that families still share.

The picture that historians have painted of Indian boarding schools has generally been a bleak one. The scenario goes something like this. Late-nineteenth-century policy makers, convinced that the alternatives facing Indians were racial extinction or forced assimilation, were determined to effect the latter. The mechanism for accomplishing this objective was education. On- and (especially) off-reservation boarding schools were deemed the ideal instruments for lifting Indian children out of the depths of "savagism" and setting them on the path to progress, that is, "civilization." Boarding schools would carry out this process by removing Indian children from their native environment, stripping away all outward vestiges of traditional identity, and then exposing them to an instructional program equally divided between academic and industrial training, supplemented by routinized chore work. All this took place in a military-like institutional setting characterized by drill and marching, constant monitoring, and harsh discipline, where the very acts of eating, sleeping, and hygiene were regulated by bugles and bells driven by the precise measurements of the white man's clock. Conceived as assimilationist hothouses, boarding schools were designed to individualize, republicanize, and Christianize the next generation of Indian youth, qualifying them as fit candidates for American citizenship. Students, meanwhile, endured heartbreaking loneliness, substandard diets, humiliating punishments, life-threatening diseases, and an unrelenting assault on their cultural and psychological selves.[1] Not an uplifting story.

But there is another, less dismal, side of the boarding school story, and it is this other side that is the focus of this essay. This essay asks: In what ways and for what reasons did Indian youth sometimes come to look upon their years at boarding school as a rewarding and even joyful experience? Before addressing this question, a few disclaimers are in order. First, the following discussion is not a revisionist attempt to argue that boarding schools were a necessary or desirable development in the evolution of federal Indian policy or that most Indian youth looked upon their school years as an overall pleasant or positive experience. Nor does this essay claim that past treatments of Indian schooling have dwelled exclusively upon the negative features of the boarding school story. In fact, most scholars who have studied the subject, however critical in their perspective, acknowledge that Indian communities and students alike saw redeeming value in the boarding school experience.[2] This essay, rather, attempts to pull together the various strands of this somewhat muted theme and to make sense of it as an important element in the boarding school story. Third, it is important to remember that the Indian student's response to boarding school was not an either/or matter. Over the course of several years, a single year, or even a single day, a given student might experience a range of emotions and respond in a range of ways, running the gamut from active accommodation, to bewilderment, to ambivalence, to overt resistance.[3] Finally, this study is offered with the frank admission that scholars are on very shaky ground when they attempt to make hard generalizations on the question of student responses. This is partly so because efforts to examine the subject are frequently and necessarily based on material collected long after the experience itself. While memoirs and oral historical accounts are invaluable, it is nonetheless true that *experiencing* an event is often quite different from *having experienced* it. As Sally McBeth has pointed out, because the boarding school experience is such an important element of what it has meant to be Indian in America—that is, Indian identity—it is imbued with shifting symbolic meanings that are often paradoxical and contradictory. Meanwhile, given the paucity of sources for uncovering the attitudes, feelings, and actions of Indian children at the time of their attendance, historians are forced to rely on these accounts recorded years later. This essay does not resolve this dilemma; it merely acknowledges it.[4]

It is important to remember that although Indian agents often resorted to force to fill school enrollment quotas, some Indian children came to boarding school willingly. Consider the behavior of an adolescent Hopi girl in 1906 when she spotted a covered wagon full of Hopis coming down the road from Second Mesa. Polingaysi Qoyawayma had heard rumors that a group of children from Keams Canyon Boarding School were to be taken to Sherman Institute, the distant school in southern California, and she thought the approaching wagon must surely be this group. When the wagon stopped at the trading post to camp for the night, her suspicion was confirmed by one of wagon's occupants, who announced: "We're going to the land of oranges faraway in California." Polingaysi, who had already defied her parents by attending the day school at Oraibi, was determined to do so again if it meant going to the school in the "land of oranges." Unable to convince her parents to sign the required permission form, the next morning she crept into the wagon in the predawn hours hoping the driver wouldn't spot her. But the plan went awry and she was ordered out of the wagon. The stubborn Hopi girl refused to budge, however, pronouncing: "I will not get out of the wagon. I am going along." Finally, it was decided to fetch the girl's parents, who would either force their daughter from the wagon or give in to her burning desire. In the end her father relented, saying: "I think we should allow her to go. . . . She will be well taken care of. She will learn more of the writing marks that are in books. I think we should sign the paper." And so they did, a gesture for which Polingaysi would be ever grateful.[5]

The fact that Qoyawayma eagerly wanted to go off to boarding school surely accounts for something in explaining her overall favorable attitude toward the whole experience. Also, it should not be forgotten that many students went off to school with strong support from tribal elders, an endorsement of the white man's school that presumably carried considerable weight with children embarking upon this new adventure. As the father of Francis La Flesche explained to his son:

> Early I sought the society of those who knew the teaching of the chiefs. From them I learned that kindness and hospitality win the love of a people. I culled from their teachings their noblest thoughts, and treasured them, and they have been my guide. You came into existence, and have reached the age when you should seek for knowledge. That you might profit by the teachings of your own people and that of the white race, and that you might avoid the misery which accompanies ignorance, I placed you in the House of the Teaching of the White-Chests, who are said to be wise and to have in their books the utterances of great and learned men. I had treasured the hope that you would seek to know the good deeds done by men of your own race, and by men of the white race, that you would follow their example and take pleasure in doing the things that are noble and helpful to those around you. Am I to be disappointed?

Likewise, Thomas Wildcat Alford relates that before he and another Shawnee boy, both designated as future chiefs, were sent off to Hampton Institute, tribal chiefs "told us of their desire that we should learn the white man's wisdom. How to read in books, how to understand all that was written and spoken to about our people and the government."[6]

But even in those instances where children were forced into school, they too, over the span of month and years, might come to appreciate aspects of their experience. In the end there were at least six reasons why students might find the boarding school experience satisfying—or at least partially so. First, some found boarding school a welcome escape from the desperate economic and social conditions in their home communities. Here we confront one of the most unpleasant realities of turn-of-the-century reservation life: in the struggle for existence, many families were only surviving by the skin of their teeth. For Frank Mitchell, a Navajo who attended the reservation boarding school at Fort Defiance, the motivation to attend the white man's school derived largely from economic factors. As he recalls in his autobiography: "The school accepted just any children, regardless of what conditions they were in. Some of those children were brought to school very badly clothed; there was just nothing clean or whole on them." He continues:

> When I entered school there was plenty to eat there, more food than I used to get at home. We had different foods at Fort Defiance, like rice and beans. And we had some dried fruit that we ate, like apples. Besides that we had meat, beef, which was bought for us at school. So I was happy about that; I was willing to go to school if they were going to feed me like that. The clothing that I got there too gave me joy. I was proud to look at the clothes and the shoes, and to walk around in them.

In spite of these material benefits, Mitchell dropped out for three years after spending one year at Fort Defiance, largely because of his mother's opposition to white education. But by then all of his school clothes were worn to a frazzle. "So I was running around with white calico pants again," he relates, "and even my shoes were worn out. When I realized what condition I was in again, I got to thinking about going back to school." And so he did.[7]

Sometimes the motivation to escape reservation communities sprang more social conditions. In communities ravaged by alcoholism, where the unraveling of village and kinship ties forced children into chaotic and violent environments, boarding schools held out a measure of physical and psychological security. The extent of this appeal is revealed in the comments of seventh-grade Haskell students in essays written on the topic "Alcohol and My Future." One student wrote: "Why is it that I am against the liquor traffic? Because whisky caused my father's death. He was an officer and the drunkards were all against him and killed him." Another wrote: "We once had a nice home but after alcohol entered it kept on going down and down until we had no home. Papa drank up everything. He caused mother to sell

her land and now mother has no home at all. She works. If I had the power,
I would crush every saloon to pieces." More than one student confessed to
having succumbed to self-destructing drinking.

> *I am sorry to say that I don't know when I took my first drink, maybe it*
> *was before I could walk, as my father and mother were both drunkards,*
> *although my mother punished me when I took some without her per-*
> *mission. . . . Today I am living without parents. This liquor is the cause*
> *of that and they [Indians] try hard to get us in this trap. My father was*
> *found under the snow by a farmer who happened to drive to town after*
> *the snow storm. What was the cause of this? Alcohol. Alcohol is the cause*
> *of nearly all crime. Let us brace up and fight against our common enemy*
> *who is killing out parents.*[8]

In such troubled environments it is understandable that some Indian
youth looked upon boarding school as a welcome relief, a safe space from
the oftentimes depressing and destructive conditions of reservation life.

Sometimes it was parents who turned to boarding schools because personal and economic circumstances made it impossible for them to care for
their children. One Kiowa woman recalled: "I wanted to go home and be
with mama, but she said, 'Well, if you come home, we'll only be eating one
meal a day, and so I think you should go.' " In *Boarding School Seasons*, Brenda Child cites several instances of parents requesting that superintendents
enroll their children in boarding school. In 1924 a recently widowed Ojibwa father wrote the school at Flandreau, South Dakota: "I have lost my wife
and left me with six children. . . . I would like to ask you to send these little
folks over to you two or three years so I can get along. It is hard for me [to]
stay here alone home because children not used home alone when mother
gone. When I am going working out it hard for them . . . and this all I ask
you if you have a place for them." That same year, another widowed father
made this appeal: "I am writing you to see if you can do me a favor by taking my daughter in your school it would be a big favor to me as my wife died
Feb. 4th and have no way to taking care of the girl we cant stay at home as
it is very lonesome for her. . . . Therefore I am asking you this favor, to turn
my daughter over in your care."[9]

The flip side of those economic factors *pushing* students into school were
the same factors *pulling* them in its direction. This second motivation for at-

tending school stemmed from the belief that learning the ways of the white man would enhance Indian youths' opportunity to make a living wage. The architects of Indian education, of course, intended for students to make the connection between schooling and economic advancement. As Merrill Gates would declare at Lake Mohonk: "Discontent with the tepee and the starving rations of the Indian camp in winter is needed to get the Indian out of the blanket and into trousers,—trousers . . . with a *pocket that aches to be filled with dollars!*" When speaking in Los Angeles at a teachers institute, Commissioner of Indian Affairs Francis Leupp took special note of the Sherman Institute banner with its bold insignia of S and I. Fluttering in a light breeze on the drill field, the banner came "pretty near being a dollar mark." Leupp continued: "Sordid as it may sound, it is the dollar that makes the world go around, and we have to teach the Indians at the outset of their careers what a dollar means. That is, in some respects, the most important part of their education." When Indians learned the meaning of a dollar, they would want to *earn* dollars, *save* them, and ultimately *spend* them. Schooling, the logic went, not only fostered self-sufficiency but also implanted that quintessential American economic value—possessive individualism. Schooling would cause Indian youth to dream material dreams. As one Phoenix merchant urged in the Indian school's newspaper, the *Native American*:

> *Early to bed and early to rise,*
> *Love all the teachers and tell them no lies.*
> *Study your lessons that you may be wise*
> *And buy from the men who advertise.*[10]

Such acquisitive sentiments were not limited to policy makers and merchants. Since the time of early contact, Indians had admired European trade goods and were eager to trade beaver pelts and deerskins to acquire them. Two centuries later, the consumer products of U.S. factories were no less alluring. In 1879 Richard Henry Pratt received a letter from Skunks-Head, who had turned his son over to Pratt when the latter was recruiting students at Fort Berthold. Skunks-Head wrote that he missed his son greatly, but "I sent my son away to learn more work so that he can buy wagons and stoves and we will live well through him." He continued: "Whenever I go hunting I only find white men and their work. There is nothing now for an *Indian* to live on, so I want my son to be a white man and sent him away. It is all right. My son is now in the midst of good works and my heart is glad. I see his picture where he has on white man's clothes which contain many places to put money in pockets, and I know that you hold my son well for me."[11]

At the most fundamental level, economic survival meant Indians' ability to negotiate the everyday economic transactions with white farmers and merchants, and this in turn required the ability to communicate with them. The schools' capacity to equip students with this most valuable skill provided school officials with a powerful tool for gaining students' cooperation in learning the language of their colonizers. Consider the following exchange between a ten-year-old Maricopa boy named Hezekia and his teacher when the former announced that he was conducting a "strike" against speaking English.

> *Teacher: Hezekia, can your father speak English?*
> *Hezekia: No sir.*
>
> *Teacher: When he wants to write a letter what does he do?*
>
> *Hezekia: He get somebody who knows English to write for him.*
>
> *Teacher: He knows Indian, why don't he write it?*
>
> *Hezekia: We can't write Indian.*
>
> *Teacher: Oh, I see; when you get to be a man you want somebody
> else to write your letter for you?*
>
> *Hezekia: No sir (and he began to look abashed).*
>
> *Teacher: When your father goes to the store to buy something,
> how does he do if he cannot tell what he wants?*
>
> *Hezekia: He has somebody talk for him.*
>
> *Teacher: But if nobody there can talk Indian what can he do?*
>
> *Hezekia: He points to what he wants.*
>
> *Teacher: But if he can't see what he wants what does he do?*
>
> *Hezekia: He don't get it.*
>
> *Teacher: So you want to do like that when you are a man, do
> you; have somebody talk for you at the store, or go around point-
> ing to this or that, holding up your fingers to show how many
> you want and saying "muncha"; then pay for one thing and get*

your change, and pay for another and get your change—all be-
cause you can't count how much they all cost, and being afraid all
the time you are being cheated and not getting all you pay for; or
have to go away without what you want, all because you cannot
talk English like almost everybody around here can do? I don't
believe your father and mother want you to do that way, and I
can't think you want to do that way yourself.[12]

Confronted with this logic, Hezekia was persuaded to learn English.

Before Indians could think about buying cookstoves or sewing machines, it was imperative to provide them with those skills and values required for economic self-sufficiency. Hence a key component of the boarding school curriculum was industrial training. While boys enrolled in classes in farming, blacksmithing, carpentry, wagon building, and tailoring, girls pursued domestic science courses in the areas of cooking, sewing, and canning. Later, normal, commercial, and nursing programs opened up further career possibilities. Even institutional chore work and so-called outing programs, policy makers reasoned, held out the promise of giving industrious youth a "leg up" in the economic struggles of life.[13] Speaking in Los Angeles, Commissioner Leupp reported on a group of Navajos from Fort Defiance who had spent the summer harvesting sugar beets in Colorado: "They came back a month or two afterwards with some $1,600 jingling in their pockets. Every one of those boys learned a lesson. Moreover, every one of those dollars has been invested in sheep; and when those boys come to make their homes they will have something to start on, something they own themselves, and something that they got by their own labor."[14]

Not surprisingly, many students shrewdly observed that there was little economic future in digging sugar beets. Thus, when Max Hanley, a twenty-six-year-old Navajo returning to Sherman Institute in the fall of 1924, was told that he was too old to continuing his schooling, "I kept pleading to let me attend. I wanted to learn a good career, and they finally agreed." Before leaving Sherman he had mastered three trades. "In the white man's words, 'I specialized,' and certificates were filled out for me which identified what I could do best." A similar faith in skill training is revealed in a letter Pratt received from one of his outing students: "I like spend my time on farm in summer and in winter in Carlisle to go to school and learn my trade in tin shop. So when I go back Montana when my time is up so I can go at it." From Galena, Kansas, a former student, making a living at plumbing, wrote Pratt: "I do most heartily thank the Indian Training School at Carlisle, for giving me an education and a trade that I can work at. I see now it comes very handy."[15]

The economic logic of schooling even seems to have insinuated itself into the thinking of eight-year-old Albert Yava. A Tewa Hopi, Yava had attended Polacca day school for two years before arriving at Keams Canyon Boarding School in 1896. Yava admits that a lot of Hopis "would rather have been anywhere but in that school," but at the same time, "a lot of us liked it and were glad to have a chance to learn the white man's way so that we'd know how to cope in later years. That was one thing that was always on my mind." After a few years at Keams Canyon, Yava expressed to a school employee his desire to attend Chilocco Indian School. His reason: "Well, I'm interested in doing something. There isn't anything for me on the reservation. We don't own much livestock to take care of. I'd like to go further in school and learn something useful." When such reasoning failed to get the necessary permission signature from his parents, Yava ingeniously informed the superintendent that by Hopi tradition his uncle (who was sympathetic to his desire to attend Chilocco) was ultimately responsible for his welfare and would sign the necessary papers. The superintendent thereby satisfied, Yava gained the necessary signature and soon climbed aboard a train bound for Chilocco, where he eventually graduated with a certificate in harness making. However, this additional schooling hardly proved to be a ticket to full employment back in Hopiland. "There didn't seem to be opportunity to earn money. We didn't have much livestock to count on, and I didn't see any way to using that learning I had gotten at school. I got little jobs here and there, and I did the best I could." When Yava landed the position of interpreter at the local Indian agency at a salary of twenty dollars a month, he felt "rich." It was a beginning.[16]

Although attending boarding school was hardly a guarantee of economic security, a significant number of students appear to have drawn upon their education after leaving school. For those who returned to land allotments, courses in agriculture, stock raising, harness making, carpentry, and blacksmithing could be of inestimable value. To be sure, the situation was more problematic for those only able to find employment as teamsters, wood haulers, and road builders or in seasonal agricultural work. Still, in reservation communities, which were all too often economic wastelands, acquiring some education probably helped even these returnees put food on the table. By the end of the century many school returnees began landing prized positions in the burgeoning bureaucracy of the Indian Office. By 1899 returned students had captured 45 percent of some 2,562 positions in the Indian School service. And while most of these were at the level of cooks, shoemakers, laundresses, and seamstresses, it is also noteworthy that 16 percent of the teaching positions and 51 percent of the engineer slots were occupied by returned students. These percentages would decline as the Indian Office retreated from a conscious policy of hiring returnees, but new, more advanced curricula, such as those in commercial and nurse training, enhanced the instrumental value of the boarding school experience. In short, while the material dividends of attending Chilocco, Haskell, Carlisle, or Sherman were not altogether forthcoming, they were not entirely insignificant either.[17]

The third rewarding aspect of the boarding school experience stemmed from the fact that it offered an opportunity for gaining firsthand knowledge about the world beyond the reservation. Getting to school itself could be an adventure. Luther Standing Bear would never forget the day in 1879 that he climbed onto a "long row of little houses standing on long pieces of iron which stretched away as far as we could see." Once the train started to pull away, "We expected something terrible would happen. We held our blankets between our teeth, because our hands were both busy hanging to the seats." The journey would take several days, taking Richard Henry Pratt's first recruits through the "Smokey City," or Chicago, where the Indians were amazed at the size of the buildings. With some of the older students saying that the Indians were being taken to "the place where the sun rises, where they would dump us over the edge of the earth," this first excursion into the white man's world was hardly anxiety free. The second night out of Chicago,

> *"Now the moon was rising, and we were traveling toward it. The big boys were singing brave songs, expecting to be killed any minute. We all looked at the moon, and it was in front of us, but we felt that we were getting too close to it for comfort. We were very tired, and the little fellows dozed off. Presently the big boys woke everybody. They said they had made a discovery. We were told to look out the window and see what had happened*

while we were dozing. We did so, and the moon was now behind us! Apparently we had passed the place where the moon rose!" But as it turned out the Indians' destination was not the edge of the earth but a whole oth- er world—Carlisle Indian school.[18]

Hampton-bound Thomas Wildcat Alford, a Shawnee from Oklahoma, was also made nervous at first by the "shrieking engine and grating noises" of the locomotive, but once he was settled he could appreciate the view from the window: "I recollect the impression made on my mind as we traveled over the beautiful country, and through well cultivated fields, past beautiful homes, and through busy, bustling cities, and small towns. All was so strange to our eyes accustomed only the western prairies and lowlands, or rolling timber hills. The deep, swift rivers, the beautiful mountain scenery, awe inspiring, marvelous. A wonderland indeed!" Similarly, Frank Mitchell recalled that the trip to Fort Defiance took four days by slow-moving wagon. But he mostly enjoyed it, partly because the young Navajos were fed well and given new clothes. "I did not feel lonesome or anything during the trip; I was just glad to going along. I guess everybody kept looking forward to the next town." And sometimes it was the mere anticipation of what lay in store. Max Henley recalled the day he was told that he would be sent away to school: "That's when I became real excited; it was during the summer. When I herded sheep I would think,'I wonder how I'll be talking English? What will I be saying?' Even at night, when I woke, I would be thinking about it. 'I wonder if they'll cut my hair? Will I still have my earrings? What will they do to me? The school children's clothes and shoes are nice. That I know I'll have.' "[19]

Boarding school brought a whole new series of adventures. As difficult as students found the first few days and weeks of boarding school—and this should not be underestimated—this period was also a time of wondrous discovery. Don Talayesva recalls that it was at Keams Canyon that he first sat on a modern toilet, "which was like a spring, and flushed. I was uneasy at first and expected the bowl to overflow; but I caught on quickly and liked it—although it was a waste of water." Flushing toilets were just one of the technological miracles to be observed in the larger off-reservation schools. At these locations students were exposed to the wonders of needle baths, electric lights, steam heating, phonographs, moving pictures, and countless other inventions of the white man. And then there was the classroom experience of struggling through their first lessons learning a new language. Max Henley recalled the pride he felt the first time he scratched on the blackboard a whole sentence: "The sun is shining." It was the first giant step among many in his quest to make sense of the strange sounds spoken by the *bilaganna*. Charles Eastman writes that "when the teacher placed before us a painted globe, and said that our world was like that . . . I felt that my foothold was deserting me." Similarly, a teacher at Hampton Institute reported that after one student completed the assigned task of filling in a map of the Western Hemisphere with pictures of vegetation, animals, and dwellings of the various regions, he "was found gazing at it with folded hands long after the bell had rung for dinner." For this student, as well as many others, the world was much larger than originally supposed.[20]

The so-called outing system was another opportunity for exploring the larger world. Originally conceived by Carlisle's founder, Richard Henry Pratt, the outing program in its purest form was designed to place selected students for extended periods of time in middle-class farm households, where, in exchange for their labor, students would earn a small wage and, more importantly, come to know firsthand the daily expectations, values, and lifeways of their patrons. Although the outing idea—especially as the idea spread to schools in the West—sometimes degenerated into little more than a program for supplying a cheap Indian labor force for employers devoid of philanthropic motives, when carefully monitored it was capable of fulfilling its original objectives. Placed with a farm family, one Carlisle outing student reported back to Pratt: "I am very much oblige to you Capt. and I did not know nothing when I first came here and this time I know everything I got to do. I like farming very well and I think I am going to be a farmer when I get home." A girl in the country wrote: "I am up in my small cozy room. I love this place, they care so kind. I have a good kind father and mother and two little sisters here. They are very sweet little sisters to me." Another girl wrote:

> *I must thank you for senting me to a nice place. I like it very much and the people I stayed with are kind enough. I used to think that I am the shortest girl than anybody else but now I don't for my mistress is a shortest woman. I am taller than her and when she looks at me telling me what to do she have to looked up, but she is very nice kind lady, I like her indeed. I am trying to do without being told and am trying to learn ev-*

ery little things. My mistress likes to have me read, she gave me a book to read and when I got through with it, she give me another one, she helps me on my studies too.

Yet another outing student wrote to Pratt: "I like to see the Ocean once. Can I? If you say my employer will let me go to see the great Ocean."[21]

Field trips were another way for students to see firsthand the land and peoples beyond the school grounds. A remarkable example is the trip some twenty students from the Navajo boarding school at Crown Point, New Mexico, took in the spring of 1937, apparently at the inspiration of the school's superintendent, Hugh Carroll. Over the course of a week or so, the students and several members of the school staff journeyed by bus to southern California, staying at other Indian schools en route, including Sherman Institute. And then it was on to the coast, where they rode on the legendary Long Beach roller coaster that stretched out over the ocean, took a boat to Catalina Island, and even did some deep-sea fishing. Fortunately for historians, these young Navajo sojourners, once home, were asked to write about their experiences. As the following extracts reveal, the Crown Point travelers saw things they could have scarcely imagined.

> **Harry Martin:** *We ride on the roller coaster I almost fall off. Look like it go thrown you into water its near ocean to. I almost lose my hart. I sure scare hear the ocean waving.*

> **Gladys Etcitty:** *The steamer came in about 6:00 clock. It looks so big. It stopped. There were so many people came out of the ship. Mr. Carroll said to us this is the ship that goint to take you to Catalina Island. We went back to Long Beach Trailer Park and there the supper was already to serve.... I didn't even sleep about our trips to Catalina Island that night. I was thinking how the ocean could look like when we get on the steamer ship.*

> **Ben Lopez:** *At zoo we saw ostrich, camels, lions, bears, crow, monkey, kanagross, peacock, turtle, antelope, zebro, badgers, and bad cat.*

> **Juan Lee:** *Most of California are a desert country.*

> **Louise Cowboy:** *And we got some oranges and on we went on until got to Riverside. We stop at Indian School. We saw all kinds of Indians and there were just a few of the Navajo girls, six of*

them.

Jose Dorrance: *After ate our breakfast we went town in Los Angeles which is so crowded that we rode in street car and elevator and escalator when going up stairs. . . . I am very much appreciate about our trip to California which we never been there. Thanks to Mr. Carroll and all others who took us Los Angeles.*[22]

For these twenty Navajo students, the world had gotten a little bigger.

A fourth source of enjoyment was the schools' extracurricular programs. Larger institutions such as Carlisle, Haskell, Phoenix, and Sherman boasted a wide range of athletic, music, and dramatic programs as well as numerous clubs and societies. By the turn of the century, for example, Haskell Institute offered students membership in the YMCA, the YWCA, the school orchestra, several instrumental and vocal groups, the marching band, the Thespian society, three literary societies, and two debating clubs as well as the opportunity to compete in track, baseball, basketball, and football. Because of the growing mystique of football in Indian and white schools alike, and because Haskell was gaining regional notoriety for its performance on the gridiron as the "Carlisle of the West," it is not surprising what the outcome would be in 1906 when one the debating clubs, the Invincibles, debated the question: "Football should be abolished as a school or college game." Just two years before, Haskell had defeated the Universities of Texas, Nebraska, and Kansas, after which it had journeyed to the World's Fair in Saint Louis to test its mettle against the famous Carlisle Indians. In spite of being humiliated by Carlisle 38–4, Haskell had tasted greatness. Hence, in the debate two years later on whether to ban the sport, the negative had a distinct advantage and easily carried the day, the judges voting 3–0 in their favor. The affirmative would have had to face a similar uphill battle in convincing judges at Carlisle, Phoenix, Chilocco, Albuquerque, Sherman, and other institutions that sent their own pigskin warriors onto the gridiron.[23]

Football appealed to students at multiple levels. In addition to providing an opportunity for Indian youth to demonstrate their prowess on the athletic field, it enabled players to travel to distant cities, earned them special treatment in the dining hall, and bestowed upon them the coveted trophies befitting gridiron warriors, including team sweaters bearing a brightly colored C, P, or S. The power of these symbols is revealed in a letter that Pete Calac, Carlisle's team captain, wrote to Superintendent Oscar Lipps in 1915.

Away for the summer on outing with several other team members, Calac wrote to express the players' concerns over rumors of a crackdown on the players' special privileges. After expressing the sentiment that the players deserved special consideration, he added: "Say Mr. Lipps, I would like to ask if you could not get us some different varsity sweaters? I would like these sweaters with big necks. The neck part being old gold and the body red, the end of the sleeves being old gold and the edge of the sweater at the bottom also being old gold." The reason for the request was simple enough: "These other sweaters, it seems, everyone is wearing." Then there is the request of John Flinchum, Carlisle's former Choctaw football captain, who, on the eve of leaving for the battlefields of Europe in 1918, asked the school to send him a school sweater and the letter "C," which he planned to stitch on the sweater. And then he added: "I wish you would send me two of those football seals and colors, one to put on my football certificate and one for my commission as lieutenant." For Flinchum, and presumably many others, these symbolic references to their gridiron victories counted for something.[24]

Then, too, because football schedules frequently pitted Indian teams against all-white ones, gridiron victories provided a forum for building race pride and even for settling old scores—if only metaphorically. Glenn "Pop" Warner, Carlisle's coach for several years, later recalled that his Indian players always displayed a distinctly "racial spirit" when the game was strictly "Indian against the White Man." In such circumstances the players "seemed to recognize the fact that it was upon the athletic field that the Indians had an even chance against their white brothers, and they wanted to show that given an even chance they were the equal of their paleface brothers."

Given Warner's assessment, imagine the emotions running through Carlisle players before a symbol-laden game against Army. Gus Welsh, quarterback in the 1912 game against Army, would later recall how Warner did his best to exploit players' embittered memories just before they took the field. "Warner had no problem getting the boys keyed up for the game. He reminded the boys that it was the fathers and grandfathers of these Army players who fought the Indians. That was enough!" But apparently the Carlisle Indians were not the only team to view football contests as a way of counting symbolic coup on their white opponents. One of Haskell's younger players wrote home: "Our football men are busy each day putting in hard practice for the coming war. We have been mobilizing our troops since the first of September and they are now trained and equipped for the coming campaign."[25]

But pride in the school's pigskin victories spread beyond the locker room. School spirit ran high in football rallies as well as in the grandstands, which reverberated with the songs and yells giving courage and support to gridiron combatants.

> *Hurrah, hurrah, Old Haskell will be there,*
> *Hurrah, hurrah, with touchdowns to spare,*
> *All the Paleface players seem afraid they'll lose their hair*
> *When we go plunging to victory.*[26]

The genuine excitement elicited by a school's gridiron victories is revealed in Esther Burnett Horne's recollection of her years at Haskell in the 1920s. As Horne, a Shoshone from Wyoming, remembers it, at home games "most of the student body attended and got carried away in the excitement of the game." When games were played at a distance from Haskell, students filled the auditorium to follow the ebb and flow of the team's progress by watching a "gridgraph" of the game. Under this system, "A diagram of the playing field was projected onto a screen in the auditorium where we all gathered at game time. There was a movable light projected onto the graph of the field, and as plays were excitedly announced over the speaker system, the light—emblematic of the football—moved to demonstrate what plays were being made. The crowd went wild! We yelled feverishly and got just as excited as when we were watching our team play at home."

Horne reveals yet another benefit that might redound to the much-heralded pigskin heroes. To help players remain in good academic standing, there were always Haskell girls willing to help them out with class assignments. She adds: "It was a combination of hero worship, supporting the team, and resistance to the noncooperative boarding school system."[27]

School officials may have looked the other way at such goings-on. Not so in the case of potentially more dangerous contact between the sexes. Other than in the classroom, and perhaps the dining room, the sexes were generally kept apart, except in carefully monitored moments, such as on Saturday evenings when smaller children tossed bean bags and played other innocent games and older ones came together for waltzes, square dances, and Virginia reels. One teacher at the Fort Mohave school recalls that on such occasions the boys dressed in uniforms and the girls in white dresses, and both conducted themselves in the finest Victorian protocol: "A boy bowed before a girl when requesting a dance, conducted her to her seat afterward and thanked her." Jim Whitewolf, a fifteen-year-old Kiowa Apache, would always remember his first "promenade." Planned by the school staff, this event involved the girls selecting their partners in advance, the boys being kept in the dark as to their partners until the evening of the performance. Somewhat nervous about the upcoming affair, all Whitewolf could do was hope that his partner would be the Comanche girl who had recently sent him a note asking him to be her sweetheart. When the big night finally came,

> We had hair oil on our hair, and we had flowers in our buttonholes, handkerchiefs in our pockets, and our neckties all tied. All of us boys marched in twos. We stood real straight and had our coats buttoned up. There were about ten of us, and we were all seated on a bench in a row. We were facing a big crowd of all the students there. I noticed that there was a chalk line drawn around the floor along the edges where we were all seated. Pretty soon, as we were sitting, all the girls came in dressed in white, with red flowers on. They were sure pretty. My heart was just shaking. I didn't know which was the girl who had invited me. The girls knew who they invited, and they each sat down by the boy they invited. A girl came over and sat down by me. I just sat there real straight. It was the Comanche girl who had written me that note before.

Whitewolf goes on to describe how he and his partner won the competition, which consisted of judging which couple was best able to promenade around the room keeping time to the music. After the prizes were awarded—a cake, a pair of gloves, and a scarf—the various couples were allowed to talk with their dates. He recalled: "I was about fifteen years old at this time. It was the first time I ever had a date with a girl and talked with her like that."[28]

Outside of participating in scripted social rituals like a Victorian promenade or interacting socially in the classroom, contact between the sexes was kept to a minimum. On the other hand, school officials were not always successful in this regard. Anna Moore, who at the age of fourteen met her future husband at Phoenix Indian School, recalled: "We wrote notes because the matron was very strict and only let us see each other at social functions. But sometimes Ross would sneak over to the girls' side of the campus, where we would play croquet until the matron discovered us and shooed Ross back where he belonged. Soon we were going together. We were truly childhood sweethearts." Meanwhile, there were much less innocent goings-on at Keams Canyon, where, according to Edmund Nequatewa, the older boys regularly gained access to the girls' dormitory late at night. "These things must have been planned ahead, because when they got around to the girls' dormitory, the girls had hung down their sheets to pull up the boys." It was the irrepressible Don Talayesva, however, who gives the clearest example of just how enjoyable life at Keams Canyon could be:

> One Saturday afternoon, as I worked alone in the kitchen, I spied Louise on the porch of her dormitory and beckoned through the window for her to come over. After feeding her, I hugged her warmly for the first time, told her that she was a sweet little thing, and that I wanted her for my wife. Then I moved with her gently into the pantry, and locked the door. The little room was crowded and we had to stand and be quick; but she knew what to expect and seemed experienced. It was the first time that I had found and given real pleasure in lovemaking. After that I cared more for her than ever.[29]

This was hardly the kind of extracurricular activity school officials had in mind when they imagined the acculturative dividends to be derived from marching bands, dramatic clubs, and athletic teams. It reminds us, however, that the social world of the boarding school was not without its pleasures, both sponsored and forbidden, whether in the form of eating up yards on the gridiron before cheering fans or silently scaling sheets hung outside a dormitory window in the blackness of night.

A fifth satisfying aspect of boarding school life was the day-to-day humorous moments that served to lighten students' hearts and spirits. Sometimes it was the moment witnessed; sometimes it was the telling of the moment in late-night dormitory whisperings; sometimes it was a carefully orchestrated prank directed at no one in particular; and sometimes it was a made-up story or joke to help them get through the day—or night. The latter was the situation at Haskell, where large rats were heard at night roaming the dormitory. "There was a lot of joking about the rats," Essie Horne recalled. "We'd say they must be carrying little shovels on their backs as they worked in the yard. Or we'd joke about them sweeping and mopping the stairs, saving us from work the next day." Understandably, the rats gave the girls the "creeps." The joking helped. All too frequently the brunt of the story was a student, most probably a new arrival who didn't know which way to pull on his pants, who didn't know what a zipper was, or who ate his first banana with the peel. Essie Horne recalled the time when a girls' group was practicing the Butterfly dance for an upcoming performance of *A Midsummer Night's Dream*: "I became so engrossed in my interpretation that I was unaware that I had fluttered down to one end of the gym while the rest of the troupe had gone the opposite direction. I was rudely jolted back to reality when by best chum . . . began to laugh hysterically."[30]

Not surprisingly, a considerable amount of student humor came at the expense of other students. On one occasion Carlisle's superintendent Pratt received this note from the victim of students' teasing: "Dear Captain Pratt: I am going to tell you something about my name. Captain Pratt, I would like to have a new name because some of the girls call me Cornbread and some call me Cornrat, so I do not like that name, so I want you to give me a new name. Now this is all I want to say." The note was signed Conrad. A bit less innocent but nonetheless funny—to onlookers at least—was the prank pulled on an unsuspecting, short, eighty-seven-pound Creek girl, Marian, newly assigned to kitchen detail at Chilocco. Marian's new job was to cook the oatmeal for nine hundred students and then afterward to clean the huge pot, a project she could only accomplish by standing on a stool. It was on one of these occasions when Marian was precariously balanced on the rim of the pot, her head nearly to the bottom, that disaster struck. One of the older girls casually walked by, removed the stool, and gave Marian a gentle shove. Her feet furiously kicking, head down in soapy water, Marian managed to extricate herself, whereupon she went to the hitherto oblivious cook with a tea towel wrapped around her head and asked to be excused. The fact that she never told on the guilty party (assuming she could identify her) would earn her the respect of the older girls, who greatly enjoyed the entire scene. Meanwhile, there was another story to tell.[31]

Other humorous moments were more public, although this story involving Mrs. William T. Bull, wife of Carlisle's football coach in 1898, was made public only because the *Indian Helper* chose to publish it. This would not be the first time the name Bull would produce smiles on the lips of Carlisle students. Two years before, when William Bull, then a player for Carlisle's arch foe, the University of Pennsylvania, was knocked to the ground, one of Carlisle's gridiron warriors pointed to the grounded Bull and was heard to remark, "Sitting Bull." Fast-forward to 1898. Coach Bull and his wife have just arrived at their new living quarters on the Carlisle campus. Coach Bull is attending to his coaching duties, and Mrs. Bull is at home awaiting the arrival and acquaintance of an Indian girl who is being sent over by the superintendent to assist her with her domestic chores. The said girl arrives. When she enters the room, Mrs. Bull immediately asks her name. But upon hearing the girl's response, she is nothing short of alarmed. In the words of the *Indian Helper*, "the lady of refinement and culture began to look around for protection." And what response would have evoked such panic? The answer lay in the girl's name itself, the only words uttered in response to Mrs. Bull's question, what is your name? The answer: Amelia Kills Bull![32]

And consider the incident at Wind River Boarding School involving Chester Yellow Hair. This crisis was provoked when Yellow Hair, apparently in a moment of frustration, declared in front of his classmates that their teacher, a Mr. Jones, was "Crazy Jones." The recipient of this declaration was so upset by Yellow Hair's act of insolence that he immediately went to the agent, Albert K. Kneale, and demanded that the boy make an apology before the entire school. When Kneale confronted Chester about the episode, he couldn't help but note the lack of remorse. Chester had difficulty seeing why his remark was problematic and simply stated that Jones "don't ought to be so crazy." Still, a carefully worded apology was crafted. The next morning Chester would stand before the entire school and utter the words: "I am sorry I said Mr. Jones is crazy." But Chester's much-anticipated recantation never came off as planned. Instead of saying "I am sorry I said Mr. Jones is crazy," Chester stood up before his Shoshone and Arapaho schoolmates and announced: "I am sorry Mr. Jones is so crazy." What had exactly gone wrong? Agent Kneale attributed the rewording of the sentence and its meaning to the boy's dullness, his inability to memorize the words correctly. But one wonders if something more was involved. Interestingly, Kneale freely admits that teacher Jones was generally regarded as being a little mentally imbalanced. In any event, the deed was done. Jones had now suffered even greater humiliation than before and was soon seen packing his bags. Meanwhile, the students at Wind River presumably were not only relieved at the departure of "Crazy Jones" but had had a good laugh to boot.[33]

A sixth source of pleasure had its origins in the capacity of students to create a social world of their own making. Sometimes the basis for this world was simple friendship; at other times it took the form of organized groups or gangs, frequently but not always drawn along tribal lines. K. Tsianina Lomawaima writes in her history of Chilocco: "Peer relationships were rich and complex and students organized interaction within a miniature society of their own creation." Whatever the organizational basis, students engaged in a host of activities ranging from innocent play, to less innocent pranks, to more politicized acts of cultural solidarity and institutional resistance. In all these activities students found ways of making boarding school life bearable and sometimes enjoyable. There is, of course, a great irony here: that the very oppressiveness of the boarding school regime indirectly contributed to some of students' greatest satisfactions. Then, too, the variety of responses reminds us that although boarding schools were "total institutions," students were not merely passive victims of institutional routine and cultural hegemony.[34]

Unsupervised play was a most welcome escape from the daily regimentation of school life. Don Talayesva tells us that when he grew depressed and considered running away from Keams Canyon, another student prescribed the same antidote to homesickness that had cured him—going down to the livestock pen and riding pigs. "He caught one by the tail and I clambered on its back and rode it about the pen. It was great fun. I felt better when I got off, and thought to myself that if my homesickness returned I would ride a pig again." Esther Horne recalled the time at Haskell when she and a friend posed in a photo group dressed like flappers, complete with "rolled-down hose and hiked up hickories." For added effect, "We rolled up white papers to look like cigarettes and stuck them in the corner of our mouths so we would appear to by worldly." It was all great fun until the photo somehow ended up on the matron's desk. The subsequent punishment of marching around the flagpole shouldering a broomstick may have taken some of the fun out of the episode, but perhaps not all of it. Meanwhile, the older boys at Chilocco took advantage of the weekends and the surrounding acres of woods to escape from the watchful eyes of matrons and disciplinarians. In the woods and along ravines they trapped squirrels and rabbits and then cooked them over campfires and homemade stoves. Stolen eggs, butter, and chickens, together with corn parched on dust pans, only added to the enjoyment.[35]

As these examples show, the lines between innocent play, creative pranks, and outright resistance are hardly distinct. While riding hogs can clearly be dismissed as a fun-filled game, stealing corn from the school silo or butter from the commissary smacks of bold defiance. The point is that students devised endless ways of extracting joy, or at least satisfaction, in an institutional setting hegemonically oppressive in so many of its features. Consider the youthful ingenuity of the so-called Big Seven, a gang of Omaha boys whose activities are so affectionately told by Francis La Flesche. During recess one day, La Flesche recalls, the group loosened the joints of the long stovepipe so that upon reentering the classroom the quick-step marching was sufficient to bring the soot-filled pipe down in a disastrous crash. This apparently accidental event won the boys a "half-holiday." On another occasion the boys discovered a particularly flimsy portion of the hog fence, which prompted them to scatter corn outside the weakened section of fence, just beyond the reach of the hogs. It was in the middle of geography, La Flesche recalls, that the superintendent burst into class shouting that the hogs had broken loose and must be rounded up. "We did not wait to be ordered a second time; but snatching our hats from the pegs in the hall, we ran down the hill with wild shouts and cries. All afternoon we chased pigs, and had a glorious time."[36]

Another means of getting through the routines of boarding school life—and a psychologically satisfying one as well—was to tag a hated member of the staff with a funny or derogatory nickname. Frank Mitchell recalled that at Fort Defiance an especially ugly woman was given the Navajo equivalent of "The-Woman-Who-Makes-You-Scream," while a "mean and skinny" woman won the appellation of "Miss Chipmunk." Anna Shaw recalled that at Phoenix one of the girls became marvelously adept at imitating a despised matron nicknamed "Ho'ok" after the legendary Pima witch. In re-creating the nightly ritual of the bed check, the talented imitator "tied some large nails together so they would jingle like old Ho'ok's keys. Then she would call out in a nasal tone, 'Girls, girls!' How she giggled when she saw us scattering in every direction like scared rabbits."[37]

While nicknaming hated school employees was satisfying psychologically and clearly illustrates that Indians were more than passive victims in the boarding school drama, such behavior was largely negative or defensive in the form of gratification. Presumably even more satisfying were those ways in which students sometimes managed to sustain or even create their cultural allegiances while away at school. Imagine the playground scene at Pine Ridge when a group of Lakota girls, with materials salvaged from sewing class, engaged in the following activity. As a teacher at the school later recalled:

> Thus equipped, following the life patterns they knew, they would set up camps in the several corners of the playground, complete with tepees made of unbleached muslin, about two feet high for the families of Indian dolls made from sticks, covered with brown cloth, with beads for eyes and real hair clipped from their own braids. Their dresses were cut Indian style, decorated with the tiniest of belts and necklaces and moccasins. Wagons would be made of the boxes and spools, to convey them and their belongings when on visits to a camp in the neighborhood corner. There a feast would be prepared from scraps brought from the kitchen. One could see as many as fifty tepees at one time. One group would be encamping, another decamping, and another moving their heavy laden wagons. Sometimes another touch of reality would be seen near a tepee, a tiny horse or dog, molded from the sticky gumbo with twigs for legs and dried in the sun, would be between the poles.[38]

The scene was so impressive that it attracted a crowd of adults just beyond the school fence. The teacher chose not to interfere.

La Flesche recalled that a somewhat similar expression of Native culture occurred at his Presbyterian boarding school when a visitor inquired as to whether the Omaha students knew any tribal songs. To the students' surprise the superintendent gave them permission to sing one of the old songs. "There was some hesitancy," La Flesche remembered, "but suddenly a loud clear voice close to me broke into a Victory song; before a bar was sung another voice took up the song from the beginning, as is the custom among the Indians, then the whole school fell in, and we made the room sing. We understood the song, and knew the emotion of which it was the expression. We felt, as we sang, the patriotic thrill of a victorious people." The visitors were horrified, exclaiming, "That's savage, that's savage! They must be taught music." So, shortly thereafter, La Flesche reports, the class was subjected to a daily singing lesson where the Omahas learned hymns and ballads more suitable to their civilized futures. Meanwhile, for a brief moment they had enjoyed the thrill of connecting with the deep cultural stirrings of their Omaha tradition and had the knowledge that they had counted coup—if ever so briefly—on the white visitors who had inquired if they knew any Indian songs.[39]

But most expressions of Native culture occurred surreptitiously, in those spaces and times of students' own making, when they were beyond the reach of the institution. Much of it was at night. One Mescalero Apache boy recalled that it was in the late-evening hours that "someone in the dormitory would start telling a Coyote story. While it was being told everyone would be quiet. Then at the end of the story, all would break out laughing." But clandestine late-night gatherings went beyond telling Coyote stories. It was at these times that students planned their pranks, concocted ingenious way of slipping off into the night to attend a tribal dance, or perhaps planned escaping the institution altogether. While the school staff at Chilocco slept, students held peyote meetings, and boys gathered in the woods to parch corn over campfires and carry on all-night stomp dances. In a remarkable statement, one former student of the Riverside Indian school in Oklahoma recalled: "I didn't learn my Indian ways at home; I learned them right here [Riverside]."[40]

As the foregoing suggests, boarding schools were complex institutions capable of evoking complex responses. The evidence suggests that many students, for a range of reasons, managed to find solace, promise, and even pleasure in an institutional setting constructed on cultural and political premises of more than dubious standing. The evidence also suggests that somewhere in the mix of ambivalence, accommodation, and resistance, some students came to forge an emotional bond with the institution that had been such an important formative element in their lives. The depth of these ties is reflected in the letter to Hampton Institute from Madeline Stevens, a former student employed as a seamstress at a school for the Osages. The purpose of the letter was to gain her children's entrance into Hampton. "I am every anxious to get them there," she wrote. "If their [*sic*] there even for a term it would be of great benefit to them in the future." She went on to explain that in remembrance of her own time spent at Hampton she had made a quilt out of pieces of girls' dresses she had brought home with her from her beloved alma mater. She called it her "Hampton quilt." Along similar lines, a former Carlisle student wrote Pratt: "I can't help but think of my dear old school days at Carlisle and the wonderful things she has done for me, and the greatest pleasure, to graduate under your leadership of that once great school for the American Indian."[41]

Meanwhile, across the continent, Dorothy Allen wrote a poem about her beloved Sherman Institute, where

Orange trees, with their fruit of gold,
The beauty of which can not be told;
The dear old buildings, grand and tall,
Seem to welcome one and all.

For this student, at least, the years at Sherman were very special ones. Once more, she suspected that other students viewed their situation similarly.

Patiently striving day by day,
Yet proud to own and proud to say
The happiest hours we could demand
Were spent as one of Sherman's band.[42]

Like Polingaysi Qoyawayma, the young Hopi girl who had defied her parents to attend the faraway school in the "land of oranges," so Dorothy Allen had come to Sherman Institute and had not been disappointed. For her and for countless others at similar institutions, the boarding school experience was about more than homesickness, mind-dulling routine, and cultural invasion. It was also about escaping desperate poverty, cheering gridiron warriors on the playing fields of Carlisle or Haskell, or suppressing laughter at a midnight dormitory meeting. We need to factor this variety into our accounts of this fascinating and important moment in Indian history. Until we do so we will have failed to fully understand what it meant to be an Indian away at boarding school.

Notes

1. General studies on the boarding school experience include David Wallace Adams, *Education for Extinction: American Indians and the Boarding School Experience, 1875–1928* (Lawrence: University Press of Kansas, 1995); and Michael C. Cole-

man, *American Indian Children at School, 1850–1930* (Jackson: University Press of Mississippi, 1993). For major case studies see Brenda J. Child, *Boarding School Seasons: American Indian Families, 1900–1940* (Lincoln: University of Nebraska Press, 1999); Clyde Ellis, *To Change Them Forever: Indian Education at the Rainy Mountain Boarding School, 1893–1920* (Norman: University of Oklahoma Press, 1996); Sally Hyer, *One House, One Voice, One Heart: Native American Education at the Santa Fe Indian School* (Santa Fe: Museum of New Mexico Press, 1990); Donal Lindsey, *Indians at Hampton Institute, 1877–1923* (Urbana: University of Illinois Press, 1995); K. Tsianina Lomawaima, *They Called It Prairie Light: The Story of the Chilocco Indian School* (Lincoln: University of Nebraska Press, 1994); Sally J. McBeth, *Ethnic Identity and the Boarding School Experience of West Central Oklahoma American Indians* (Washington DC: University Press of America, 1983); Scott Riney, *The Rapid City Indian School, 1898–1933* (Norman: University of Oklahoma Press, 1999); Robert A. Trennert, *The Phoenix Indian School: Forced Assimilation in Arizona, 1891–1935* (Norman: University of Oklahoma Press, 1988); and Genevieve Bell, "Telling Stories Out of School: Remembering the Carlisle Indian Industrial School, 1879–1918" (Ph.D. diss., Stanford University, 1998).

2. In particular see Lomawaima, *They Called It Prairie Light*, 124–25; Child, *Boarding School Seasons*, 24–25, 100; Ellis, *To Change Them Forever*, 96; Trennert, *Phoenix Indian School*, 207–8; and Riney, *Rapid City Indian School*, 221.

3. For the complexity of student response see Adams, *Education for Extinction*, chaps. 7 and 8; Coleman, *American Indian Children at School*, esp. chaps. 4, 8, and 9; Michael C. Coleman, "The Symbiotic Embrace: American Indians, White Educators, and the School, 1820s–1920s," *History of Education* 25 (1996): 1–18; McBeth, *Ethnic Identity*, chaps. 6–8; and Lomawaima, *They Called it Prairie Light*, 123–25.

4. See McBeth, *Ethnic Identity*, chap. 6. For a different view see Coleman, *American Indian Children at School*, 197–98.

5. Polingaysi Qoyawayma [Elizabeth White], *No Turning Back: A True Account of a Hopi Indian Girl's Struggle to Bridge the Gap between the World of Her People and the World of the White Man*, as told to Vada F. Carlson (Albuquerque: University of New Mexico Press, 1964), 49–54.

6. Thomas Wildcat Alford, *Civilization, and the Story of the Absentee Shawnees*, as told to Florence Drake (Norman: University of Oklahoma Press, 1936), 90. Also see his account on pp. 104–7. Alford goes on to say that the chiefs were adamant on the point that two youths must not abandon their Shawnee religion for that of the white man's or they would forfeit their right to become chiefs. This was a promise Alford was unable to keep. Francis La Flesche, *The Middle Five: Indian School Boys of the Omaha Tribe* (1900; reprint, Madison: University of Wisconsin Press, 1963), 127–28. Coleman, *American Indian Children at School*, 60. Coleman calculates that of the 69 out of 109 narrators providing information on the reasons for attending school the breakdown is as follows: compelled by "authorities"—17; sent by tribal members—33; overlapping influences—9; and personal choice—10. For the variety of parental and tribal attitudes see Adams, *Education for Extinction*, 210–22, 244–55.

7. Charlotte J. Frisbie and David P. McAllester, *Navajo Blessingway Singer: The Au-

tobiography of Frank Mitchell, 1881–1967 (Albuquerque: University of New Mexico Press), 56, 62, 68.

8. *Indian Leader,* March 1915, 4, 6.

9. McBeth, *Ethnic Identity,* 109; Child, *Boarding School Seasons,* 15–16. The appeal of boarding schools must have been especially strong for orphans who found in the institution a degree of material and physical security increasingly unavailable in tribal societies, many of which had seen their kinship systems and economies vitiated by long-term contact with whites. See Marilyn Irvin Holt, *Indian Orphanages* (Lawrence: University Press of Kansas, 2001), 37–40, 48.

10. The quote is found in *Native American,* April 10, 1915, n.p. Also see *Proceedings of the Lake Mohonk Conference of Friends of the Indian,* 1896, Lake Mohonk, New York, 11–12; *Native American,* October 19, 1907, 331.

11. *Southern Workman,* April 1879, 43–44.

12. *Native American,* October 28, 1916, 295–96. Although this exchange took place at a day school, the logic of the teacher's appeal would have applied to the boarding school environment as well.

13. For descriptions of boarding schools' industrial and outing programs see Adams, *Education for Extinction,* 149–63; Trennert, *Phoenix Indian School,* 46–47, 51–54, 68–76, 87–92, 100–101, 123–24, 136–38, 167–68; Robert A. Trennert, "From Carlisle to Phoenix: The Rise and Fall of the Indian Outing System, 1878–1930," *Pacific Historical Review* 52 (August 1983): 267–91; Riney, *Rapid City Indian School,* chap. 3; Child, *Boarding School Seasons,* chap. 6; Lomawaima, *They Called It Prairie Light,* 65–90; Jean A. Keller, *Empty Beds: Native American Student Health at Sherman Institute,* 1902–1922 (East Lansing: Michigan State University, 2002), chap. 3; and Bell, "Telling Stories Out of School," chap. 5.

14. *Native American,* October 19, 1907, 331.

15. "Max Hanley," in *Stories of Traditional Navajo Life and Culture,* ed. Broderick H. Johnson (Tsaile az: Navajo Community College Press, 1977), 41; *Red Man,* September 1891, 2; *Indian Helper,* September 27, 1889, 2.

16. Harold Courlander, ed., *Big Falling Snow: A Tewa-Hopi Indian's Life and Times and the History and Traditions of His People* (Albuquerque: University Press of New Mexico, 1978), 12–21.

17. Adams, *Education for Extinction,* 283–92; Wilbert H. Ahern, "The Returned Indians: Hampton Institute and Its Indian Alumni, 1879–1893," *Journal of Ethnic Studies* 10 (winter 1983): 101–24: and Ahern, "An Experiment Aborted: Returned Indian Students in the Indian School Service, 1881–1908," *Ethnohistory* 44 (spring 1997): 263–304.

18. Luther Standing Bear, *My People, the Sioux* (1928; reprint, Lincoln: University of Nebraska Press, 1963), 131. The entire story is found on pp. 128–32.

19. Alford, *Civilization,* 95; Frisbie and McAllester, *Navajo Blessingway Singer,* 59; and "Max Henley," 31.

20. Don Talayesva, *Sun Chief: The Autobiography of a Hopi Indian,* ed. Leo Simmons (New Haven: Yale University Press, 1942), 107; "Max Hanley," 33; and Charles A. Eastman, *From the Deep Woods to Civilization* (Boston: Little, Brown, 1923), 47.

21. Quotations taken from the *Red Man,* September 1891, 2–3. Needless to say, not

all outing placements were successful, and Carlisle students appear to have been quite willing to express their discontent in letters to Pratt, just as patrons sometimes voiced their displeasure with students. In addition to the above see the *Red Man*, June 1895, 1–4.

22. Records of the Bureau of Indian Affairs, Record Group 75, Eastern Navajo Agency, Central Classified Files, 1926–1939, file 806 Miscellaneous, box 67, National Archives, Laguna Niguel, California.

23. *Indian Leader*, October 26, 1906, 1. On the importance of clubs and societies to the school program see *Annual Report of the Superintendent of Indian Schools, 1897*, in *Annual Report of the Commissioner of Indian Affairs, 1897*, 55th Cong., 2nd sess., House Document no. 5, Serial no. 3641. The role of athletics—especially football—in Indian schools has recently received a good deal of scholarly attention. See Michael Oriard, *Reading Football: How the Popular Press Created an American Spectacle* (Chapel Hill: University of North Carolina Press, 1993), 229–47; David Wallace Adams, "More Than a Game: The Carlisle Indians Take to the Gridiron, 1893–1917," *Western Historical Quarterly* 32 (spring 2001): 25–53; John Bloom, *To Show What an Indian Can Do: Sports at Native American Boarding Schools* (Minneapolis: University of Minnesota Press, 2000); Bloom, "'There Is Madness in the Air': The 1926 Haskell Homecoming and Popular Representations of Sports in Federal Indian Boarding Schools," in *Dressing in Feathers: The Construction of the Indian in American Popular Culture*, ed. S. Elizabeth Bird (Boulder: Westview Press, 1996), 97–110; Keith A. Sculle, "'The New Carlisle of the West': Haskell Institute and Big-Time Sports, 1920–1932," *Kansas History* 17 (autumn 1994): 192–208; and Linda Peavy and Ursula Smith, "World Champions: The 1904 Girls' Basketball Team from Fort Shaw Indian Boarding School," *Montana: The Magazine of Western History* 51 (winter 2001): 2–25.

24. Records of the Bureau of Indian Affairs, Record Group 75, Carlisle Indian School Student Records, 1879–1918, Entry 1327, file nos. 4550, 5638, National Archives, Washington DC.

25. Glenn Warner, "The Difference between Red and White Football Material," *Literary Digest*, May 11, 1920, 78–79. Also see Warner, "The Indian Massacres," *Colliers*, October 17, 1931, 7. Welsh is quoted in Robert W. Wheeler, *Jim Thorpe: The World's Greatest Athlete* (Norman: University of Oklahoma Press, 1975), 128. The Haskell player is quoted in *Indian Leader*, October 9, 1914, 3.

26. *Indian Leader*, January 2, 1914, 5. Also see Claude Maxwell Stauffer, comp., *Songs and Yells* (Carlisle: Carlisle Indian Press, n.d.); and *Sherman Bulletin*, November 10, 1922, 4.

27. Esther Burnett Horne and Sally McBeth, *Essie's Story: The Life and Legacy of a Shoshone Teacher* (Lincoln: University of Nebraska Press, 1998), 46.

28. Minnie Braithwaite Jenkins, *Girl from Williamsburg* (Richmond VA: Dietz Press, 1951), 261; Jim Whitewolf, *The Life of a Kiowa Apache Indian*, ed. Charles S. Brant (New York: Dover, 1969), 91–92. For a discussion of gender relations in boarding schools see Adams, *Education for Extinction*, 173–81.

29. Anna Moore Shaw, *A Pima Past* (Tucson: University of Arizona Press, 1974), 137; Edmund Nequatewa, *Born a Chief: The Nineteenth Century Boyhood of Edmund*

Nequatewa as told to Alfred F. Whiting, ed. P. David Seaman (Tucson: University of Arizona Press, 1993), 92; and Talayesva, *Sun Chief*, 111, 117–18.

30. Horne and McBeth, *Essie's Story*, 38–39, 43.

31. Quoted in Richard Henry Pratt, *Battlefield and Classroom: Four Decades with the American Indian, 1867–1904*, ed. Robert M. Utley (New Haven: Yale University Press, 1964), 293; Lomawaima, *They Called It Prairie Light*, 130.

32. *Indian Helper*, March 18, 1898, 4.

33. Albert H. Kneale, *Indian Agent* (Caldwell ID: Caxton Printers, 1950), 124–25.

34. Lomawaima, *They Called It Prairie Light*, 130; Coleman, *American Indian Children at School*, 130–32. Coleman, however, makes a valuable point when he argues that historians run the risk of misrepresenting the reality of the boarding school environment when they "over-empower" students' responses. See Coleman, "The Symbiotic Embrace," 3, 17.

35. Simmons, *Sun Chief*, 97; Horne and McBeth, *Essie's Story*, 40–41; Lomawaima, *They Called It Prairie Light*, 135–38.

36. La Flesche, *The Middle Five*, 67–68.

37. Mitchell, *Navajo Blessingway Singer*, 66; Moore, *A Pima Past*, 135. Also see Lomawaima, *They Called It Prairie Light*, 48; and McBeth, *Ethnic Identity*, 129.

38. Thisba Huston Morgan, "Reminiscences of My Days in the Land of the Ogalalla Sioux," *Report and Historical Collections* (South Dakota State Historical Society) 19 (1958): 28–29.

39. La Flesche, *The Middle Five*, 100.

40. Morris E. Opler, *Apache Odyssey: A Journey between Two Worlds* (New York: Holt, Rinehart, and Winston, 1969), 87; Lomawaima, *They Called It Prairie Light*, 139–40; and McBeth, *Ethnic Identity*, 176.

41. Reprinted in *Southern Workman*, June 1897, 11; George E. Balenti to Richard Henry Pratt, December 1, 1920, Richard Henry Pratt Papers, Beinecke Rare Book and Manuscript Library, Yale University.

42. *Sherman Bulletin*, December 21, 1910, 1.

2. "We Had a Lot of Fun, but of Course, That Wasn't the School Part"

Life at the Rainy Mountain Boarding School, 1893–1920

Clyde Ellis

Clyde Ellis, professor of history at Elon University, is a well-known scholar of American Indians on the Great Plains. He has published many books
and articles, including *A Dancing People: Pow Wow Culture on the Southern Plains*. Ellis spends a good deal of his time among Kiowas, Comanches,
and Apaches of southwestern Oklahoma. Through his writings he helps
us understand American Indian history and culture from within Native
communities. He is best known for his classic work *To Change Them Forever: Indian Education at the Rainy Mountain Boarding School, 1893–1920*.
Using secondary sources, archival documents, and extensive oral histories, he offers us the present essay.

The Office of Indian Affairs operated the Rainy Mountain Boarding
School in the shadow of Sepyalda, a sacred mountain. Unlike Carlisle,
Sherman, Haskell, and other better-known schools, the Rainy Mountain school was situated on a reservation. Ellis points out that students
at Rainy Mountain suffered the same loneliness, harsh punishments, and
cultural assaults found at other Indian boarding schools. However, he
offers oral histories which confirm that many former Indian students at
Rainy Mountain gained a great deal from their education and found their
boarding school days "well worth the time." Some Kiowas have called the
school the backbone of the Kiowa nation because it became an "Indian"
school where children learned to combine two worlds. Former students remember dancing, enjoying Christmas and other holidays, singing, playing
sports, and conducting a student circus complete with a gorilla and buffalo. The school is gone, but elders say the souls of the children remain at the
site, where one former student buried marbles to mark his childhood.

On a clear, windy afternoon in August 1990, ninety-two-year-old Parker
McKenzie, a Kiowa from Mountain View, Oklahoma, pointed to the ramshackle remains of the Rainy Mountain Boarding School and told me, "That
was where I got my start in life." The ruins to which he pointed lay in the

center of what had once been a reservation boarding school where hundreds of young Kiowas endured what federal officials hoped would be a transformative experience. In a remote corner of southwest Oklahoma's sprawling Kiowa-Comanche-Apache Reservation, government teachers struggled for nearly three decades to make the vision of a new Indian race a reality. Crowded into the dormitories and classrooms that lay in the shadow of the place they called Sepyalda, Kiowa children toiled to learn the lessons that officials believed would make them indistinguishable from whites. It was an ambitious plan, for schooling meant more than simply learning English and industrial skills; it was to be the definitive moment in the metamorphosis of a people. Writing to the commissioner of Indian Affairs in 1899, Rainy Mountain's superintendent, Cora Dunn, put the matter bluntly: "Our purpose is to change them forever." Places like Rainy Mountain, to echo David Wallace Adams's insightful phrase, proposed to use education for extinction.[1]

But a funny thing happened on the way to assimilation via the ABCs. As a generation of scholarship has revealed, schools became places where the construction of identity was deeply contested, where time and time again Indian people proved both more receptive to learning and more resilient in culturally contextualizing that learning than policy makers ever imagined. As K. Tsianina Lomawaima has reminded us, places like Rainy Mountain truly became "Indian schools," for more often than not it was students—not administrators—who determined the day-to-day routines. This is not to suggest that boarding schools were anything less than wrongheaded experiments that wagered with students' lives as if they were dice to be rolled. Schools were too often the sites of cruel, even horrific, treatment. But looking only at that side of the experience tells what we have known for decades and tends to obscure the more complicated realities of school life. This is not to dismiss the stories of abuse and misery, but it is to suggest that another line of inquiry, one based in this case on conversations in the Kiowa community with former students and their relatives, suggests somewhat more complex narratives than the ones typically offered up. Three things form the core of my comments: the tribe's somewhat unexpected but deeply rooted support for the school, the experiences of students themselves, and the school's long-term legacy for the Kiowa community.[2]

Conversations about school days with members of the Kiowa community offered compelling, often contradictory, and always complicated accounts of their life as boarding school students. As with all sources, some caveats are in order. Because much of what follows rests on memories that reach back to the early twentieth century, the question of reliability is legitimately raised. Despite the caution with which these sources must be used, it is nevertheless true that they have a potency and resonance that are absent in the school's official records. Certainly, they tell us a great deal about how some members of the community have negotiated their own accounts of the past. And as Michael Coleman reminds us, oral accounts are credible sources in their own right: "The school obviously was such a radically new experience that it imprinted itself deeply upon the minds of the narrators—they recalled the arrival with special vividness. Further, most of them began life in oral cultures, where accurate recall and the faultless performance of ritual and other duties were seen as vital to survival. This is not to claim that memory is infallible in such cultures, merely that the deeply ingrained need to remember accurately did not dissolve the moment the narrators entered the school gates."[3]

Lomawaima makes the same argument in her work on Chilocco. The sixty-one former students who spoke to her expressed different opinions and memories, but collectively they created a mosaic that captured the rhythms of boarding school life more completely than official sources alone ever could. "Marked inalterably by the communion of shared experience," she writes, former students knew that "the memories one has been entrusted with cannot be laid aside or relegated to the attic of the soul or the mind."[4]

As Coleman and Lomawaima suggest, Indian schools were complicated places. And as with so many other culturally loaded encounters, Indian education could be—and often was—used by Native people to serve multiple ends that included maintaining identity. That Indian people used the schools to suit their needs and purposes is an important consideration, for it raises the often-overlooked notion of agency. I am not suggesting that Indian children somehow gained control of every school or were always able to avoid the abuse and misery that seem to have been constants at every school, but the fact that schools largely failed to destroy Indian identity begs questions about how and why that failure occurred. It can be explained in part by a lack of support from federal bureaucrats, but it can also be explained by what Indian children and their parents were doing to counteract the assimilationist agenda under which schools ran. Contrary to policy makers' ideas, schooling was *not* an example of how to successfully implement an assimilationist blueprint.

Indeed, quite the opposite occurred time and time again. From the most remote day schools to the largest off-reservation schools, assimilation failed. Indian schools were not laboratories in which children were simply remolded into copies of white, middle-class America. Instead, schools were a cross-cultural encounter in which Indians and whites alike negotiated a complicated set of cultural boundaries. And because Indian schools never achieved assimilation (as federal policy makers understood the term), shouldn't we should resist the temptation to employ assimilation models to frame our discussions? Such models do little more than tell us what bureaucrats *hoped* would happen, and they often ignore what *did* happen. Writing from the vantage point of assimilation models tells us about policy and its failures, but it tells us almost nothing about experience. From an ethnographic point of view, multiple strands of experience are at work here. Some of them confirm our widely held ideas about how schools did more harm than good. Others suggest that, like Parker McKenzie, many students lived in a world of competing interests and influences in which they found it possible to maintain important connections to their tribal life. Listening to these voices reveals experiences, attitudes, and encounters that add immeasurably to our understanding of the contours of boarding school life. They reveal the low moments that characterized the life of every student, and they give us an important perspective on the loneliness and desperation that afflicted many children. But they also suggest experiences that are plainly at odds with conventional wisdom and widely held ideas about boarding school life. It wasn't a perfect life, and it wasn't what they deserved, but by any measure, conversations in the Kiowa community suggest that life at a place like Rainy Mountain was more than an exercise in resistance, oppression, and misery.

Perhaps the most obvious place to begin is at that wrenching moment when parents saw their children taken off to the schools. While popular opinion holds that most Indian families resisted enrolling their children at every turn, the reality was usually somewhat less clear cut. When we listen to the Kiowa community's conversations about enrolling their children, a very different narrative emerges. While there were always families that resisted the schools, families in the Rainy Mountain district were generally willing and often eager from the very beginning to have their children enrolled.

Some families believed that education and training meant a more secure future. Others hoped the schools would provide the food, clothing, and shelter that were too often in short supply on the reservations. Some children went to be with relatives or because they had no other viable choice.[5] Myrtle Ware, for example, said that she was enrolled at Rainy Mountain in 1898 because her family was poor. Living at the time with an aunt and uncle in a tipi near Anadarko, Ware recalled being told "I can't be taken care of down this way . . . [my aunt] took me up there to Rainy Mountain. She asked my dad, 'I wanta put her up to school there, where I'll go and see her,' and I went up that way." Annie Bigman, born in 1900, arrived at Rainy Mountain between 1904 and 1905 for similar reasons. "Daddy started me to school when I was about four years old," she stated. "He was sick then," she added. "He don't want to take care of a little one so he pushed me to school."[6]

Guy Quoetone (pronounced "kwee-tone") was born in 1885 and attended John Jasper Methvin's Methodist Institute south of Anadarko before switching to Rainy Mountain. He would have gone to one of the agency schools in Anadarko, he said, "if my father hadn't already have joined the Methodist church." However, Quoetone explained that "when we started to school" his father "wanted me to go to that school [Methvin] and dedicated me and sent me." When asked why he transferred to Rainy Mountain, he replied, "Well . . . we lived closer to Rainy Mountain." He also recalled that he told his father, "Maybe they might give me better grades, but they didn't."[7]

Lewis Toyebo (pronounced "toy-bow") got to Rainy Mountain because a relative prevented missionaries from carrying him away to another school. In 1897, at the age of five or six, Toyebo and a playmate were on horseback headed for a mission school when a relative "chased us down and made us get off." Pondering the incident nearly ninety years later, Toyebo mused, "We might have been preachers." He recalled that "Daddy and Mother told me they were to take me to Rainy Mountain School," where Toyebo spent the next decade, eventually becoming an assistant disciplinarian. Interestingly, his father, Edward, attended school with his son after Cora Dunn granted him permission to stay on the school grounds and attend classes: "While his progress has been slow, as might be expected at his age, during his three years . . . at school he has learned to read and write and can speak English with sufficient ease to make a very acceptable interpreter for the missionary." Deprived of educational advantages in his boyhood, Toyebo late in life determined to educate himself. For several years he struggled along with no other help than his little boy during vacations.[8]

Sarah Long Horn, born in 1902, entered Rainy Mountain in 1910 with a cousin:

> We mostly was raised together, and I always want to be with her. . . . I went down there to see that girl. They say she's going to school, so I went to visit her and she begged for me to stay. So I thought to myself, I'll stay for a few days and then I'll go back. Then when the time came, well I was already in school. So I just stayed there and never did go back home . . . that's how I got to school. I went to school myself. By going visiting, she asked me to stay, so I just stayed with her.[9]

James Haumpy entered Rainy Mountain in the fall of 1913 at about the age of thirteen when his parents sent him to school to be with "those other boys they was schooling out there." Haumpy found little solace in that fact: "I was a little boy. I don't know how to talk English. They put me in school. Well, I ain't used to it. And I cried and cried, I wanna go home." Like other young Kiowas, Haumpy went because his parents wanted him to and because other Kiowa children were there as well. He also remembered that once he got over his initial displeasure, Rainy Mountain was not entirely unpleasant: "I seen pretty girls at that school," he remembered. Parker McKenzie said that by the time his parents enrolled him and his brother Daniel in 1904, "most of the Kiowas already were impressed of the benefits of education and took advantage of schooling." The Rainy Mountain school was well known to the Kiowas, he added, and "no one had to inform them about the schools, they were on hand and saw them."[10]

The willingness of the Kiowas and Comanches to enroll their children compels us to reconsider the conventional wisdom that tribes usually resisted the schools and used any means available to keep their children out of the hands of government teachers. Although resistance did occur on the Kiowa-Comanche-Apache Reservation, parents showed a surprising willingness to enroll their children. Ironically, one of the most common complaints lodged with the agent concerned the lack of schools, not the fact that they were being forced to enroll their children. When Agent James Haworth turned students away in 1875 because he lacked adequate space and teachers (he could accommodate only about sixty of the reservation's nearly six hundred school-age children), Kiowas bitterly objected. Some parents offered to pay for schooling, and one headsman reportedly offered a pony to get his child into school. "They are now very anxious to know when the school will commence again," Haworth wrote. "I will be glad if I could tell them soon." Twenty-one years later, a delegation of Kiowas reminded the commissioner of Indian Affairs that "we have placed our children in schools provided by the government. . . . We point to these facts as evidence that we are striving in the right way to fit our people for the day when we realize we must come to the end of the reservation." Individual students echoed this sentiment. Eugenia Mausape entered the schools because her parents "think it's good way." Cecil Horse attended both the Methvin Institute and Rainy Mountain to learn what his father called "the right way of living."[11]

Important support for the school also came from well-placed authorities inside the tribe. In August 1905, Big Tree, an influential Kiowa and former opponent of reservation life (he eventually became a Baptist), dictated a letter to Agent James Randlett after the agent had solicited the chief's help in getting the school filled. Big Tree replied, "I will tell the people to put these children in school. . . . We are going to the Ghost Dance Friday and I will let the people know about the school and tell them to put these children in school." Jim Whitewolf remembered that Henry Brownbear, a Kiowa Apache chief, told the agent that all of the tribe's school-age children ought to be enrolled and that any parent who resisted should not receive rations.[12]

Not every Kiowa parent was anxious to surrender a child, however, and some doggedly refused to comply. In September 1900, for example, allotment negotiations prompted embittered parents to keep their children at home in an attempt to force concessions. Superintendent Dunn reported only two dozen students on campus at the end of the opening week; in past years opening week had brought in an average of seventy-five children. "The Kiowas are in an ugly frame of mind over the terms of the allotment treaty," she reported, "and are determined to be as annoying as possible. If the children do not come in by the first of the coming week," she concluded, "some coercive measures will have to be used to fill the school." A group of Kiowa parents remedied the situation when they collected enough children to open the school. On another occasion, Dunn reported to the agent that disputes over annuity payments had led Kiowas and Comanches to hold their chil-

dren out of school. Quanah Parker, Big Tree, and local bankers interested
in "stirring up the Indians," wrote Dunn, had convinced Kiowa parents to
"keep their children out of school altogether." Unable to convince parents
to comply with regulations ("persuasion is worse than useless in the present state of mind," she wrote), Dunn concluded that "all I can do is to wait
until the pending questions are adjusted" and hope that some of the "right-
minded Indians" would enroll their children.[13]

Once they enrolled at Rainy Mountain, Kiowa youngsters entered a new
world designed to replace all that they had known. For nearly forty weeks a
year they lived according to a regimen rooted in white, middle-class models
of diligence, individualism, and discipline. It was to be a wholly transforming experience in which no detail was too small to be spared, no lesson too
limited to be ignored. What Indian children learned, and how they learned
it, observes Bruce David Forbes, had enormous implications: "More than
simply offering an education in certain subjects, the boarding school lifted
young people out of native contexts and immersed them in white, American culture. The intention was to raise godly, civilized, educated children,
with all the implications that those words carried. The goals were difficult
to achieve if the child remained in touch with old ways and life-styles; the
separation of the boarding school made children more educable in new
patterns."[14]

The change began immediately upon arrival. Because officials linked
physical appearance to a civilized life, the children went through a process
designed to sever their physical and material connections to their tribal
world. Guy Quoetone recalled that he was "still in my Kiowa costume" the
first time his parents left him at the Methvin Institute. Before the hour was
over, he had been subjected to a series of humiliations that he remembered
years later in an interview. After assuring his parents, "You don't have to
worry. Just don't come back for about a month or two. . . . He'll be alright,"
staff members ushered Quoetone into a room where two men and a woman waited for him:

> They shut the door and about that time I get excited and they got a chair.
> This man set me there and they commence to hold me. He set me down
> in that chair and that lady talked to me and tried to get my attention.
> While I was talking at her . . . this barber . . . he come from behind and
> cut one side of my braid off. . . . About that time I jumped up and they

grabbed me and hold me down. And I turned tiger! I commenced to fight and scratch and bite and jump up in the air! They had a time, all of them, holding me down. Cut the other side. Two men had me down there and that white lady tried to hold my head and then that barber cutting all the time. It was almost an hour before he finished cutting my hair. And you ought to see how I looked. I sure hate a haircut![15]

All the students received uniforms that, like haircuts, deliberately subordinated Kiowa culture and imposed new forms of discipline and order. At Methvin, Guy Quoetone remembered getting "a suit—jeans—kind of grey." During Annie Bigman's Rainy Mountain years, the girls wore gray uniforms that resembled sleeveless jumpers. A white blouse, black shoes, and stockings completed the ensemble. Boys wore "little brown suits. Boys' knee pants. Brown caps." Sarah Long Horn's uniforms had a distinctly military look and included hair ribbons identifying them as members of company A, B, or C. Lewis Toyebo also remembered a martial look to his clothes: "Our school uniforms were grey with red stripes. . . . We were a sight on earth." Juanita Yeahquo, a Kiowa who attended the Riverside School in Anadarko, described her uniforms as "awful clothes. . . . I guess we got prison uniforms and didn't know it." She especially disliked the fact that girls wore heavy boots.[16]

For many students, the transformation also included a new name. Because administrators and teachers thought tribal names a babble of indecipherable syllables, they translated them whenever possible or used what John Wesley Powell described as "suitable or euphonic" replacements. Kiowa surnames were often anglicized and combined with new first names, as with Guy Quoetone, who was named after the principal at the Methvin Institute. Eugenia Mausape was named after Mrs. Methvin's sister. Isabel Horse was named after Isabel Crawford, the missionary at nearby Saddle Mountain Mission. Her surname was the English translation of *tsatoke*, the Kiowa word for horse. Sometimes the transition was not very smooth, and more than one student remembered being disconcerted by the fuss over new names. Ethel Howry, for example, remembered being confused when summoned by a name she neither recognized nor understood.[17]

As part of a plan designed to replace familiar customs with a bewildering array of new cultural looks and practices, Rainy Mountain students were strictly separated by age and sex in all aspects of life. Matrons hovered over their wards and were unstinting in their punishment when students crossed the line. "Keeping the sexes apart was routinely strict," said Parker McKenzie. "We were under strict discipline, we were never free." Boys and girls maintained separate living quarters, ate at separate tables, occupied different portions of the same classrooms, and were kept apart at chapel services. School officials allowed them to mix only at the school's carefully chaperoned social functions, and even then it was not quite an open field. Students "all marched to and from such events in military order—and separately, too."[18]

Students flirted, but they also recognized the line separating boys and girls, and "most feared to cross it," McKenzie recalled. Sarah Long Horn remembered that boys often tried to find ways around the wall of separation by attempting an occasional daring foray into the girls' dorm. The odds of success were long, however, and there were more auspicious moments. For example, when students made the trek to Boake's Trading Post, about a mile from the campus, they often tried to sneak away with their sweethearts. Staff members guarded against such escapes, however, and often foiled the best-laid plans. "They watch us real close," Sarah Long Horn said. "There's got to be one teacher up in front and there's got to be somebody else in the back that will watch the boys and the girls." Fred Bigman grumpily recalled that "we never did get to talk to any girls."[19]

Like all boarding schools, Rainy Mountain ran according to a military regimen. William Collins Jr., a Ponca who attended the Pawnee Boarding School in the 1930s, recalled that "the most profound aspect of my sojourn at the Pawnee Indian School is the specter of discipline. Discipline in its most rigid, non-yielding, almost brutal, shocking and galling state. Non-Indian was the order of the day."[20] Administrators organized students into companies or squads and designated older pupils as cadet sergeants. A former Riverside student said that boarding school "was really a military regime. . . . Every year an official from Fort Sill would come down and review our companies and our drilling maneuvers. We marched everywhere, to the dining hall, to classes; everything we did was in military fashion. We were taught to make our beds in military fashion, you know, with square corners and sheets and blankets tucked in a special way. . . . On Sundays we had an inspection . . . just like the military."[21]

Those who stepped outside the bounds received quick lessons. "Everything you do, you get punished," recalled a former Riverside student. Another Riverside student remembered that school officials openly distrusted students, "treated you like a criminal," and allowed the older girls to "slap them [younger girls] around." Disciplinary responses ran the gamut from stern lectures to sadistic whippings. William Collins Jr. remembered feeling like "a lamb ready for the slaughter. We were like dumb driven cattle— unable to help ourselves and no help forthcoming."[22]

By far the most common infraction was speaking Kiowa. Getting caught meant enduring a variety of punishments, including soapy toothbrushings, extra drill duty, carrying stepladders on the shoulders for several hours, or restriction from social events. One former Rainy Mountain student remembered being forced to hold quinine tablets in her mouth for speaking Kiowa. Sarah Long Horn said that boys caught speaking Kiowa had to wear sandwich boards reading "I like girls." At other schools administrators forced boys to wear dresses. Jim Whitewolf's punishment for speaking his language was two days in the laundry with the girls, wearing an apron and washing socks. Rainy Mountain girls stood face-first in room corners for speaking Kiowa. Myrtle Ware said that getting caught speaking Kiowa brought demerits that restricted trips and outings: "There's one of the matrons, you know, she goes around and listens . . . when one of them gets six marks, they don't let them go to the store."[23]

For all of the attention given to eradicating the Kiowa language, however, the campaign rarely succeeded. Children carried on conversations in Kiowa "when the matron ain't listening," said Myrtle Ware. Despite the punishments they had to endure, McKenzie said that Kiowa "nevertheless remained the dominant language away from the campus, particularly with the younger boys." McKenzie wooed his future wife, Nettie, by passing her messages in phonetically written Kiowa, a practice that prevented teachers from confiscating the notes and reading them out loud. McKenzie's syllabary led eventually to the first written form of the Kiowa language. Others carried on what amounted to whispered courtships that escaped the attention of matrons.[24] Away from school, Kiowa remained the language used in the majority of Indian homes where the children went for holiday visits and the summer break. Many (if not most) students became bilingual and never relinquished their native tongue, a costly failure in light of the school's mission. The survival of the Kiowa language meant that an important barrier to assimilation remained in place. The full meaning of this became clear in the decades that followed when the generations of young people who went through the school became a galvanizing force in the continuation of Kiowa culture and took a central role in transmitting crucial knowledge and traditions.

By far the most serious offense short of violence or sexual misconduct was running away. According to its official records, Rainy Mountain suffered only about two dozen runaways during its twenty-seven-year history. It is unlikely that this is an accurate count; school officials were reluctant to admit that runaways even occurred and tended to consider only repeat offenders as true runaways. Moreover, if children returned within a reasonable amount of time (usually several days), the offense was not recorded as a runaway. In March 1918, for example, Rainy Mountain superintendent R. W. Bishoff nonchalantly reported to the agent that one of his students "deserted from our school about a week ago and I have heard that he is with his mother at Anadarko. If not too much trouble will you have your police find out if he is around there and let us know."[25]

Some runaways were lonely, others were scared, and a few simply did not intend to stay in school. A Wichita girl who attended Riverside in the late 1910s said, "I don't exactly know why, but I was all the time running away. There were two older girls who at the end of the week would say, 'let's go home.' And since I was the little kid, I'd always say, 'Okay.' Whenever we'd run home, my folks would just bring us back the next day. I don't ever remember getting punished for that."[26]

James Haumpy gained a reputation at Rainy Mountain for running away and was probably typical of the boys who would not stay put. He usually ran away because the older boys tried to pick fights with him. "I don't fight," he said. "You know how it is." But he discovered that the girls did not particularly like him either, and that was too much for him to take. "Young and got to go to school," he said, "and some girls they don't like you. That's why I wanna go home."[27]

On the other hand, anyone who doubted the harshness of a reservation boarding school had merely to witness how some runaways were treated. On balance, boys were treated more harshly than girls, but both sexes were subjected to humiliating and painful punishments that included being shackled to a ball and chain, forced to stand on tiptoe with arms outstretched, whipped across the palms of the hand, and made to kneel on two-by-four boards for extended periods. Some schools locked children in darkened closets while others humiliated boys by shaving their heads or making them wear dresses. One former student recalled runaways being forced to eat their own vomit after being subjected to a meal of spoiled food. The most draconian punishment was whipping. Students genuinely feared such occasions, because they occasionally ran out of control. "The men . . . do it," Annie Bigman recalled. "When they whip 'em, some would half kill them." Bert Geikoumah remembered, "Well, they whip you hard. Boy they don't monkey with you. They whip you."[28]

Order and discipline, then, lay at the core of the boarding school experience, but the true test of the civilizing program came in the classroom, where Kiowa children would be molded into citizens freed from the temptations of life on the plains. At least that was the plan. Students at Rainy Mountain were expected to matriculate through the sixth grade and to acquire industrial and vocational skills in the form of farming and industrial arts for the boys and domestic training for the girls. To these were added lessons in the rudiments of history, grammar, arithmetic, civics, the English language, and Christianity. The 1902 annual report for the superintendent of Indian schools summarized the government's goals in a discussion of papers delivered at a summer seminar for Indian school teachers. In "Essentials of Indian Education," for example, the Most Reverend John Ireland argued that above all "the Indian needs a practical education. It is well for him to know that he must live as a white man, and consequently he must learn to work." Because "work is the basis of all civilization," continued Ireland, Indians must be exposed to strict lessons of industry and discipline in the classroom:

> Teach the boys a trade of some kind, and teach them farming, which is, of course, the most important of all. Teach the girls the ordinary industries for which they are fitted . . . and I believe it will do much more for the elevation of the race than teaching boys. Let the spirit of the home be what it should be, and the father and son will be all right. Teach the girls to take care of their homes and make them attractive. Teach them cooking, teach them neatness, teach them responsibility. Teach the girls to milk and take care of poultry; and teach them how to serve a nice appetizing meal for the family; do this and I tell you you have solved the whole question of Indian civilization.[29]

All that was necessary, policy makers insisted, was enough general knowledge to instill respect for Anglo-American values. The result was a curriculum of limited expectations and goals that according to Sally McBeth was
"not intended to meet any specific Indian problems or needs."[30]

How well did all of this work at a typical reservation school? A 1914 report from Rainy Mountain provides some answers. (The curriculum and
schedule it detailed had not changed significantly since the school's opening in 1893; the most notable additions were evening classes and activities,
otherwise it was much like the curriculum that Cora Dunn had perfected
in the 1890s.) The day began at 6:00 a.m. with drilling and cleaning. Morning roll call came at 6:45. Breakfast followed from 7:00 to 7:30, after which
students returned to their rooms to do routine chores. Classes began at 8:00
and ran until 11:45. Lunch came at noon. Instruction resumed at 1:00 and
continued until 5:00. Supper was served at 6:10. Evenings were filled with
more classes, vocational training, reading circles, recreation and free time,
lectures, and various programs.[31]

The calendar also indicated numerous evening socials for "small, middle, or large-sized" boys and girls, as well as lectures on topics ranging from
the humane treatment of animals to patriotism. Evening roll call came at
7:15 for young pupils and at 8:00 for the older ones. At 9:00 it was lights out.
Weekends brought some respite from the routine. Saturday mornings usually found students engaged in chores or work from 8:00 to 11:00, but afternoons were considered free time. On alternate Saturday afternoons groups
made the trip to nearby Gotebo or to Boake's Trading Post to buy treats and
see the sights.

It was a long and arduous schedule, and many children went to bed ex-
hausted from the frantic pace. One former Rainy Mountain student recalled
how much she look forward to going to sleep:

> *I think that in remembering I treasure most the last half hour of each
> busy day. Scrubbed and in their pajamas each girl sat up in the middle of
> her cot hugging her knees and with bowed head chanted: "Now I lay me
> downtosleep. I pray the Lord my soultokeep. If I should die beforeIwake,
> I pray the Lord my soultotake." Each word was spoken in unison, sharp-
> ly and without expression, then the last three words of each phrase were
> run together as one word in a lower tone. One loud Amen and then Plop!*

they fell back upon their pillows. There was a long sigh and rustle of sheets and all was still.[32]

Sunday meant worship services from 10:00 a.m. to noon, recreation and free time for much of the afternoon, and church service from 5:00 to 6:15. Because officials believed that lessons learned from the Scriptures ought to be interwoven with those learned in the classroom, religious training was a standard component in the boarding schools. "The Sabbath must be properly observed," the Indian Office reminded administrators. "There shall be a Sabbath School or some other suitable service every Sunday, which all pupils shall be required to attend." Interestingly, employees were encouraged to attend but could be excused on personal or doctrinal grounds. As for students, however, "you went to church; there was no *not* going." Juanita Yeahquo remembered that "we had to go. Some girls would hide under the beds to get out of going. But you would get punished if you weren't there. They took a count."[33]

Yet what occurred at the missions was hardly the conversion envisioned by policy makers. Instead, communities often used the missions to underscore their own notions about kinship, belief, and identity. At mission after mission, schoolchildren and their families created a new and vibrant form of Christianity that more often than not was rooted in Kiowa institutions and values. Headsmen became deacons, missionaries learned to speak Native languages, and rituals were adapted to suit Kiowa needs. At the Saddle Mountain Mission, for example, missionary Isabel Crawford had the hot rocks from sweat lodges brought to the mission's baptismal pool, where they were dropped in. A rich and vibrant hymn tradition was inaugurated at the Rainy Mountain Mission in the 1890s, and Kiowa men and women—many of them boarding school graduates—took active roles as lay readers, deacons, and ordained ministers. As one former student of Fort Sill Boarding School said, "I learned to read the Bible at the boarding school, and that helped me in my life. But I never forgot my Comanche ways—my language, my relations, my obligations to those old people. Jesus reminds me every day to be a good Comanche, and to take care of my people. That boarding school—it gave me the tools to do that."[34]

It all sounded fine in theory, but in reality most schools never had a chance of putting such plans to work, at least not consistently. Rainy Mountain was no exception, and its limited facilities and understaffed teaching corps meant that in good years it might be able to provide students with parts of the program, but rarely with all of it. A 1911 inspection, for example, revealed a distressing lack of critical facilities, including a dairy barn, carpenter shop, and industrial cottage. Worse, because of the lack of teachers, classes were terribly overcrowded. In December 1912, Rainy Mountain's attendance stood at 146, but the school employed only two academic teachers plus an industrial teacher. Rosters showed that 47 percent of the student body (67 pupils) were in the first grade and 28 percent (41 pupils) were second and third graders. Thus, 108 of 146 students attended grades one through three with one full-time teacher. In September 1913 the situation was no better. With 108 students on campus (soon to top out at 166), 85 pupils were assigned to the first grade with one full-time teacher. A 1915 inspection report revealed that 10 percent of the school's first and second graders had been at Rainy Mountain for as long as seven years. By 1917, Rainy Mountain also had the highest trachoma rates in the entire Indian school system; in March 1916, for example, medical logs revealed that an astonishing 163 of 168 students were infected. To give students some measure of relief, administrators purchase fifty pairs of dark glasses in late 1915 and another thirty pairs in late 1917. In a masterful show of understatement, the agent described the situation to the commissioner's office as "somewhat difficult."[35]

Alarmed by such statistics, field matron Mary Clouse recommended in 1916 that the agency add "another teacher and two more grades to our boarding schools" in order to prepare the children more fully for what lay ahead. Concerned that the schools were not adequately training the children, and alarmed that former students often fell into disreputable habits after school days were over, Clouse concluded that the schools could combat such conditions with more thorough instruction. Kiowa-Comanche-Apache agent C. V. Stinchecum's reply was a masterpiece of official rhetoric. Clouse's suggestion was "impracticable for the reason that . . . schools are conducted in accordance with well defined plans laid down by the Commissioner of Indian Affairs. The reservation schools are only expected to take the boys and girls through the first six grades."[36] That Rainy Mountain could hardly be counted on to do even that much seems not to have crossed the agent's mind.

The language barrier represented one of the chief causes of poor advancement rates. Strictly forbidden to speak Kiowa, the children encountered se-

rious difficulties from the first day in class. The transition was especially
grueling for very young pupils, many of whom were so frightened that according to McKenzie they "just clammed up." McKenzie recalled an experience that helps to illustrate the difficulties involved. Resolute in her determination to teach the children English, his teacher plunged into an intensive
program to demonstrate the use of articles. Placing a boy's hat on a stool,
she told the children it could be "a" hat or "the" hat. "Some of us were puz-
zled," said McKenzie, "because she was seeing two hats where we only saw
one. . . . How she managed to get it across to us still mystifies me."[37] Fred Bigman discussed the difficulty of learning English. "Boy, I had a hard time,"
he said. "When they start talking English I don't know what they are talking about." Once, when he was called to the board for spelling and grammar
exercises, he panicked: "And when I went to school in class . . . that teacher
told me to come up to the blackboard, write something on it. I didn't know
what to write. I didn't know what she said. So I ask a guy . . . what'd she say.
. . . She said for you to run out. Boy I jumped up and grabbed my cap and
away I went. I went plumb back to our boy's building." Bigman eventually improved "to where I got to learn to talk English pretty good. Wasn't extra good." Indeed, he admitted, his limited language skills meant he never
did "get to that Bible" study required of more advanced students. As a result he went only as far as the third grade. Looking back on the experience,
he commented that "I had a hard time. I think about it sometimes myself.
Oh, it was painful."[38]

Ethel Howry had similar experiences at the Methvin Institute. Years later how she recalled the mysteries of boarding school life and a language that
she did not yet understand:

> So she [the teacher] says, "Come here Ethel." Here I went. Oh, she was
> so glad and she says "Good, Good," she says. I didn't even know what
> she wanted. So she picked us all up and took us back to the school. To
> our building. Just then I didn't know what she done but that was where
> she cleaned us up and we had the clothes on and she named us. And we
> went and oh we just cried and our brothers would come over and put us
> to bed, and we'd go to sleep, and they'd have to go back to their quar-
> ters. First thing in the morning they'd come [back to help the girls]. We
> didn't know nothing.[39]

Students also occasionally received unexpected lessons with unintended consequences, as with one young boy whose introduction to English at Rainy Mountain came from the school's farmer. As the man tried to harness several uncooperative horses, the youngster heard him scowl "stand still" at the animals, a command he punctuated immediately with several obscenities. Asked to share his beginning knowledge of English in class later that day, the boy enthusiastically stood up and said "Stand still, you son of a bitch!" By all accounts the teacher was not amused.

Because many students took several years to attain even minimal fluency in English, academic training remained remedial. Vocational training overshadowed academic skills almost without exception. Former students often said relatively little about their academic experiences (except for language lessons), but they had quite a bit to say about vocational training. Most believed that they learned valuable skills but often regretted that they were forced to learn in an environment where, said Juanita Yeahquo, "they worked us like dogs." When asked if she remembered any of the classes she took in school, Sarah Long Horn said no, but she commented at length on her vocational training. She remembered that girls were assigned to the school's bakery, laundry, and ironing room and that kitchen work was standard for all girls. "That's where I got all my work, my neatness and my sewing, most of my cooking, things like that, because we stay there and do all that work."[40]

Myrtle Ware's memory of the classroom was that her teacher taught them "how to write and sing and read and spell." Beyond that she offered no specific information on academic training except to say, "I like to go to school in the morning 'cause I feel a little fresh to learn something. . . . At a certain time you go to school, you know, so many hours, and then you're out to work so many hours, too." She spent much of her time working in the laundry, where she was so proficient that after several years as a student she took a job as an assistant matron.[41]

William Lone Wolf, who enrolled at Rainy Mountain in 1905, remembered that "mostly they teach us how to work; it was a nice school, I learn some—I learn to work there." Students from the reservation's other schools made similar comments. "We were taught practical things such as sewing and cooking, laundry and how to care for a family," said a former Riverside student. "All the things we learned were things we needed to know for our immediate living." Some students regretted not getting more academic training. "It didn't take me long to realize how far behind I was," noted a former Fort Sill student. "I had a little math and science . . . compared to those who attended public school." One Riverside student lamented the lack of academic instruction, while a Fort Sill student said, "I don't think it was good because it was really academically inferior to the public school." Parker McKenzie put it a bit more bluntly and characterized one man's teaching qualities as "mostly bossing." Jim Whitewolf said that he "didn't like the jobs they gave me, but I knew that if I did them all right they wouldn't bother me. But if I didn't they might whip me."[42]

For their part, Rainy Mountain students held mixed opinions about their teachers. Fred Bigman, who matriculated under teachers in both public schools and reservation schools, saw no real distinction between the two. "I don't see any difference," he said. "Teachers always teachers. . . . I do what they tell me. I mind them." Guy Quoetone schooled under missionary teachers prior to enrolling at Rainy Mountain. He preferred missionaries because "I think that they were really more interested that we learn."[43] Some Rainy Mountain students genuinely admired a number of their teachers. Flora A. DeLay, for example, was still alive in 1963 when former Rainy Mountain students held their first-ever reunion. They invited DeLay, said Parker McKenzie, because she was "a dedicated teacher and well liked." At the time of her death two years later, McKenzie sent his condolences to DeLay's niece: "The hearts of many Kiowa men and women . . . were made very sad when they learned of her passing. . . . We Kiowas are indebted much to our former teachers and counselors. They were most assuredly dedicated individuals, as demonstrated by the very 'raw' material they molded into the stream of American life."[44]

Thankfully, there was more to school life than the training that dominated students' lives. A wide variety of extracurricular activities offered welcome diversions. On the campus students could participate in reading circles, evening meetings, lectures, club meetings, and other group activities. Dances and socials were especially popular and often featured prizes for the best performances. Juanita Yeahquo remembered many such dances at Riverside, but she also recalled that some students found such occasions awkward. "It's like we've got our feet in two paths," she observed, one Indian and one white. Forced to "dance all those white man's dances—like the boogie-woogie," Yeahquo found that socials were not always enjoyable affairs.[45]

The schools celebrated important holidays, especially Christmas, when a week's vacation allowed children to go home for virtually the only time during the school year. The vacation was not automatic, and in some years Cora Dunn queried the agent about whether or not the children could be released. In 1905, for example, she noted that parents were "very anxious to have a Christmas vacation . . . though in my judgment it is not advisable." Rainy Mountain sponsored an annual Christmas dinner, complete with turkey (or pork in years when the budget was tight) and small gifts. Students observed Halloween, New Year's Day, and Easter ("the only time I ever saw eggs," said Parker McKenzie). Indeed, to encourage "the inculcation of patriotism," the Indian Office regularly issued guidelines reminding the schools to observe appropriate holidays. In 1891, for example, Commissioner Morgan called attention to all of the usual holidays plus Washington's Birthday, Arbor Day, and Franchise Day.[46]

A number of other pursuits kept students occupied. Playing in the band was one of the school's most popular diversions. Dunn started the band sometime in the late 1890s, and it became an institution unto itself. A bandstand was built in the center of the campus in 1906, and Dunn personally directed rehearsals and performances. Music played an integral role in the introduction of Anglo-American culture at Indian schools across the country, and in Dunn's opinion no other aspect of Rainy Mountain's curriculum was as effective in that process. In 1895 she requested funds for a piano, justifying the purchase in part on the grounds that it would greatly improve the school's ability to cultivate the students' sense of advancement. "I attend personally to the instruction of the music pupils," she wrote, "and find them more enthusiastic and responsive in this than in any other branch of study." She was counting on the Indian Office's support "to make the musical features of this school a power in the intellectual and moral elevation of the pupils." The government agreed and in late November 1896 approved funds for a piano.[47]

The band proved to be a huge success. "The proficiency of the Rainy Mountain band is a matter of pride and no school influence has contributed more to the advancement of the pupils," Dunn wrote in 1907. Indeed, students eagerly participated and showed impressive talent. Parker McKenzie said that Dunn produced "wonderful school bands from fourteen-to twenty-year-olds who learned to play the masterpieces even before some mastered the fourth grade." On a visit to the campus in the summer of 1990 he stood by the remains of the principal's cottage, motioned in the direction of the bandstand, and said that he could still see Dunn striding purposefully toward her waiting students, baton in one hand and sheet music in the other.[48]

Athletic teams were among the school's most popular extracurricular activities. Rainy Mountain sponsored a variety of teams for both sexes. Like the band, these were a source of school pride and offered the chance to get away from campus. Policy makers also regarded sports as another way to impart American values and ideals to the children. The hard work of sports, for example, and the stress laid on individuality could tear down traditional cultural identity. Cora Dunn endorsed sports at the school (though not as enthusiastically as the band) and always included athletic equipment in her annual request for supplies. Baseball games against neighboring reservation schools and local teams began around 1902. "The boys are taking great interest in playing ball," Dunn reported that year, "and have arranged match games with the ball clubs of the surrounding towns." Lewis Toyebo played shortstop for the team and remembered that "about the only other team we played was Gotebo, then we just played among ourselves, just to have some exercise." He recalled that his dream was for the New York Yankees to discover him. Girls were especially fond of basketball and started their own teams around 1910.[49]

The failure to destroy the Kiowa language occasionally paid dividends at athletic events. One Kiowa who attended boarding school in the early 1930s recalled a revealing episode from his days as a member of the football team. As a Kiowa at the predominantly Comanche Fort Sill School, his assignment during games against Riverside (largely Kiowa in those days) was to linger around the line of scrimmage and eavesdrop on the plays being called in Kiowa by the Riverside players. He would then quietly translate the plays from Kiowa into English for his Comanche teammates, and they would then plan their defensive strategy accordingly. Sixty years later he chuckled at the memory and smiled ruefully at the thought that "for once, it was okay to talk Kiowa!"

After James McGregor's arrival as superintendent at Rainy Mountain in 1910, the school's athletics program grew rapidly. "Principal McGregor," recalled Parker McKenzie, "knew such extra-curricular activity was not only of physical benefit to the students, but also provided a sane outlet for their excess energy." By 1912 he had arranged a meet between Rainy Mountain, Fort Sill, Riverside, and St. Patrick's School that included baseball, high jumping, running, and pole vaulting. To this was joined an academic meet with contests in writing, reading, spelling, and arithmetic. The event proved to be so popular that in 1913, 1914, and 1915 it was expanded to three days and moved to Anadarko, where the city's opera house was used for oratorical contests and nightly entertainment provided by students.[50] In addition to baseball, which seems to have been the most popular sport at the school, students eagerly participated in volleyball, tennis, and track. At the age of ninety-two, Parker McKenzie once playfully jogged in place and attributed his good health to the fact that he had once been a member of the Rainy Mountain track team.

The athletics program rallied the students together, gave them a sense of identity, and fostered real pride in their school and teams. School songs and yells, popularized during McGregor's tenure, exalted Rainy Mountain's teams. One favorite made fun of the archrival Fort Sill School:

> *A big long train comes 'round the bend,*
> *good-bye Fort Sill, good-bye;*
> *It's loaded down with Kiowa men,*
> *good-bye Fort Sill, good-bye;*
> *We got your goose, so what's the use,*
> *good-bye Fort Sill, good-bye;*
> *We got your scalp, that makes us yell,*
> *good-bye Fort Sill, good-bye.*

Another song extolled Rainy Mountain's character:

> *You may talk about your baseball team of Riverside and Fort Sill;*
> *the Anadarko Boarding School, you mention if you will.*
> *The Rainy Mountain Kiowa Kids are going to do all this;*
> *we're from the place of knowledge, honor and grace;*
> *For we are jolly students of this Indian land;*
> *We've got to send our colors o'er the white and blue;*
> *We make cheers and yells of our dear old school;*
> *We're the kind who play the game.*

Yet another song declared Rainy Mountain "the place most dear to me. It's where we all get in the game—where the Kiowas eat gravy."[51] It worked a bit hard for the rhyme, but the meaning was clear just the same.

Finally, a rich and often closely guarded private world kept students busy when they were not in class or otherwise occupied. Although administrators tried to control the lives of students, the children inevitably found ways to create space between themselves and their superiors. On one level such activities were meant simply to retain some level of autonomy. James Silverhorn said that after the school day was over "the boys used to all go up on the hill—up on Rainy Mountain and stay up there until supper time. Just to take a walk."[52] Likewise, clandestine conversations in Kiowa preserved an important measure of identity.

Other activities combined mischievousness with a determination to make do for themselves. Parker McKenzie recalled late-night raids on the kitchen after "gravy day" when the boys would break into the dining hall, fill their hats with gravy and biscuits, and then sneak back to their rooms for a feast. Jim Whitewolf did the same during his years at the Kiowa school in Anadarko. He and his friends often stole food when they worked in the kitchen and would slip away on Saturday afternoons and cook it. "We wanted to cook it in our own way," he recalled. There were other diversions as well. On mornings when a heavy frost or rare snowfall came to Rainy Mountain, the older boys sometimes borrowed the fire-escape ladders and dashed to the top of the mountain for a ride down that was as exciting as it was dangerous.[53] Such activities relieved the monotony of school life and enabled students to maintain some sense of autonomy.

McKenzie reported that students also engaged in a wide variety of games and self-made amusements. In addition to the usual pursuits of baseball, tag, and marbles (the impending showdown of self-designated world champions caused eager anticipation. "We regarded it almost as much as the World's Series now is regarded," he noted), students maintained a circus behind Rainy Mountain. Cast-off furniture and other junked odds and ends were scavenged and put to use as props. A band provided accompaniment on imaginary instruments made from wooden sticks and drums fabricated from discarded tubs. Aerialists, tumblers, and acrobats wearing long-handle underwear for tights performed on mattresses, while cowboy rope artists and clowns entertained the crowd. A menagerie of rabbits, possums, "a rat or two," squirrels, and snakes was a popular attraction. One boy won acclaim for his gorilla act, which featured a fur suit crafted from a worn-out mohair mattress and wooden teeth, and during which he growled and hung from a chain. Two others created a buffalo complete with cow's skull and horns. Admission was a uniform button, preferably brass.[54]

School administrators probably knew about the circus, but there is no indication that they ever tried to close it down or restrict it. But there were moments when Dunn and her staff must have wondered what their students were up to in their spare time. Matrons and disciplinarians fumed over the mysterious wholesale loss of the uniform buttons required for admission and waged a never-ending battle to keep students properly clothed. School supply invoices from May 1909 and April 1910, for example, show orders for a total of six gross of coat and vest buttons, and a note in Dunn's hand on one such invoice asks plaintively why so many uniform buttons were constantly missing.[55]

Once school days were over, most students disappeared back into the local Kiowa communities. Agency records show that relatively small numbers went onto Chilocco, Phoenix, or Carlisle, but the total never amounted to more than a handful of those who went through the reservation's schools. Trained only in agricultural, mechanical, or domestic skills, students faced limited prospects, so returning to their old homes and towns was about all that most could look forward to. Military careers took some away, and others like Parker McKenzie successfully parlayed their education into professional careers. At least one, Martha Napawat, returned from Carlisle to become a Rainy Mountain employee. For the most part, however, Rainy Mountain sent its students back to their communities.

Agents attempted to track the movements of former students and sent detailed questionnaires to field matrons to ascertain the whereabouts and occupations of former students. In 1914, for example, the Indian Office notified James McGregor of its wish "to know something of the success you have achieved in following up the careers of Indian boys and girls who have attended only reservation schools." The letter noted the importance of securing meaningful work for former students "so that they may have opportunity to practice the training they have received at school and become self-supporting." The office was especially interested in McGregor's "ideas and plans for placing these youths at work, also of their responsiveness in availing themselves of the opportunities presented for their benefit."[56]

A series of field matron's reports from 1915 offers some evidence on life after school days. Asked to survey her district's "returned students," Mary Given wrote that "most of our young people are married soon after coming out of school. We have a cooking club for girls. Good books and magazines [are] lent to boys and girls." Mary Clouse added that "we assist them, invite them to our Sunday School, encourage them to be workers, are planning a Summer School of ten days, and a camp meeting." Anna Heersma "attempted to interest boys and girls in the work of their homes, suggesting good reading matter," and Mary Wilkin reported that "some have done well with their crops and caring for their homes. Have given out good reading and had little social times for them." Above all, field matrons and missionaries tried to keep former students on the straight and narrow path and energetically opposed the introduction of peyote or of practices that might lead students away from the lessons and values championed in the schools.[57]

From the perspective of former students, Rainy Mountain represented a collection of contradictions. When measured against the government's expectations, it did not succeed in erasing the cultural identity of Kiowa students; at the same time, however, despite its numerous limitations, it did provide a level of education that most students said was useful after their school days were over. Some students learned well and left the school with advantages they would otherwise have missed. "If it hadn't been for Rainy Mountain School, I probably would not be typing this account," wrote Parker McKenzie. "Despite the hardships we encountered there, they were well worth the time.... It provided us the opportunity for an education, though rudimentary for most of us. We had a lot of fun, but of course, that wasn't the school part."[58] Yet McKenzie, who spent nearly forty years of his adult life as a Bureau of Indian Affairs employee, never gave up his Kiowa identity. He originated and perfected a written system for the Kiowa language and gained prominence as a tribal historian. Other former students also carried fond memories away from the school, despite its often unpleasant circumstances. "But I really did, I really did like that school," said Sarah Long Horn. "I'm always thankful that I went to that school because that's [sic] lots of things that I had ... learned from that place." On his ninetieth birthday, Lewis Toyebo told his descendants that he had "fond memories" of Rainy Mountain: "I now see the Kiowa people have made rapid progress from the tipi to the halls of higher education. . . . That was the wish and prayer of our ancestors who have gone on."[59]

Perhaps the most revealing set of comments came in early 1920 when news reached the Kiowas that Rainy Mountain would close at the end of the school year. Deeply troubled by the prospect of losing their school, a group of tribal leaders sent a petition to Washington imploring the government to reconsider. "To discontinue the institution would mean the removal of the very backbone of the tribe," they wrote. "The best Indian pupil in every respect . . . is the one that has been in attendance at a Government school long enough to learn to speak English, understand the necessity of cleanliness, good health, right living, and the general habits of the whites." The petition closed with a plea for more education, not less: "We need more education and better education . . . the welfare of the tribe ought to be paramount. The Kiowas need their school; they cannot very well get along without it."[60] The petition failed, and in the fall of 1920, for the first time in twenty-seven years, the Rainy Mountain Boarding School sat empty. Except for a brief stint as a work camp during the New Deal years, it was never used again. The main buildings fell into disrepair, and local Kiowas eventually dismantled the stone buildings and used the materials in new construction at the nearby Rainy Mountain Baptist Mission. In time, ranchers opened the grounds to cattle, and the campus slowly disappeared beneath the grass of the Oklahoma prairie.

As Parker McKenzie wandered across the ruins of the Rainy Mountain campus that afternoon in August 1990, he came across the school's old concrete flagpole base, hidden in the grass. McKenzie did not see it until he stepped on it. Looking down to see what he had found, he said, "How about that," immediately snapped to attention, and placed his hand over his heart, a lesson learned at Rainy Mountain almost a century ago. A moment later he resumed our conversation about his life as a young boy on the Kiowa-Comanche-Apache Reservation. The contradiction of those two experiences struck me with considerable force. An hour earlier McKenzie had been giving me driving directions in the Kiowa language with careful explanations about differences in tense, inflection, and tone. He talked easily of this or that Indian family and of the survival of various Kiowa cultural traditions. At the nearby Rainy Mountain Church cemetery he gave me a lesson in Kiowa genealogy and carefully pointed out the graves of former students. Finding the flagpole base, however, took him back to a time and place that stood in stark relief to all that he had been so busily telling and showing me. Indeed, that earlier era had been intended to prevent conversations like the one we were having from ever occurring.

Like many other former students, McKenzie is an example of how the boarding schools simultaneously failed and succeeded. They failed inasmuch as they did not destroy Kiowa identity or culture. Cutting children's hair, dressing them in new clothing, and teaching them to farm, bake, or sew did not necessarily transform identity. Given the circumstances at Rainy Mountain, it was unlikely that such a transformation could have been achieved anyway. Yet the school succeeded in important ways—another contradiction considering the conditions that usually prevailed. Hundreds of young Kiowas attended the school and gained important experience and skills that they used after leaving. Fluency in English, for example, was a critical factor. Students left the school with varying levels of proficiency, but they had enough knowledge to survive. The vocational instruction they received likewise made it possible for them to make their way in the world that lay outside the campus. It was not a perfect preparation, and it was not what they deserved, but it helped to ease the transition from a life their parents had led to the very different one that they faced.

The irony is that most students began their new lives by combining two worlds. And it is here that the contradictory nature of schools like Rainy Mountain is most clearly revealed. Yet the seeming contradiction of going to boarding school and staying Indian was not so much a conundrum as it was simply a fact of life. Kiowas had changed many times during their history; the boarding schools were only the latest in a long series of events. Learning English, for example, or learning a trade—these were the very things that made it possible to function in the modern world, but not at the cost of losing important cultural foundations. Indeed, it was the maintenance of their cultural base that enabled many Kiowas to endure the world around them. Cora Dunn was mistaken in her belief that she could change them forever. She might mold them into English-speaking Christians, but she could not transform them into exact replicas of Anglo-Americans.

In later life former students revealed the limits of change. James Silverhorn went through the boarding schools but remained closely associated with important tribal institutions. He joined the Native American Church in the early 1930s and assumed prominence as one of its leaders in the Kiowa community. As an adult he kept four of the Kiowa sacred medicine bundles. Former Rainy Mountain student Fred Bigman also joined the Native American Church, and like many other former students he used it as an avenue to maintain his culture. Lewis Toyebo was never discovered by the New York Yankees, but he became a renowned songwriter during and after World War II and was one of the driving forces behind the creation of a new genre of songs called War Mother songs. Another Kiowa man who graduated from Fort Sill served in the military for nearly thirty years, came home to Oklahoma at his retirement, and became a stalwart in the Native American Church and powwow communities. When asked if the schools took his cultural identity away, he replied, "They couldn't, I didn't let that happen. People are all the time asking me who I am. Who am I? I am a *Kiowa*."[61]

Rainy Mountain Boarding School can now barely be seen from the road. The mountain is there, an enduring landmark, a landscape, writes N. Scott Momaday, "that is incomparable, a time that is gone forever, and the human spirit, which endures."[62] The campus itself is largely gone, save for the tumbledown ruins of a few buildings. Its outlines are faintly visible from the top of the mountain, but unless one knew with certainty what had once existed there it would be impossible to recognize the campus of a reservation boarding school. Yet Rainy Mountain—the place and the school—remains a powerful force for Kiowa people. Most Kiowas have relatives who attended the school, roamed its campus, and felt its forces—good and bad. Kiowas visit the mountain regularly to cut sage and cedar for ceremonial use. For many of them the trip is akin to a pilgrimage; the combination of the mountain's historic cultural importance and of the school's role in their lives and in the lives of their kinsmen is palpable. Visitors to the mountain invariably talk about the school and what it must have been like for the grandparents, great-aunts, cousins, nephews, or friends who went there. And they always speak with reverence about those people and about what happened a century ago in this lonely corner of a vast reservation.

A trip to the school in May 1994 with Yvette Zotigh, the granddaughter of two former students, reminded me of how indelible the place is. Lingering at the top of the mountain, taking in its broad vista, Yvette quietly told me that coming to Rainy Mountain was important because she knows her grandparents were here. "They were *here*. And they're still here. I know my grandfather came to this spot where I'm standing, because he buried his marbles here one time so that the older kids wouldn't take them." She dug her shoe into the soil and wished quietly that she could find the marbles. "The marbles are here, somewhere," she said. "And so is he. When I come here I know he's here." The Kiowa people have never forgotten this place, and they venerate the memory of relatives who went to the Rainy Mountain Boarding School. It is a memory that celebrates survival during a troubling time as well as the precious cost of that survival. And those who go to the mountain today understand the advice given to me when I made my first trip to that tumbledown campus and its slowly disappearing buildings: "Walk quietly at that place, son," an elderly Kiowa man told me, "because the souls of those small children are still there."

Notes

1. Cora Dunn to William A. Jones, September 4, 1899, Rainy Mountain School files, Records of the Kiowa Agency, Indian Archives Division, Oklahoma Historical Society, Oklahoma City [hereafter cited as RMS]. Many scholars have addressed the history of the Indian schools, but David Wallace Adams's *Education for Extinction: American Indians and the Boarding School Experience, 1875–1928* (Lawrence: University Press of Kansas, 1996) remains the indispensable treatment. For a brilliant commentary on the deeper meaning of education see Adams's "Fundamental Considerations: The Deep Meaning of Native American Schooling, 1880–1900," *Harvard Educational Review* 58, no. 1 (1988): 1–28. For a comprehensive account of Indian education see Margaret Connell-Szasz, *Indian Education in the American Colonies: 1607–1783* (Albuquerque: University of New Mexico Press, 1988); and Connell-Szasz, *Education and the American Indian: The Road to Self-Determination since 1928* (Albuquerque: University of New Mexico Press, 1977).

2. For discussions of Rainy Mountain see Clyde Ellis, *To Change Them Forever: Indian Education at the Rainy Mountain Boarding School, 1893–1920* (Norman: University of Oklahoma Press, 1996); Ellis, "Boarding School Life at the Kiowa-Comanche Agency, 1893–1920," *Historian* 58, no. 4 (1996): 777–93; Ellis, " 'There Are So Many Things Needed': Establishing the Rainy Mountain Boarding School, 1891–1900," *Chronicles of Oklahoma* 72, no. 4 (1995): 414–39; and Ellis, " 'A Remedy for Barbarism': Indian Schools, the Civilizing Program, and the Kiowa-Comanche-Apache Reservation, 1871–1915," *American Indian Culture and Research Journal* 18, no. 3 (1994): 85–120.

   For accounts of boarding school education see Sally J. McBeth, *Ethnic Identity and the Boarding School Experience of West-Central Oklahoma American Indians* (Washington DC: University Press of America, 1983); Robert A. Trennert Jr., *The Phoenix Indian School: Forced Assimilation in Arizona, 1891–1935* (Tucson: University of Arizona Press, 1988); Devon A. Mihesuah, *Cultivating the Rosebuds: The Education of Women at the Cherokee Female Seminary, 1851–1909* (Urbana: University of Illinois Press, 1993); Michael C. Coleman, *American Indian Children at School, 1850–1920* (Jackson: University Press of Mississippi, 1993); K. Tsianina Lomawaima, *They Called It Prairie Light: The Story of Chilocco Indian School* (Lincoln: University of Nebraska Press, 1994); Donal Lindsey, *Indians at Hampton Institute, 1873–1923* (Urbana: University of Illinois Press, 1994); Brenda Child, *Boarding School Seasons: American Indian Families, 1900–1940* (Lincoln: University of Nebraska Press, 1998); Scott Riney, *The Rapid City Indian School, 1898–1933* (Norman: University of Oklahoma Press, 1999); Amanda J. Cobb, *Listening to Our Grandmothers' Stories: The Bloomfield Academy for Chickasaw Females, 1852–1949* (Lincoln: University of Nebraska Press, 2000); Jacqueline Fear-Segal, "Nineteenth-Century Indian Education: Universalism versus Evolutionism," *Journal of American Studies* 33, no. 2 (1999): 323–41.

3. Coleman, *American Indian Children at School*, 197–98.

4. Lomawaima, *They Called It Prairie Light*, xvi.

5. McBeth identifies six reasons for attending the boarding schools. (1) It would enable children to cope more effectively with a changing cultural environment. "Now," said one Kiowa-Apache man, "we in White man's world. Today. We got to go that way." (2) Schools provided clothes and other necessities. "I wanted to go home and be with momma," recalled one former student, "but she said 'Well, if you come home we'll only be eating one meal a day, and so I think you should go to Riverside.' " (3) Death of a parent often meant the child was sent away to school. (4) They went because their friends were there. (5) Difficulty in the public schools, especially embarrassment over poor performance. (6) Opportunity to associate with other Indians. McBeth, *Ethnic Identity*, 108–11. See also Lomawaima, *They Called It Prairie Light*, 32–44.

6. Myrtle Paudlety Ware interview, November 11, 1967, T-76, p. 2, Doris Duke Oral History Collection, Western History Collections, University of Oklahoma Library Archives, Norman [hereafter cited as DDOH]; Annie Bigman interview, June 14, 1967, M-1, p. 3, DDOH.

7. Guy Quoetone interview, March 23, 1971, T-637, p. 16, DDOH.

8. "Happy 90th Birthday Lewis Toyebo, February 28, 1982," Commemorative birthday celebration reminiscence, courtesy of Mrs. Ruby Williams of Fort Cobb, Oklahoma [hereafter cited as "Lewis Toyebo Birthday"]; Cora Dunn to John Blackmon, January 30, 1906, RMS.

9. Sarah Long Horn interview, June 27, 1967, T-62, pp. 6–7, DDOH.

10. James Haumpy interview, July 11, 1967, T-81, p. 6, DDOH; Parker McKenzie to the author, August 1, 1990.

11. *Annual Report of the Kiowa Agency* [hereafter ARKA] in *Annual Report of the Commissioner of Indian Affairs* [hereafter ARCIA], 1875: 775; ARKA, 1896: 255; Eugenia Mausape interview, September 14, 1967, T-138, p. 200, DDOH; Cecil Horse interview, June 21, 1967, T-27, pp. 191–92, DDOH.

12. ARKA, 1891: 351; ARKA, 1896: 254; Big Tree to James Randlett, August 30, 1905, RMS; Inspection Report of the Kiowa Agency, June 10, 1897, Agents' Reports, Records of

the Kiowa Agency, Oklahoma Historical Society; Jim Whitewolf, *Jim Whitewolf: The Life of a Kiowa Apache Man*, ed. Charles Brant (New York: Dover, 1969), 83.

13. Cora Dunn to Randlett, September 5 and 14, 1900, RMS.

14. Bruce David Forbes, "John Jasper Methvin: Methodist Missionary to the Western Tribes (Oklahoma)," in *Churchmen and the Western Indians, 1820–1920*, ed. Clyde A. Milner and Floyd A. O'Neil (Norman: University of Oklahoma Press, 1985), 56.

15. Guy Quoetone interview, T-637, p. 17, DDOH. For an interesting comparison, see Jim Whitewolf's account of his first day at the Kiowa school in 1891, *Jim Whitewolf*, 83–84.

16. Guy Quoetone interview, T-637, p. 21, DDOH; Annie Bigman interview, June 15, 1967, T-57, p. 16, DDOH; Sarah Long Horn interview, T-62, p. 9, DDOH; Juanita Yeahquo interview, June 21, 1967, M-2, p. 8, DDOH; "Lewis Toyebo Birthday."

17. Powell cited in Francis Paul Prucha, *The Great Father: The United States Government and the American Indians*, 2 vols. (Lincoln: University of Nebraska Press, 1984), 2:674; see also Daniel F. Littlefield Jr. and Lonnie E. Underhill, "Renaming the American Indian, 1890–1913," *American Studies* 12 (fall 1971): 33–45; "Lewis Toyebo Birthday"; Forbes, "John Jasper Methvin," 56–57. Some students also received birth dates. Parker McKenzie remembered that most students were assigned a birthday on either the first or the fifteenth of a particular month.

18. William T. Hagan, *United States–Comanche Relations: The Reservation Years* (Norman: University of Oklahoma Press, 1990), 198; Parker McKenzie to Randle Hurst, October 23, 1987, copy in possession of the author; McBeth, *Ethnic Identity*, 99–100. In 1890 the Indian Office issued "Rules for Indian Schools," which stated that "in play and in work, as far as possible . . . they must be kept entirely apart," see ARCIA, 1890: cl–clii.

19. Sarah Longhorn interview, T-62, p. 10, DDOH; Fred Bigman interview, T-50, p. 24, DDOH.

20. William Collins Jr. interview, October 23, 1969, "Ponca Oral History Material," M-45, p. 31, DDOH.

21. McBeth, *Ethnic Identity*, 102–3.

22. McBeth, *Ethnic Identity*, 105; William Collins Jr. interview, M-45, pp. 31–32.

23. Juanita Yeahquo interview, M-2, p. 8, DDOH; Sarah Long Horn interview, T-62, p. 10, DDOH; Myrtle Ware interview, T-76, p. 5, DDOH; Whitewolf, *Jim Whitewolf*, 87–90.

24. Fred Bigman interview, June 14, 1967, T-50, p. 24, DDOH; Parker McKenzie, "How Written Kiowa Came into Being," typescript, n.d., in the possession of the author; Myrtle Ware interview, T-76, p. 10, DDOH; McKenzie to Hurst, October 23, 1987.

25. R. W. Bishoff to C. V. Stinchecum, March 20, 1918, RMS.

26. McBeth, *Ethnic Identity*, 86–87.

27. James Haumpy interview, T-81, p. 6, DDOH.

28. Annie Bigman interview, June 15, 1967, T-57, p. 9, DDOH; Fred Bigman interview, T-50, pp. 27–28, DDOH; Bert Geikoumah interview, July 8, 1967, T-86, p. 9, DDOH. One former Rainy Mountain student told me that after one student was whipped so savagely that he died, administrators covered the incident up by attributing

the death to pneumonia. The most infamous event associated with whippings at the Kiowa-Comanche-Apache schools occurred in the winter of 1891 when three schoolboys ran away from the Kiowa school in Anadarko only to be found some miles from the school, frozen to death in a blizzard. Relatives of the three boys found the man responsible, and according to Bert Geikoumah "they whipped him and they pretty near kill him. His eyes, too, they knock out. . . . A lot of these Indians didn't want to send their kids to school." Geikoumah interview, T-86, p. 7.

29. *Annual Report of the Superintendent of Indian Schools*, in ARCIA, 1902: 420–21.

30. McBeth, *Ethnic Identity*, 89. Lomawaima makes the revealing argument that the Indian school curriculum was not only poorly administered and planned but also "ran counter to developments in mainstream America." The craftsmanship and apprenticeship programs typical of Indian schools were decades out of line with prevailing attitudes in American business and education. See *They Called It Prairie Light*, 65–72. For evaluations of what those attitudes were see Lawrence Cremin, *American Education: The National Experience, 1783–1876* (New York: Harper and Row, 1980); Cremin, *American Education: The Metropolitan Experience, 1876–1980* (New York: Harper and Row, 1970), especially chap. 3, "Patterns of Diversity"; Cremin, *The Transformation of the School: Progressivism in American Education* (New York: Random House, 1961); Michael Katz, *Class, Bureaucracy, and Schools: The Illusion of Educational Change in America* (New York: Praeger, 1975), especially chap. 3, "Twentieth-Century School Reform: Notes toward a History"; and Joel Spring, *The American School, 1642–1990: Varieties of Historical Interpretation of the Foundations and Development of American Education*, 2nd ed. (New York: Longman, 1990), especially chap. 7, "Schooling and the New Corporate Order," and chap. 9, "Meritocracy: The Experts Take Charge."

31. Rainy Mountain Indian School Calendar, 1913–1914, RMS. This regimen was typical of other schools as well. For a discussion of the similarities at a Choctaw mission school, for example, see Christopher J. Huggard, "Culture Mixing: Everyday Life on Missions Among the Choctaws," *Chronicles of Oklahoma* 70 (winter 1992–93): 432–49.

32. Geneve Albright Burford, "Prairie Lore," quoted in "Rainy Mountain School Experiences," *Anadarko Daily News*, August 15–16, 1987, 2.

33. Juanita Yeahquo interview, M-2, p. 8, DDOH; "Rules for Indian Schools, 1890," quoted in Francis Paul Prucha, *The Churches and the Indian Schools, 1888–1912* (Lincoln: University of Nebraska Press, 1979), 161–62; McBeth, *Ethnic Identity*, 100.

34. Luke E. Lassiter, Clyde Ellis, and Ralph Kotay, *The Jesus Road: Kiowas, Christianity, and Indian Hymns* (Lincoln: University of Nebraska Press, 2002); see also Marvin Kroeker, *Comanches and Mennonites on the Oklahoma Plains: A. J. and Magdalena Becker and the Post Oak Mission* (Hillsboro KS: Kindred, 1997); Luke Lassiter, " 'From Here On, I Will Be Praying to You': Indian Churches, Kiowa Hymns, and Native American Christianity in Southwestern Oklahoma," *Ethnomusicology* 45, no. 2 (2001): 338–52; author's field notes, May 1999.

35. F. H. Abbott to Stecker, February 11, 1911; Quarterly Report for Indian Schools, December 1912; Cato Sells to Stecker, February 15, 1913; C. F. Hanke to Stecker, March

10, 1915; Physician's Semi-Annual Report, December 31, 1916, and March 31, 1917; C. V. Stinchecum to Dr. D. V. Hailman, February 9, 1916; all in RMS.

36. Mary Clouse to C. V. Stinchecum, November 17, 1916, and Stinchecum to Clouse, December 15, 1916, Field Matrons' Files, Records of the Kiowa Agency, Microfilm KA 74, Oklahoma Historical Society.

37. McKenzie to the author, August 1, 1990.

38. Fred Bigman interview, T-50, pp. 24–25, DDOH.

39. Ethel Howry interview, T-78, p. 154, DDOH.

40. Juanita Yeahquo interview, M-2, p. 5, DDOH; Sarah Long Horn interview, T-62, pp. 8–9, DDOH.

41. Myrtle Ware interview, T-76, pp. 3, 5, DDOH.

42. William Lone Wolf interview, March 31, 1967, T-42, p. 8, DDOH; McBeth, *Ethnic Identity*, 92–93; McKenzie to Hurst, October 23, 1987; Whitewolf, *Jim Whitewolf*, 94.

43. Fred Bigman interview, T-50, p. 29, DDOH; Guy Quoetone interview, September 26, 1967, T-149, n.p., DDOH.

44. McKenzie to the author, August 1, 1990; McKenzie to Mrs. Henry T. Choquette, April 2, 1965, copy in the possession of the author.

45. Juanita Yeahquo interview, M-2, p. 4, DDOH.

46. Parker McKenzie, interview by the author, August 1, 1990, Mountain View OK; Morgan to Indian Agents and Superintendents of Indian Schools, October 22, 1891, RMS; Cora Dunn to Dunn, December 12, 1905, RMS.

47. Cora Dunn to Browning, December 19, 1895, RMS.

48. Cora Dunn to Blackmon, April 25, 1907, RMS; McKenzie to Hurst, October 23, 1987; McKenzie interview, August 1, 1990.

49. Cora Dunn to Randlett, April 23, 1902, RMS; "Lewis Toyebo Birthday." For insightful accounts of how students used sports in the boarding schools to affirm their own ideals and identity, see John Bloom, *To Show What an Indian Can Do: Sports at Native American Boarding Schools* (Minneapolis: University of Minnesota Press, 2000); and David Wallace Adams, "More Than a Game: The Carlisle Indians Take to the Gridiron, 1893–1917," *Western Historical Quarterly* 32, no. 1 (spring 2001): 25–53.

50. "Development of Extra-Curricular Activities at Rainy Mountain," n.d., from a packet compiled for a school reunion in June 1963, copy in the possession of the author; Unknown writer to McGregor, October 29, 1912, and R. W. Bishoff to Stinchecum, March 16, 1917, RMS.

51. Rainy Mountain School Songs, ca. 1910–1914, photocopies in the possession of the author, courtesy of Parker McKenzie.

52. James Silverhorn interview, September 28, 1967, T-146, p. 4, DDOH.

53. McKenzie to Hurst, October 23, 1987; Whitewolf, *Jim Whitewolf*, 96.

54. McKenzie to Hurst, October 23, 1987.

55. Supply invoices, May 25, 1909, April 25, 1910, RMS.

56. E. B. Meritt to McGregor, February 21, 1914, RMS.

57. "Field Matron's Quarterly Reports": Mary Given, June 30, 1915; Mary Clouse, July 14, 1915; Anna Heersma, June 30, 1915; Mary Wilkin, July 14, 1915; all in Field Ma-

trons' Files, Microfilm KA 74. In September 1915 Mary Clouse issued a stinging in-
dictment against what she called the "Dance Element," charging it with corrupting
the morals of the tribe's young people and tearing down the work of the schools.
"These dances are one of the breeding places of illegitimate children," she wrote,
"which is [sic] becoming the shame of the tribe. Lust is on the increase." Clouse to
Stinchecum, September 15, 1915, Field Matrons' Files, Microfilm KA 74.

58. McKenzie to Hurst, October 23, 1987.

59. Sarah Long Horn interview, T-62, p. 14, DDOH; "Lewis Toyebo Birthday."

60. Petition of the Kiowa Tribe, January 1920, Kiowa Agency Classified Files, 1907–
39, Record Group 75, National Archives, Washington DC.

61. James Silverhorn interview, T-146, p. 1, DDOH; Fred Bigman interview, T-50, p. 1,
DDOH; McKenzie to the author, August 1, 1990.

62. N. Scott Momaday, *The Way to Rainy Mountain* (Albuquerque: University of New
Mexico Press, 1993), 4.

3. The Man on the Bandstand at Carlisle Indian Industrial School

What He Reveals about the Children's Experiences

Jacqueline Fear-Segal

Jacqueline Fear-Segal is a professor of American Studies at the University of East Anglia in England, where she teaches several courses on Native American history and race relations. She has published many articles on American Indian history and education. In this article she discusses a mysterious character who wrote weekly articles in the *Indian Helper, For Our Indian Boys and Girls,* the newspaper at Carlisle Indian Industrial School. Administrators at Carlisle controlled the newspaper. "Articles and stories carried in the *Indian Helper* were slanted, sanitized and clearly subjected to strict editorial control," Fear-Segal writes. She uses the newspaper and the articles anonymously written by the Man on the Bandstand to assess the administration's spying, all-seeing, and all-knowing gaze.

Fear-Segal points out that Richard H. Pratt, the founder of the Carlisle school, had once worked at a prison where the government had incarcerated Indians, and he patterned the boarding school after a prison. Fear-Segal carefully deconstructs the physical plant, which greatly resembled that of prisons, asylums, factories, and workhouses. Carlisle had a six-foot fence surrounding the physical plant and a jail for truant students. In the heart of the campus, school officials placed a large, white bandstand where Pratt and his staff often observed the actions of students. They used the bandstand as a metaphor to symbolize white control of the place and its inhabitants. The Man on the Bandstand often commented on the language, dress, deportment, manners, and appearance of Indian children at the school. The all-seeing observer on the bandstand used administrative power to regulate the behavior of students at Carlisle.

The first generation of Native American children channeled through the government Indian school system left behind almost no record of their experiences. Today, the violent nature of this aggressive educational campaign and its long-term consequences for families and communities are beginning to be understood, but we still know very little about the lives of individuals

who experienced it, especially in the early days.[1] The few who published accounts provide invaluable insights, but these were the most articulate and
confident, and almost all wrote with the benefit of hindsight.[2]

To deepen our understanding of what it was like to live in these institutions and feel the day-to-day impact of their "civilizing" mission, scholars
have begun to interrogate a variety of different sources. Those close to Native communities still have access to "living documents," and interviews
with survivors have shed new light on how they lived and subsequently came
to view their school years.[3] But representatives from the first generation of
children sent away to school are no longer with us to tell their stories. Taken
from homes mostly untouched by American culture, they passed through
the schools with no one ahead to lead the way and in an era when white
determination to eradicate their cultures was at its height. Some of their
stories were never told.[4] Others were recounted privately and then passed
down from generation to generation, carried in the living memory of Native
American communities. Many have been lost or buried. But traces of some
have been preserved within the written record and can be unearthed from
the archives.[5] Fragments uncovered and interpreted can be pieced together to create a mosaic. For the early years of government schools the detail
is still very abbreviated. Owing to the scarcity of surviving material, every
available source needs to be thoroughly explored to cede any information
that can contribute to our knowledge of daily life at Indian schools.

To contribute to this mosaic, this essay will interrogate a traditional written source, examining it within the physical context of its production. At the
Carlisle Indian Industrial School, the first federally funded boarding school,
a four-page newspaper was published weekly between 1885 and 1900: the *Indian Helper*. In the guise of a school magazine, the *Indian Helper* reported
events, handed out admonitions and advice, printed letters, and document-
ed the activities of staff and students. A white-controlled newspaper source
such as this comes freighted with some obvious problems, particularly when
used as a source to hear from the children and understand their experiences. Nevertheless, although strictly censored, the *Indian Helper* carries a
detailed record of everyday life at the school and supplies the fullest available documentation of daily interactions between white educators and the
children they sought to transform. By interweaving traditional analysis of
this publication with a study of the spatial layout of the built environment

of Carlisle, this essay will frame the propagandized version of events relayed by the *Indian Helper* within the physical context of the school and reveal a previously indiscernible shadow narrative. This narrative brings us telling detail about how the "civilizing" campaign was conducted and also supplies evidence to deepen our understanding of the children's responses.

Established in 1879 in Carlisle, Pennsylvania, the Carlisle Indian Industrial School was a living experiment conducted on Indian children. It supplied the blueprint for the system of federal Indian schools that was set up by the government over the following twenty years. Many of these schools would long outlive their prototype, which was closed down in 1918. Carlisle's founder and first superintendent, from 1879 to 1904, was Captain Richard Henry Pratt, who was confident that his rigorous five-year program of academic, vocational, military and Christian training would sever Indian children's attachment to family, community, and all aspects of their past and teach them to dress, talk, behave, and think like white Americans. Winning and holding the support of white Americans was essential to Pratt, so the school published a large monthly newspaper to expound its philosophy and trumpet its achievements; this was the public voice of Carlisle.[6] The *Indian Helper* was a second and far more modest publication, and both its title and subtitle (*For Our Indian Boys and Girls*) made clear that this little paper's targeted audience was the Indian children themselves. The paper's main readers were students at the school, children who had gone "out" to work for families in the Pennsylvania area, and a growing body of Carlisle-educated Indians who had returned to their reservation homes.[7]

Articles and stories carried in the *Indian Helper* were slanted, sanitized, and clearly subjected to strict editorial control. Information about the paper's editor is therefore essential to our understanding of how to read the *Indian Helper* as a historical source. But the identity of its editor was the *Indian Helper*'s most distinctive and baffling characteristic. Each week a notice on the second page announced: "The INDIAN HELPER is PRINTED by Indian boys, but EDITED by The-man-on-the-band-stand, who is NOT an Indian."[8] This anonymous, invisible, white, male persona brazenly located himself on the school bandstand, claiming it as both home and editorial site. From here he watched the children and commented on their activities. To understand his purpose and the relationship he tried to cultivate with the children through the pages of the *Indian Helper*, we need to look closely at the buildings and grounds of the Carlisle campus and at the bandstand in particular.

The *Indian Helper* was consciously tied into the very fabric of the Carlisle school. Analysis of the interplay that was fostered between this publication and the physical environment of the campus lays bare some of the daily detail of Carlisle's oppressive program as well as the secret of some of the children's responses. First, it allows us to see the intense scrutiny to which the children were subjected as they went about their lives. This mimicked and parodied a system of surveillance pioneered in prisons and was intrinsic to Carlisle's mission to destroy Native cultures. Second, it reveals that the Man on the Bandstand, who combined characteristics of God, Uncle Sam, and grandfather with those of prison officer, spy, and dirty old man, was created as an active component in Carlisle's program, working to substitute *his* creed and code for values and beliefs the children had learned at home. Finally, it demonstrates that in the pages of the *Indian Helper*, despite its overt purpose, it is possible to uncover concealed evidence to help us document and understand some of the ploys and strategies the children used on a day-to-day basis to withstand the force of Carlisle's mission.

For fifteen years, no one besides the Man on the Bandstand claimed editorship of the *Indian Helper*. From his bandstand in the middle of the school grounds, this "man" supposedly watched the children, eavesdropped on their conversations, and then reported and spoke out in the pages of the *Indian Helper*. Sometimes he would analyze or critique an issue, but he did not restrict himself to a traditional editorial column. His preferred style was to interject his comments and opinions all through the paper, briefly but unexpectedly, in little homilies and asides: "How nicely the girls go through with their gymnastic drill!! They must not forget to stand as erect when out of class as they do when exercising."[9] His attention always focused on the children. Few things about their dress, deportment, manners, physical appearance, or behavior escaped his comment. Interspersed among commonplace school news, the minutiae of their lives were described and placed on public display. The children were his subjects, observed and reported on, as well as exhibits to demonstrate the success of the educational experiment. All-seeing and all-hearing but selectively revealing, in the columns of the *Indian Helper* this imaginary persona strutted across the pages that allowed for his construction: a commanding, authoritative, omnipotent, but illusory presence. Full appreciation of how he claimed and wielded his power requires knowledge of the school's layout, and we will return to consider this later. Nothing about the powerful but elusive Man on the Bandstand was straightforward or stable. Every week in the *Indian Helper* there was a "Puzzle Corner," with conundrums, enigmas, and riddles for readers to solve. Placed at the end of the paper, it appeared to be the Man on the Bandstand's signature, because the biggest, ongoing mystery was the question of his identity.

Who was this invisible, ubiquitous, unnamed, and secretive Man on the Bandstand, and what was his function in a school ostensibly committed to helping Indian children find a place in American society? For readers living far from Carlisle or with few links to the school, the identity of the Man on the Bandstand remained a perpetual puzzle, and their letters, printed in the *Indian Helper*, were used to further this sense of mystery. Reporting that "a little girl in Iowa would like to know what we mean by the Man-on-the-band-stand," he confided, "That is what a great many people would like to know, but that is the Man-on-the-band-stand's own secret."[10] Ten years later he was a little more forthcoming but equally cryptic in answer to the same question, explaining, "The Man-on-the-band-stand is the NEWS personified."[11] But anyone who lived and worked at the school or who spoke to the Indian boys who worked at the print shop was well aware that for twenty-five years supervision of all school publications lay in the hands of the white woman who ran the print shop and lived in the teachers' building, which stood just fifteen yards from the bandstand: Marianna Burgess.

So, was Marianna Burgess the Man on the Bandstand? This question was posed directly one week and then answered negatively, in a section of the *Indian Helper* called "Question Box":

> Q: Who is the Man-on-the-band-stand? Is it Miss Burgess? L.D.
> Ans. The Man-on-the-band-stand is the editor of the INDIAN HELPER, who sees everything, but does not print all he sees. The Man-on-the-band-stand is not Miss Burgess.[12]

This answer was confusing, but it contains a truth. One week, when Burgess was away from the school, she teasingly revealed to readers of the *In-*

dian Helper the part she regularly played in the production of the paper as well as her intimate association with the Man on the Bandstand: "The Indian printer boys received many deserved compliments on last week's HELP-ER which they issued in the absence of the Man-on-the-band-stand's chief. The old man *thought* they would do well if they tried."[13]

Marianna Burgess shared his initials, M.B., and she played on this in the paper. Her relationship to the M.O.T.B.S., as he was often called in the *Indian Helper*, was intense, complicated, and shifting. She generally described herself as his "Chief Clerk." On occasions, however, a Mrs. M.O.T.B.S. was mentioned, with the suggestive implication that this was Burgess. It was certainly she who constructed his multiple personalities and developed his voice. He was her creature. In the pages of the *Indian Helper*, where she created, paraded, operated, played, and flirted with him, we find her delighting in his power, ambiguity, and numerous roles. Through him she attempted to control, intimidate, and manipulate the children, and from behind the safety of his facade she claimed the freedom to report, uncensored, her own version of all that went on in the school. He allowed her to live a vicarious life. But although Burgess might wield the editorial hand, call herself his "Chief Clerk," and constantly energize the mystery surrounding his identity, she and the Man on the Bandstand were not one and the same person. The Man on the Bandstand was a constructed persona, claiming more ubiquity and power than Marianna Burgess could ever hope for.

The *Indian Helper*, like the Carlisle Indian School, was under the authority of Captain Richard Henry Pratt. Pratt had been discharged from the U.S. Army by the War Department in order to conduct the Carlisle experiment in Indian education. His army uniform, which he often wore when going about his duties at Carlisle, was a constant reminder of the source of his authority.[14] Pratt would sometimes position himself on the bandstand in the middle of the campus, seen and seeing. Although he was not the Man on the Bandstand, his imposing six-foot-tall figure, silhouetted on the bandstand, gave a shadowy reality to this imaginary man. And Pratt's presence at Carlisle was essential to the Man on the Bandstand's existence. Behind Pratt and the campaign to expunge Native cultures stood the full apparatus of the American state.

Carlisle was spawned by the expansionist territorial ambitions of the United States. As the United States commandeered and engulfed Indian lands, Indian nations were concentrated on reservations and their children packed off to white-run schools. The first pupils at Carlisle came to the school after spending three years as prisoners in Fort Marion, Florida, where Pratt had been their jailor. Most of those who followed might not strictly have been prisoners, but they were hostages for their parents' good behavior out west, participating in an educational experiment approved, bolstered, and financed by the federal government. It is within this power structure that the *Indian Helper* and the persona of the Man on the Bandstand have to be configured. This constellation of power transformed what might have been only an imaginary, laughable, chameleon-like editorial voice into a sinister and threatening force.

The Man on the Bandstand's traffic in enigmas, evasions, and secrecy cloaked a monstrous power game. The Man on the Bandstand claimed, as he frequently reminded his readers, to be unknowable, and he chided them for believing otherwise. "How smart some people think they are when they are sure they know all about the Man-on-the-band-stand!" "The fact is," he continued, "no one but the old man himself knows anything about him, except that he tells the truth."[15] Reveling in his own mystery, he gave away tantalizing hints and tips about his identity, teasing and tormenting his readers. Perhaps the most bizarre was a small diagrammatic drawing of a face, published under the heading:

THE MAN-ON-THE-BAND-STAND
WOULD LIKE TO KNOW

Who took this picture of him.[16]

The picture was meaningless, an apparently harmless enigmatic joke, but within the context of the Carlisle Indian School it carried a ominous message about power and visibility. This supposed "photograph" of the Man on the Bandstand divulged nothing about its alleged subject. The mocking request suggested indignation that someone might have caught a glimpse of him and even had the audacity to take a photograph. The sketched lines of this diagrammatic cipher, however, teasingly confirmed his identity as both unknowable and invisible. By contrast, every feature of the children and their new American identities was regularly exhibited in the many photographs taken by local photographer J. R. Choat.

Photographs were one of the main weapons in the armory of the Carlisle school. Pratt used them to illustrate the children's transformation from "savage" to "civilized" which the school boasted it could accomplish.[17] The *Indian Helper* was one of the vehicles by which they reached the outside world. Repeatedly offered for sale or handed out to readers in exchange for securing subscriptions to the paper, these photographs of the children presented them scrubbed, dressed, arranged, and displayed for the public eye. A series of "before" and "after" photographs of both individuals and groups was also made to exhibit the transformation wrought by a Carlisle education. While close-up photographic images of the Indian children, as products of Carlisle's civilization program, were paraded for all to examine, an enigmatic drawing was all that was seen of the Man on the Bandstand. It was a mask for his shifting and multiple personalities and a mocking boast about his invisible and indecipherable power.

In the pages of the *Indian Helper*, the Man on the Bandstand repeatedly referred to his physical presence on the Carlisle campus and bragged that he could see all that went on. The layout of the school buildings provides an important key to understanding this claim. When one Indian subscriber allegedly asked, "Will you please explain why you are called the 'Man-on-the-band-stand'?" the answer came back: "If the questioner were at Carlisle, he would know why. The Band-stand commands the whole situation. From it he can see all the quarters, the printing office, the chapel, the grounds, everything and everybody, all the girls and the boys on the walks, at the windows, everywhere. Nothing escapes the Man-on-the-band-stand. . . . Already he sees into the homes of the boys and girls who go out upon the farms."[18] Situated at the symbolic as well as architectural hub of Carlisle, the bandstand commanded panoramic views of the whole school, but its full potential for voyeurism was realized only when it was made the permanent "home" of an invisible, vigilant observer.

When the Carlisle Barracks became home to the Carlisle Indian Industrial School, the bandstand was already there, standing in the middle of the parade ground.[19] Pratt ordered it renovated and painted.[20] The other buildings, which lay along three sides of a quadrangle around the bandstand, he readily adapted to his purposes.[21] From photographs and maps we are able to reconstruct how the school looked. On the eastern side, the two-storied, double-verandaed house of the superintendent faced in a straight line across the parade ground, past the flagpole, directly up the bandstand steps.[22] To the north lay the girls' dormitory, then the boys' quarters, the industrial shops, and beyond them the school cemetery.[23] There are no photographs of the cemetery, but its triangular plot doubled in size and became rhombus-shaped when the school expanded into new farmlands in 1887, and its location is clearly marked on surveyors' maps.[24] On the southern side of the quadrangle stood the teachers' house and the school building, and in the far southeast corner was the low, stone guardhouse, with its four dank prison cells. Only the western side of the quadrangle lay open when the Carlisle Indian School was first established.[25]

Within five years, Pratt had ordered the construction of a huge, three-story dining hall opposite the superintendent's quarters, closing in the quadrangle.[26] This dining hall is critical to our understanding of the visual grammar of the campus. Its location completed the enclosure of the central area of the school, blocking off views of both road and exit from inside the campus. In the very first weeks of the school's existence, Pratt had organized the building of a six-foot-high fence around the outer perimeter of the entire campus.[27] The children could not look out, but anyone standing on the bandstand's raised, covered platform had a complete, panoramic view of the whole school. Pratt could easily oversee the children at meal times, gaze through the windows of the girls' rooms, or stare at the heavy, grilled door behind which Indian boys suffered their punishments in solitary confinement.[28]

When not stationed at his post, the Man on the Bandstand led his readers to believe that he moved unseen among the children, observing their activities and eavesdropping on their conversations. He could drop in, undetected, on any event, innocent or otherwise. In fact, the more apparently innocent his visitations, the more menacing they feel: "The Man-on-the-band-stand pricked up his ears when he heard strains of music on Friday evening. Then looking toward the sewing room, and seeing a bright light shining through the window, he stepped over to see what might be going on. . . . He stole in so quietly that no-one saw or heard him."[29] Sometimes he singled out individual children, although he did not always name them. On these occasions he described his view from the bandstand and movements around the grounds in such minutiae that they could be tied to specific people and events: "The Man-on-the-band-stand sometimes looks right over the dining-hall. If he should tell the girls' names who do some very silly things back there, they might be ashamed."[30] Not only was he spying and eavesdropping, but he also recruited the children as informants: "Some one whispered in the ear of the Man-on-the-band-stand that if he had taken a peep into the Teacher's Club kitchen he would have seen Carrie Cornelius working faithfully."[31]

When good behavior was reported, the implication was that bad behavior would be too. From his privileged vantage point, the Man on the Bandstand observed and then reported and discussed the lives of Indian children while they attended the school, and then, when they left Carlisle, using the *Indian Helper* and the U.S. postal services, he followed them back to their reservation homes. His location at the center of the school transformed an innocent bandstand into an inspection tower. Had he been a silent observer, his presence might have been disturbing but without threat. His ability to publish his sightings made the Man on the Bandstand menacing.

Today it is impossible to imagine the Man on the Bandstand stationed at his post without being reminded of both the design and purpose of Jeremy Bentham's panopticon.[32] Bentham envisioned a radical new method for simultaneously punishing and reforming prisoners, and he went further, suggesting that asylums, factories, workhouses, and even schools could also be successfully run using the same plan and principle. In *Panopticon* (1791) he presented his design for this innovative penitentiary, where order would be maintained without resort to physical violence; surveillance and recorded evidence would be substituted for force.

Fundamental to Bentham's design was the inspection tower, constructed at the center, from which the subduing gaze of authority would look out and observe the prisoners in the tiered cells organized around it. The prisoner could not see into the tower, but under the ever-vigilant eye of a superior power that watched and recorded his every move he was compelled to examine his conscience, acknowledge his guilt, and mend his ways.[33] This was a surveillance more intrusive than mere policing. It regulated, but it also demanded an inner change in the prisoner, enlisting him in the enactment of his own transformation. Although the tower might not be occupied full-time, its physical presence would create the impression of continuous surveillance.[34] In England, Bentham's twenty-year campaign to construct a panopticon penitentiary failed, but he had provided prison architects with a design deemed capable of promoting discipline thorough surveillance. In the United States, when the Eastern State Penitentiary opened on the outskirts of Philadelphia in 1821, its debt to Bentham was obvious and it became internationally acknowledged as a landmark experiment in reform, building technology, and prison architecture.

Two hundred miles from Philadelphia's pioneering prison, the Carlisle Indian School represented a later and more circumscribed reform movement than the one that inspired the penitentiary. Yet the task of civilizing Indian children, as projected by reformers, shared something in common with earlier schemes to reform prisoners: both relied for their success on the subject's imbibing a new morality. To experience the demanded inner transformation, Indian students, like prisoners, were required to participate in the process of their own correction and consciously reject their previous lifestyle and behavior. At Carlisle no carefully crafted inspection tower looked out over the pupils, but in the pages of the *Indian Helper* the bandstand was commandeered to perform this function.

Before the Carlisle Barracks were handed over to Pratt, they had been used by the U.S. Army to train young cavalry recruits to fight Indian tribes in the West. At this time the bandstand seemed a commonplace, innocuous structure and a far cry from the inspection tower we have been discussing.[35] Its location in the middle of the parade ground reflected its social and musical functions and carried no ominous connotations. When the Indian school took over the barracks, the bandstand retained its innocent demeanor. But, by a series of ingenious strategies, this inoffensive gazebo was converted into an inspection tower, claiming greater potency than Bentham ever dreamed of and powers more diverse than those enforced at the Eastern State Penitentiary.

The invention of the invisible man who made the bandstand his home and watched the children continuously from its raised platform turned this roofed structure into a quasi inspection tower. Unlike Bentham's panopticon, the bandstand's architecture did not immediately declare its purpose. To the uninformed eye, it still looked like a pretty, pagoda-shaped bandstand. To anyone made aware of its unseen resident and his reports in the *Indian Helper*, its open-sided, octagonal shape and elevated platform could never look the same again.

This "inhabited" bandstand was perfectly equipped for both visual and auditory surveillance. Bentham, in his first version of the panopticon, had planned to supplement visual surveillance with a parallel system of acoustic surveillance, made possible by a system of pipes leading from the prisoners' cells to the central tower. The difficulty of ensuring that sound traveled only in one direction and therefore prevented the prisoners from listening to the inspectors had forced Bentham to abandon this part of his scheme.[36] Bentham, when designing his panopticon, was bound by the constraints of real life. For the Man on the Bandstand, who resided in a world of fantasy and make-believe, issues of feasibility imposed no such limits. Capable of single-handedly maintaining his constant vigil from the center of the school, he also claimed the power to *listen* to the children.

In him the voyeuristic, eavesdropping powers of the panopticon reached new phantasmagoric heights, which he flagged and indulged in the *Indian Helper* in a column entitled "What I See and Hear." Although supposedly living on the bandstand in the center of the school, he also trumpeted his ability to step down from his home to spy on the children wherever they might be. He could mingle unseen among them on the grounds, prowl through the classrooms and dormitories, or crash a school picnic undetected. To understand the Man on the Bandstand's claim to possess special powers, we need to turn our attention both to the particular historical and social circumstances that allowed for his creation and to ongoing life at Carlisle. Here it is the differences between Bentham's prisoners and Carlisle's Indian children that is instructive.

While neither Bentham nor the Philadelphia Quakers ever doubted that the gaze of authority, directed from the panopticon onto the prisoner, possessed the power to induce guilt and contrition, this was a supposition rooted in a Christian notion of conscience and the individual soul. Many Indian children did not share this Christian cosmology. Despite wide differences in their separate tribal cultures, they had grown up in societies where community and kinship lay at the core of all definitions of good. For them, the concept of individual salvation or damnation was completely alien because their lives were inseparable from that of family and kin. The gaze of authority, as envisaged by Bentham, might be able to intimidate them, but it would fail to trigger the personal remorse and guilt deemed essential for inner transformation. At the Carlisle school, therefore, inspection would have little effect unless it was accompanied by an interpretive voice that was able to furnish this inner narrative for Indian children. In the pages of the *Indian Helper* the Man on the Bandstand labored to outline and impose this narrative in its daily detail, to instill in each and every Carlisle pupil that inner voice of Christian conscience.

In the aching silence experienced by every far-from-home child, where the voices of grandfathers and elders would have been heard, the Man on the Bandstand sought to make his own voice resound. He wanted to subvert loyalties as well as values. Through innumerable references to the school, its staff, individual children, and the activities of Carlisle alumni, he strove to create a new "imagined community" of educated Indians, with Carlisle at its center.[37] He tried to draw the children into a world no longer shared by elders and relations. Reading the *Indian Helper*, whether at school, on "outing," or back home on the reservation, was meant to provide a link between each subscriber, Carlisle, the Man on the Bandstand, and a broad-based Indian world very different from the one embraced by tribal affiliation. At this level, the Man on the Bandstand struggled ingeniously and consistently to further the goals of the Carlisle Indian School. To achieve his purpose, his voice was as vital as his gaze.

Voice, of course, was the Man on the Bandstand's only tangible feature—or, to be more accurate, voices, because his shifting personality was echoed in the numerous voices he used to address the children in the pages of the *Indian Helper*. He would abandon his posture of authority, step from his bandstand, and assume a variety of different personae as he moved among the children, matching these identities with the range of styles and voices that simultaneously created them. He availed himself of a dizzying array of personalities and voices.

Sometimes, like a wise grandfather, he gave counsel, pointing out the children's frailties as Indians and suggesting the best way for them to live their lives: "Horace Greeley's advice to the young white man was, 'Go west, young man!' but the advice of the Man-on-the-band-stand to all *Indian* young men who have had but little experience in caring for themselves, is 'Stay *east*, young man, till you get *strong* in experience.' "[38] Often, sounding like a Horio Alger novel, he lectured them from his podium about the proper conduct and manners necessary for achieving success in America: "The Man-on-the-band-stand would like to hear the pupils say, 'Yes, sir,' and 'No, sir,' every time when they answer a gentleman. Politeness goes a long way with a person wishing to make a success in life."[39] Employing instructive and slightly threatening tones, he could assume the role of school monitor and outline or reiterate the school rules: "The Man-on-the-band-stand would like to see all our workers present at morning services."[40] When giving praise and approval to reinforce the lessons of "civilization" taught at Carlisle, he could sound like a patronizing uncle: "The girls are buying rugs for their rooms when they have a little spare cash and the Man-on-the-bandstand is pleased to see the bright, cheery and home like effect it has upon their rooms."[41] Just as easily, in the semblance of a disappointed parent, he could single out students for humiliation or embarrassment. On one occasion it was one of "his" own printer boys who was the focus of his attention and "his" bandstand that was used as the site of punishment: "The Man-on-the-band-stand felt so disgraced and ashamed when one of his clerks was placed on the band-stand for punishment last Sabath [*sic*] that he could not hold his head up."[42] Using wheedling and insinuating tones, he also invited the children to inform on their compatriots when they left Carlisle and returned to their reservation homes: "Let the boys and girls who go home, write to the Man-on-the-band-stand something about what our other pupils are doing who returned before."[43]

A dramatic change of style took place when the Man on the Bandstand moved openly into fantasy. He was always located in a realm of semi-make-believe, but when he became privy to the thoughts of Father Christmas or struck up conversations with fairies, the world of whimsy he inhabited progressed one stage further in its mix of the weird and infantile: "The Man-on-the-band-stand stood for a few moments with closed eyes, one warm day this week, and as he was thus apparently in deep thought, a little fairy came along and called out to him, 'Grandpa, what are you thinking about?' "[44] In soft, intimate tones a world apart from his booming voice of authority, the Man on the Bandstand told the fairy a story, a fable of Christian morality. Whether cajoling, persuading, hectoring, or instructing, he incessantly alerted the children to how they should behave and what they should become.

He was always indefatigably upbeat, particularly when his focus moved from the children to their physical environment and his delight in improvements and physical changes to the campus. He detailed the construction of buildings, the laying of paths, and the introduction of modern conveniences such as lighting and steam central heating. But in all his portrayals of the Carlisle campus he assiduously avoided any description of the cemetery and its extending lines of gravestones.[45] This was the most tragic and least publicized aspect of Carlisle's history. Nearly a hundred children died at the school during its first decade. Single-line reports of their deaths appear in the *Indian Helper*, disconcertingly intermingled with news about the social activities of staff and pupils. During a period when children were dying weekly and a large number were lying sick in the school hospital, the Man on the Bandstand took the unprecedented step of addressing the subject directly.[46] In buoyant tones he recommended willpower as a means of recovery, instructing the children to "Will yourself to get well! Many people cure themselves of sickness now by using their WILL power. It is easy to die if we just give up to all our pains and aches and think we are more sick than we really are."[47] Even sickness and death were turned into grist for his moralizing, educational mill.

The Man on the Bandstand could, as we have seen, veer between different moods and voices: from congratulatory to instructional, from teasing to critical, from open to secretive, and from friendly to sinister. When much of the *Indian Helper*'s readership was in the process of acquiring both literacy and the English language, the Man on the Bandstand's antics inevitably generated some bewilderment. It was hardly surprising to learn that "Somebody asks, 'Is the man-on-the-band-stand you speak of a real person?'" Predictably, the answer given was both unenlightening and enigmatic: "Perhaps he is, perhaps he is not, we will leave you to guess that conundrum."[48]

During the years when the Man on the Bandstand was up to his tricks, approximately five thousand children passed through the Carlisle Indian School. When so much in their lives was new and terrifying, it is difficult to assess how the majority responded. Was the Man on the Bandstand an intimidating presence haunting the campus? Did they find him menacing?

Were they confused by his various guises? Or could they disregard him and dismiss his games as the silly pastime of a batty white woman? On one occasion Marianna Burgess published a letter that clearly titillated her. An Apache girl, Nellie Carey, had been savvy enough to join Burgess in her game and addressed a letter to her as "Mrs. M.O.T.B.S." before quickly and jokingly correcting herself and referring to "the Man-on-the-band-stand's Chief Clerk."[49] Examples of sophisticated engagements with the Man on the Bandstand such as this are rare. Nevertheless, his antics in the *Indian Helper* furnish us with a wealth of covert information about the children's response to Carlisle and its program.

Often this is reported as wrangles between him and the children. For a number of weeks these focus on the children's marching and their refusal to keep time with the piano as they leave the school chapel. Although it is apparently a small thing, in the pages of the school newspaper the Man on the Bandstand returns to it again and again, while at chapel the children persist in their rebellion. The boys are worse than the girls, the Man on the Bandstand notes disdainfully, reminding them that it is the boys who benefit from the most drilling. Week after week he mocks and tut-tuts, giving verbal instruction: "We can't learn to be soldiers till we learn to march to music. Right foot on accentuated note looks rather funny."[50] The boys were clearly having fun; their public show of insubordination gave them a small opportunity for revolt in an area deemed of key importance in a military school. A similar wrangle erupted over the children's refusal to keep off the grass and stay on the straight paths that crisscrossed the campus. Sometimes he tried to put the frighteners on them, warning how wet feet would lead to pneumonia and death.[51] More often, he gave a detailed description of the "crime." On one occasion he criticizes the lines of desire and defiance the children have, quite literally, stamped onto the face of the campus: "The attention of the Man-on-the-band-stand has been called by one in authority to two paths that are being worn across the grass plot in the shop court, by people who are too indifferent to go around. One is across the center from center door to center door, and the other is a short cut to the dining room and town. Come! Come!"[52] Encapsulated in his constant complaints and lists of infractions is a revealing record of the many different ways the children found to flout the rules or oppose the school. Marching out of time, walking on the grass, going barefoot, stealing apples, spilling whitewash on the croquet lawn, and chipping paint off the bandstand were fairly minor infractions. "Talking Indian" was considered more serious. The Saturday ritual of naming and shaming those who had offended was regularly reported by the Man on the Bandstand, and it stands as detailed record of both the children's determination to speak their own languages and the failure of Carlisle's boasted English-only policy.

In the pages of the *Indian Helper*, one of the schools most serious and persistent problems went almost unmentioned. Runaways plagued the authorities at Carlisle. If the students were caught and brought back, they were punished by being locked in the guardhouse.[53] Yet the Man on the Bandstand was only able to approach this problem indirectly. One week he told "A True Story of Three Indians Lads Who Tried Running Away from School." Although he named the boys—Ben Stumpfoot, Harry Shortneck, and Ed Buffalo Horn—he reassured readers that they were not from Carlisle. They had attended a western school in a previous decade. The story was told for a moral rather than informative purpose, because these boys reportedly ended up not in the guardhouse but with frostbite.[54] At many different levels, both individuals and groups of children challenged the proprieties of the school and offered both active and passive resistance to its "civilizing" program. The most serious of their offenses were ignored or referred to obliquely, but nevertheless the pages of the *Indian Helper* provide dozens of details about the many, tiny, and ingenious ways the children thwarted school authority.

On occasion the children's acts of resistance and rebellion engaged the American legal system. Theft and arson brought trials and prison sentences, accompanied by detailed coverage in the local press. When two Sioux girls, Fanny Eaglehorn and Lizzie Flanders, tried to burn down the girls' dormitory twice in the same evening, they were caught, put on trial, convicted of arson, and sentenced to eighteen months in the Eastern State Penitentiary in Philadelphia. The Man on the Bandstand could not turn a blind eye to such a public offense, and the *Indian Helper* gave a full description of their crime. Readers learned how the two girls had first set fire to papers in the reading room after supper on a dark Sunday evening in November.[55] Then, after this blaze was discovered, they secretly climbed to the top floor of the girls' building and, while the rest of the school attended chapel, lit a second fire in a clothes closet. This fire was also detected, and the girls were caught.

In relating a story that so obviously reflected badly on Carlisle, the Man on the Bandstand took the opportunity to praise the speed and efficiency of the school's firefighting force. Yet in detailing their actions, he had also inadvertently exposed the planning and determination that accompanied Fanny Eaglehorn and Lizzie Flanders's attempt to burn down their dormitory. Rarely discussed publicly, arson was a common occurrence at all Indian schools and one of the most dramatic ways the children found to express their resistance. The Man on the Bandstand condemned the girls, insisting they "had a bad record before they came and have been stubborn and ugly ever since they arrived, no amount of kindness shown them having any effect." For this he blamed the depravity of their home lives.[56]

Always at his harshest when discussing the children's traditional histories and cultures, the Man on the Bandstand missed few opportunities to teach the master narrative of U.S. history. At a school debate on "Whether or not the treatment of the Indians by the early settlers caused King Philip to war," Marianna Burgess was one of the three judges who, predictably, decided that "the best argument was on the negative side."[57] In the pages of the *Indian Helper*, all aspects of the children's home lives were consistently vilified. After a trip to Dakota Territory, Burgess even felt qualified to stage a conversation with the Man on the Bandstand to discuss the filth she saw and infer the immorality behind it:

> M.O.T.B.S.: *"Did you really find the Indians so filthy as you would have us believe from you last letter?"*
>
> M.B.: *"Yes, indeed! Why if I should describe the worst things I saw you would not allow such a letter to be published in your little paper."*[58]

Yet despite all efforts to quash the children's cultures and to denigrate their home lives, it was clear these could be expunged from neither their memories nor their hearts. Their letters, poems, and stories printed in the *Indian Helper* often reveal a message quite different from the one the Man on the Bandstand wished to convey. Published to demonstrate how they profited from and endorsed Carlisle's program, they often carried another covert message. In an English class a Lakota boy, Frank Lock, wrote a letter that the Man on the Bandstand entitled "Exchanging Books for Ponies." While ostensibly about his new aptitude with books, the boy's memories of his life in Dakota, as well as his respect for the elders whose values he is supposed to be rejecting, shine through in the letter he wrote to a friend back home:

> *I am enjoying the fair weather here and the good time, but often thought of the old places, where we have had lots of fun in training and lassoing young ponies and how we were often unhorsed, and how we used to set traps to catch foxes and wolves and how we would go to fish and search bird nests and how we used to come home with big hearts, having plenty of game and how we made old folks happy, how I used to try to have my ponies run faster than yours, and how we tried to have fat ponies; but I have now adopted the school books as my ponies, and so if I desire to have my books run fast, I study them harder and there is no doubt that you can't beat me in that race.*[59]

The energy and detail of the early writing belies the message carried in the last two lines. Despite rigorous policing and the watchful eye of the Man on the Bandstand, the children's pleasure and attachment to their home lives and values could not be totally erased, even from the pages of the *Indian Helper*. Indian schools faced their greatest challenge when children returned to their communities. Critics of the educational experiment spearheaded by Carlisle constantly reported that when students went home they reverted to traditional ways—or, as they put it, went "back to the blanket." Although Carlisle encouraged its students to remain in the East, the vast majority returned to their reservation homes. In an attempt to maintain a hold over these returnees, remind them of the standards and values taught by Carlisle, and counteract the influence of their families and communities, the *Indian Helper* was sent west to thousands of reservation homes. Going one step further, in 1891 Marianna Burgess published a little book entitled *Stiya: A Carlisle Indian Girl at Home*, using her own initials as a thinly disguised pseudonym, Embe.[60]

Written in the first person, *Stiya* is ostensibly the story of a Pueblo girl's return home and her courageous efforts to live the lessons learned at Carlisle. Burgess had been on an extensive visit to the Pueblo Indians, and she utilized the information and observations she had collected on this trip to denigrate the homes, dress, and all aspects of Pueblo life. She portrays Stiya as disgusted by the meanness of her home and the filth and superstition that pervaded it and describes her homecoming as traumatic, not joyful:

> *Was I as glad to see them as I thought I would be?*
>
> *I must confess that instead I was shocked and surprised at the sight that met my eyes.*
>
> *"My father? My mother?" cried I desperately within. "No, never!" I thought, and I actually turned my back upon them.*
>
> *I had forgotten that home Indians had such grimy faces.*
>
> *I had forgotten that my mother's hair always looked as thought it had never seen a comb . . .*
>
> *I rushed frantically into the arms of my* school-*mother, who had taken me home.*[61]

Burgess anticipated the situations a returning student would encounter and then wrote the script for how they should respond. She appropriated their experiences and emotions in a deliberate attempt to manage and direct them both. The voice of the Man on the Bandstand might be able to command and even commiserate, but his was the male voice of white authority, emanating always from his bandstand and located far away in Carlisle. In the voice of Stiya—female, intimate, guileless, and fresh—Burgess sought a way to bring the Carlisle message closer to home using a very different messenger. By purportedly identifying and empathizing with a Pueblo girl, she claimed the opportunity to speak as an Indian, from inside Pueblo society.

Sold for fifty cents through the pages of the *Indian Helper* and carried home by many returning students, *Stiya* was the closest Burgess could come to creating a portable bandstand, one capable of carrying Carlisle's message back to the children's homes. Laguna Pueblo author Leslie Marmon Silko tells us that *Stiya* caused "the only big quarrel my great grandmother ever had with her daughter-in-law, Aunt Susie." These two Pueblo women were in complete agreement about the offensive nature of the book's contents. Their intense feelings centered instead on what its fate should be. Aunt Susie thought the defamatory text should be preserved as "important evidence of the lies, racism and bad faith of the U.S. Government with the Pueblo people." Grandma A'mooh thought the book should be burned, "just as witchcraft paraphernalia is destroyed." The story of this family row was passed down orally through three generations of Silko's family. Written down and then published in 1994, it gives us a unique glimpse of two Pueblo women's impassioned response to Burgess's written words and the campaign to crush Indian cultures.[62]

Regrettably, we have yet to discover a comparable record that tells us directly how the Carlisle children reacted to Burgess when she spoke to them through the Man on the Bandstand. But if we are able to cut through the *Indian Helper's* propaganda and read it within the physical context of Carlisle, this white-edited school magazine can enable us to reconstruct aspects of day-to-day life at the school, meet some of the Indian children, uncover tiny fragments of their lives, and even hear the whisper of their voices.

Notes

1. Margaret L. Archuleta, Brenda J. Child, and K. Tsianina Lomawaima, eds., *Away from Home: American Indian Boarding School Experiences, 1879–2000* (Phoenix: Heard Museum, 2000); Joel Spring, *The Cultural Transformation of a Native American Family, 1763–1995* (Mahwah NJ: Erlbaum, 1996). For a comprehensive study of schools in Canada that exposes the abuses within a parallel school system, see J. R. Miller, *Shingwauk's Vision: A History of Native Residential Schools* (Toronto: University of Toronto Press, 1996).

2. For an annotated list of autobiographies see H. David Brumble III, *An Annotated Bibliography of American Indian and Eskimo Autobiographies* (Lincoln: University of Nebraska Press, 1981); for an analysis of school autobiographies see Michael C. Coleman, *American Indian Children at School, 1850–1930* (Jackson: University Press of Mississippi, 1993); for autobiographies by a former Carlisle student see Luther Standing Bear, *My People the Sioux* (Lincoln: University of Nebraska Press, 1975) and *Land of the Spotted Eagle* (Lincoln: University of Nebraska Press, 1978).

3. K. Tsianina Lomawaima, *They Called It Prairie Light: The Story of Chilocco Indian School* (Lincoln: University of Nebraska Press, 1994); Henrietta Mann, *Cheyenne-Arapaho Education, 1871–1982* (Niwot: University Press of Colorado, 1997); Sally McBeth, *Ethnic Identity and the Boarding School Experience of West-Central Oklahoma American Indians* (Washington DC: University Press of America, 1983).

4. Some students never returned to their own people to tell their stories, and others found their experiences too painful or difficult to tell, even to family and friends.

5. Brenda J. Child, *Boarding School Seasons: American Indian Families, 1900–1940* (Lincoln: University of Nebraska Press, 1998); Scott Riney, *The Rapid City Indian School, 1898–1933* (Norman: University of Oklahoma Press, 1999).

6. This monthly newspaper, published continuously from 1880 until the school was closed down in 1918, appeared under a series of changing names—*Eadle Keatah Toh, The Morning Star, The Red Man,* and *The Arrow.*

7. Readers paid twenty-five cents for an annual subscription. Their numbers peaked at twelve thousand in 1898.

8. This as nearly as possible reproduces the style of the text as it appeared in the *Indian Helper*.

9. *Indian Helper*, January 21, 1887.

10. *Indian Helper*, February 8, 1889.

11. *Indian Helper*, January 20, 1899.

12. *Indian Helper*, April 29, 1887.

13. *Indian Helper*, May 20, 1887.

14. Photograph by J. R. Choat, "Captain Richard Henry Pratt mounted on horseback," c. 1885, 14–32–4, Cumberland County Historical Society, Carlisle, Pennsylvania.

15. *Indian Helper*, May 20, 1887.

16. *Indian Helper*, February 12, 1886. The picture is half an inch high.

17. For an analysis of these photographs see Lonna Malmsheimer, "'Imitation White Man': Images of Transformation at the Carlisle Indian School," *Studies in Visual Communication* 2, no. 4 (fall 1985): 54–74.

18. *Indian Helper*, March 9, 1888.

19. "Map of the Carlisle Barracks," 1870, Record Group 75, subgroup c, Map 320, National Archives, College Park, Maryland.

20. Photograph by J. R. Choat, "The Bandstand," 1879, Cumberland County Historical Society; J. R. Choat, "Indian Girls in First Uniforms," October 1880, Cumberland County Historical Society, shows the renovated bandstand.

21. "Ground Plan of Carlisle Barracks, U.S. Cavalry Depot," showing location and use of buildings, made by U.S. Quartermaster's Department, 1877, Cumberland County Historical Society.

22. Photograph by J. R. Choat, "Superintendents's Quarters," c. 1880, Cumberland County Historical Society.

23. Photograph by J. R. Choat, "Girls' Quarter," c. 1885, shows the girls' dormitory, the bandstand, and the perimeter fence; photograph by J. R. Choat, "Boys' Building," c. 1880; photograph by J. R. Choat, "The Workshops," c. 1880; all in the Cumberland County Historical Society.

24. Survey map of "United States Indian Industrial School for Proposed Borough Sewer," 1884, and "Map of the United States Barracks," 1909, Record Group 77, subgroup b, Records of the Office of Chief Engineers, National Archives, College Park, Maryland.

25. Jacqueline Fear-Segal, "Mapping the Carlisle Indian School," http://www.uea.ac.uk/eas/People/fear-segal/carlisleindiansch.htm

26. Photograph by J. R. Choat, "Dining Hall," 12–8–1, Cumberland County Historical Society.

27. This whitewashed fence is visible in many of the photographs.

28. Photograph by J. R. Choat, "Guardhouse," 1880, Cumberland County Historical Society. A 1980 reconstruction of the bandstand stands in its original location. Today, visitors to the remnants of the Carlisle Indian School, which now forms part of the U.S. Army War College in Carlisle, Pennsylvania, can stand on its platform and survey the surrounding buildings.

29. *Indian Helper*, January 13, 1888.

30. *Indian Helper*, February 12, 1886.

31. *Indian Helper*, November 22, 1895.

32. For Michel Foucault's reflections on panopticism see *Discipline and Punish: The Birth of the Prison* (New York: Vintage Books, 1975), 195–228.

33. The panopticon thus allows seeing without being seen. For Foucault this asymmetry is the essence of power, because ultimately the power to dominate rests on the differential possession of knowledge. Cf. Foucault, "The Subject and Power," afterword in Hubert Dreyfus and Paul Rainbow, *Michel Foucault: Beyond Structuralism and Hermeneutics*, 2nd ed. (Chicago: University of Chicago Press, 1983), 208–26.

34. Jeremy Bentham, *The Panopticon*, in *Writings*, ed. Miran Bozovic (1791; London: Verso, 1995), 1.

35. In one of history's unsettling symmetries, the children of these same tribes would later attend school at the Carlisle Barracks.

36. Foucault points this out in a footnote. *Discipline and Punish*, 317.

37. Benedict Anderson, *Imagined Communities: Reflections on the Origins and Spread of Nationalism* (London: Verso, 1983).

38. *Indian Helper*, April 1, 1887.

39. *Indian Helper*, January 20, 1888.

40. *Indian Helper*, October 7, 1887.

41. *Indian Helper*, October 15, 1897.

42. *Indian Helper*, August 13, 1886.

43. *Indian Helper*, June 18, 1886.

44. *Indian Helper*, May 24, 1889.

45. If photographs of the cemetery were taken they have not survived or have not yet been unearthed, but its location is marked on old maps of U.S. General Hospital, No. 31, Carlisle PA. "General Map," October 18, 1918, Military History Institute, Carlisle, Pennsylvania.

46. *Indian Helper*, February 3, 1888.

47. *Indian Helper*, April 6, 1888.

48. *Indian Helper*, February 3, 1888.

49. *Indian Helper*, January 13, 1888.

50. *Indian Helper*, February 10, 1899.

51. *The Red Man and Helper*, January 15, 1904. The school newspapers combined and offered this new name.

52. *Indian Helper*, July 21, 1899.

53. Genevieve Bell, "Telling Tales Out of School: Remembering the Carlisle Indian Industrial School, 1879–1918" (Ph.D. diss., Stanford University, 1998), 209–48.

54. *Indian Helper*, March 10, 1893.

55. Photograph by Frances Johnson, "Girls' Reading Room," c. 1900, J0-1-8, Cumberland County Historical Society.

56. The quotation is from *Indian Helper*, November 19, 1897. For information on the poor home life of Indian students, see *Indian Helper*, November 18, 1898.

57. *Indian Helper*, January 21, 1898.

58. *Indian Helper*, August 19, 1887.

59. Frank Lock, "Books as Ponies," *Indian Helper*, March 16, 1888.

60. Embe, *Stiya: A Carlisle Indian Girl at Home* (Cambridge: Riverside Press, 1891).

Opposite the title page is written, "The story of Stiya and her trials is woven out of the experiences of girls at various times members of the Indian Industrial School at Carlisle, Pennsylvania. The fundamental facts, therefore, are true. Different Indian villages have contributed incidents and served for the pueblo of the story."

61. Embe, *Stiya*, 2–3.
62. Leslie Marmon Silko, "Introduction," in *Native American Literature: Catalog I* (Lopez Books, 1994), http://www.lopezbooks.com/articles/silko.html

4. Putting Lucy Pretty Eagle to Rest

Barbara C. Landis

Barbara C. Landis is the Carlisle Indian School biographer for the Cumberland County Historical Society in Carlisle, Pennsylvania. Scholars best know her for creating and maintaining an extensive and detailed website, http://www.carlisleindianschool.org, and for her work with American Indian people, tribes, and communities interested in researching relatives who once attended the Carlisle school. Landis also worked with Native Americans to have the school cemetery marked with a Pennsylvania State Marker. One of the first graves found in the cemetery was that of Take the Tail, better known to non-Indians as Lucy Pretty Eagle. In this essay, Landis offers a moving analysis of the short life of this Lakota student. Born and raised among Lakota people before the Battle of the Little Big Horn, Lucy was taken to Carlisle Indian Industrial School by the government in 1883. Within months she died of unknown causes, and school officials buried her in the school cemetery.

Landis uses Lucy's life as an example of the thousands of children the government took from their families, clans, communities, and tribes to Pennsylvania. Like too many Indian people, Lucy suffered a fatal illness that took her life. Even in death, she received little rest. Officials at Carlisle Barracks moved her remains to another site, and non-Indians spread tales that she had been buried alive. Her ghost, they said, haunted an old building at the former Indian school that people mistakenly identified as the girls' dormitory. Over the years, Lucy became a regional legend. Landis corrects the false information about Lucy, who died at the age of ten, never returning to the people of the Rosebud.

In August 2003 a group of descendants of Carlisle Indian Industrial School students gathered just outside the wrought-iron fence bordering the Indian cemetery to dedicate a historic marker. Passersby watched as people in the group took turns talking. Amid the uniform military markers that identified the remains of those children who were left behind, they remembered stories of rage and comfort, pride and shame, sorrow and laughter. Barely conspicuous in the first row of the government-issue stones was the grave of Lucy Pretty Eagle.

In 1879 the United States established the first off-reservation Indian boarding school at Carlisle, Pennsylvania. Between 1879 and 1918 thousands of Native children passed through the doors of the best-known U.S. Indian school, among them a Lakota girl from the Rosebud Agency who was known to her people as Take the Tail. At Carlisle her name was changed to Lucy Pretty Eagle, the name that appears on her headstone: "Lucy Pretty Eagle, Sioux, May 9, 1884." She became one of the earliest casualties of the federal government's culture war on Indian children, and she suffered the fate of countless Native children who died at the dozens of off-reservation boarding schools throughout North America that were modeled after Carlisle.

As Luther Standing Bear remembered, "I could think of no reason why white people wanted Indian boys and girls except to kill them. I thought we were going East to die."[1] The U.S. government shipped the remains of many of the children home in wooden boxes, but others, like Lucy, were buried in segregated Indian cemeteries like the one at Carlisle. She later became the victim of a "historical" novel, as a leading character in a fictionalized diary published for Scholastic's popular "Dear America" series. Even in death, this Lakota child could not escape those determined to distort her identity.

On November 14, 1883, Take the Tail stepped off the train that had carried her from the Dakota Territory to Carlisle. The ten-year-old had traveled thousands of miles from her parents, grandparents, and home at the Rosebud Agency. The train had taken her out of the rolling hills and grassy flatlands of the Great Plains and across the Mississippi River into a strange environment. After her journey she found herself on a strange platform in a strange place, walking toward her new school home, a victim of an experiment designed to save her. That experiment would, ironically, destroy her.

Richard Henry Pratt, the architect of the off-reservation boarding school movement, designed his school for utmost efficiency in order to transform Indian children from their perceived savagery into useful citizens—"civilized" Indians who would champion European-American values such as progress, materialism, and Christianity. Long before Lucy arrived at Carlisle, Pratt set his grand experiment into motion as a way to free Indian people from the deprivation of the reservations and mainstream them into the dominant society. He cultivated his assimilationist policies and earned his reputation as a reformer after commanding a group of Indian prisoners of war in St. Augustine, Florida, in 1875. His strong admonition to "feed the Indian to America, and America will do the assimilating and annihilate the problem" formed the cornerstone of his program for educating the children at Carlisle.[2] Pratt zealously pushed his agenda, proclaiming, "In Indian education I am a Baptist. We like to hold these children under until they are thoroughly soaked, and when they come out, they will be civilized."[3] Unfortunately, Lucy Pretty Eagle and 189 other children buried in the Carlisle cemetery drowned in the waters of assimilation, symbolizing the innocent victims of Pratt's violent metaphors.

Take the Tail's daily life at Carlisle began with the undignified removal of everything familiar. All new recruits were scrubbed down and deloused from head to toe. Their long hair was cut short and their clothes and blankets replaced with military uniforms. All of Take the Tail's activities were chaperoned, and she learned to drill, marching in formation on the parade ground at Carlisle. She was assigned to a dormitory room with girls who did not speak Lakota. She was strictly confined to the fenced-in compound of the Carlisle Barracks. Loneliness and sadness filled her days as she pined for her home and family, and she retreated inwardly. Lucy's condition at the school did not cause her illness, but it made her more susceptible to bacteria and vulnerable to viruses, respiratory ailments, trachoma, and mental anguish.[4]

Take the Tail had known cold winters on the plains with snow and wind, but the unfamiliar winters of Pennsylvania were especially dangerous for the sickly child because of the heavy, moist air of the Cumberland Valley. The bone-chilling, damp climate and cold surroundings of buildings, policies, and programs designed to "kill the Indian and save the man" were debilitating compared to the warm and familiar comforts of family and community at home.[5] According to her student folder found in the National Archives, Take the Tail arrived at Carlisle in poor health. Less than three months after she arrived at Carlisle—on March 9, 1884—she died. Although children's remains were sometimes returned to their families, Lucy was buried at Carlisle.

Take the Tail's time at the boarding school made her more vulnerable to disease for many reasons, including depression brought on by homesickness. Lucy's health declined in part because of radical changes forced on her.

In *My People, the Sioux*, Luther Standing Bear wrote about the first groups of children to attend Carlisle from the Rosebud Agency, describing how school administrators assigned the children Christian names.[6] After her arrival to Carlisle, the school staff translated Take the Tail's name from Lakota to English. They changed her name and its meaning. At Carlisle, Take the Tail became Lucy Pretty Eagle. Pretty Eagle was her father's name, and Lucy became her Christian name.

Even though Lucy met other Lakota children at Carlisle, including others from the Rosebud, teachers, administrators, matrons, and disciplinarians forbade her from speaking her own language, and she would not have roomed with students who understood her language. Of course, school officials did not single out Lucy for such policies as forbidding her from fraternizing with students who spoke Lakota; those rules applied to every student at every boarding school modeled after Carlisle. Her isolation was a universal condition shared with others at Indian boarding schools. Had her language not been taken from her, she would have been able to draw on the comfort and familiarity of her traditions to help ease into the transition of boarding school life.

In 1879 the United States buried the first Carlisle Indian School students in the soldiers' graveyard, which was then situated near the present-day grandstand at the north end of the school grounds. The last child was buried there in 1905. Lucy Pretty Eagle was the thirty-second child to be buried at Carlisle—within the first five years of the school's existence. In the late 1920s, a full decade after the closing of the Carlisle school, the students' remains in the old cemetery were reburied in a tiny plot at the eastern edge of the campus. Ultimately, the relocated Carlisle school cemetery held the remains of the 190 schoolchildren originally buried there, although school officials shipped home the remains of dozens of other children who had died. Most, including Lucy, passed away within the first two decades of the school. Lucy Pretty Eagle's grave has the distinction of being the first stone placed in the first row of the first section of the relocated Carlisle school cemetery.

According to the school newspaper, the *Morning Star*, Lucy's father responded to news of his daughter's death by saying: "She had died the year before but had come back to life again."[7] Researchers and writers have interpreted this statement in many ways. Some have suggested that Lucy reappeared after death as a ghost.

Lucy's first "reincarnation" came nearly a hundred years after her father's lament in the form of ghost story by Katherine Mock that appeared in a club newsletter published by the Officer's Wives of the U.S. Army War College. Mock had been asked to submit a whimsical Halloween tale, and she set her story in her home at the Coren Apartments, one of the buildings at the army base. In 1974 she wrote:

> *Is it imagination that seems to glimpse a movement out of the corner of my eye when no one is home but me? Can the door that slams every night between 10:00 and 10:30 really be a coincidence? Can footsteps heard overhead by your own mother be another such figment—or giant squirrels? Did the children set the bag of walnuts in the basement—they say they didn't? The sounds of the downstairs being carted off by burglars (no one was there, of course,) is just the tail end of a dream. Surely! Why is the kitchen window closed? I just opened it. What made Tweety, the bird, squawk in the middle of the night? Why do I feel my bed rocking, I haven't been to the club? Oh well. I love you Coren Apartments. Goodnight Lucy.*[8]

Four years later, picking up on Mock's theme of Lucy's unsettled spirit, a high school student, Kendra Smith, developed an essay that further exploited the young girl's presumed ghostly presence. Smith wrote: "The Indians frequently referred to fainting or having epileptic convulsions as 'dying.' But could this not also have some `ghostly' insinuations?"[9]

In 1984 Elizabeth Cromer submitted and published Lucy Pretty Eagle's ghost story for the locally prestigious Lamberton Essay contest. "Children willed themselves to die rather than live away from home. After only four months at the school, Lucy Prettyeagle was among those students that died for no apparent reason." Cromer hinted at the absurd notion that Lucy had been buried alive, attributing that theme to Cromer's distorted interpretation of Lakota cosmology: "Lucy's reported symptoms of illness show signs of her being an epileptic. Indians referred to fainting or epileptic convulsions as dying. All of these explanations link the possibility that she may have been in a trance or unconscious state when buried, and therefore not actually dead. Accordingly, questions surrounding Lucy's death may be explained in this way. The mystery surrounding her death could have been a great influence affecting her people and their acceptance of the Ghost Dance."[10]

We don't know what influenced Lucy's father's letter. We don't know what he may have meant when he suggested that his young daughter died during the previous year. But we do know that his response to his daughter's death had nothing to do with his daughter becoming a ghost, forever haunting the buildings at the Carlisle school. And his response never suggested that Lucy had literally been buried alive, although non-Indians have seized on the communication to claim as much.

The Lucy Pretty Eagle ghost story garnered national attention with the publication of Barbara Stevens's article in the July 1990 issue of *Army* magazine. Stevens further exploited the mysterious aspects of Lucy's death: "Tuberculosis was prevalent at the school when Lucy died in 1894 [*sic*], and that disease compounded by homesickness, may have killed her. Just as there are no documents or photographs verifying Lucy's enrollment, there is also no record of the actual cause of her death. The disappearance of Lucy's records in itself is an unsolved mystery."[11] The disappearance of more than two thousand student records compounds this mystery, but ghost stories seem to swirl only around Lucy Pretty Eagle. In reality, Lucy's record does exist among the eight thousand student folders at the National Archives.

Over the years, Lucy Pretty Eagle has taken on a new life created by non-Indians who have concocted the legends surrounding her demise. After Carlisle closed its doors in 1918, the army reclaimed the barracks, and in 1951 it became the home of the U.S. Army War College.[12] Soldiers and their families lived and worked in the old Indian school buildings, and many visited the school cemetery. Some of them perpetuated the myth that ghosts haunted the old school buildings.

The story quickly captured the imagination of other residents at the Carlisle Barracks, most notably the wives and children of military personnel stationed there. For them the ghost became real, a playful presence in their lives. Residents today continue to claim that Lucy haunts the Coren Apartments. Although some believe that these apartments once served as the girls' dormitory, neither Lucy nor any other Indian girl who attended Carlisle ever lived there. In 1996, using old postcards and maps, researchers proved that the Coren Apartments were not used as the girls' dormitory but rather as quarters for teachers. Still, the stories about Lucy Pretty Eagle persisted and grew. Compelling tales were spread of finding tennis shoes mysteriously tied together after a restless night or of pictures being rearranged and turned toward the walls. One of the stories described cooking smells wafting from an empty kitchen and doors being opened and closed during the night.

In the 1990s, residents of the Coren Apartments who were interviewed by the local Carlisle newspaper said they had experienced "hauntings." As of this writing, the apartment building still bears the historic plaque mistakenly identifying it as the girls' dormitory during the Indian school years. In a 1996 interview a resident told a reporter, "Most of us in this building believe (Lucy) roams the entire length of Coren." According to this resident, "records indicate Lucy was epileptic. Some people speculate she may have gone into an epileptic trance in 1884 and, thought to be dead, was buried alive. 'It's like her soul's not at rest.' "[13] All of these examples of the ghost story's proliferation are made available to researchers in archives at Carlisle.

But the most widespread dissemination of the theme of Lucy's having been buried alive is in Ann Rinaldi's 1999 book, *My Heart Is on the Ground: The Diary of Nannie Little Rose, a Sioux Girl*. In the story, Lucy goes into a trance, is presumed dead, and is buried. Her friend, Nannie, knows of her predisposition to fainting spells but is unable to rescue her. The book, targeted to a young audience, is written as a journal. Rinaldi came under sharp criticism in 2002 for having taken "a well-known ghost story that has been circulating around Carlisle for several decades, embellished it further with her own interpretation of Lakota cosmology, and crafted a children's book around this 'event.' Whether Rinaldi did this unconsciously or not, an Indian girl being buried alive is a gruesome metaphor for colonization and the spiritual, cultural and psychic suffocation and trauma Indian children suffered at Carlisle and other boarding schools."[14]

Take the Tail or Lucy Pretty Eagle never intended herself to be a metaphor for the government's off-reservation boarding school system. She was simply a little girl caught up in a national campaign by non-Indians to "uplift" and assimilate American Indian children. She lived during a time and in a place that made her vulnerable to these events. The United States forced her to travel away from her home and family to the Carlisle Indian Industrial School, where teachers could "tame" and "civilize" her so that she could be saved in this life and the next. Instead, the experience killed her, just as it did many thousands of Indian children, some of whom are still buried at the former Carlisle school.

Lucy lies in the cemetery tucked away in the corner of the Carlisle Barracks' campus adjacent to the soccer fields where she and all the Carlisle

Indian students were honored and remembered at a powwow held in May 2000 over the Memorial Day weekend. As fancy and traditional dancers moved to the beat of the drums, one granddaughter of a Carlisle student commented that for the "first time since the school children had left their homes, the children buried in the Carlisle Indian Cemetery were hearing the drum." Perhaps the echo of the songs and drums brought some measure of peace to the ten-year-old girl born for and of the people of the Rosebud.

Notes

1. Luther Standing Bear, *Land of the Spotted Eagle* (Lincoln: University of Nebraska Press, 1978), 230–31.
2. Richard Henry Pratt, *The Indian Industrial School, Carlisle, Pennsylvania: Its Origins, Purposes, Progress, and the Difficulties Surmounted* (Carlisle PA: Cumberland County Historical Society Publications, 1979), 57.
3. Pratt, *The Indian Industrial School*, 5.
4. Jean A. Keller, *Empty Beds: Indian Student Health at Sherman Institute, 1902–1922* (East Lansing: Michigan State University Press, 2002), 148–49.
5. Margaret L. Archuleta, Brenda J. Child, and K. Tsianina Lomawaima, *Away from Home: American Indian Boarding School Experiences, 1879–2000* (Phoenix: The Heard Museum, 2000), 10.
6. Luther Standing Bear, *My People, the Sioux* (Lincoln: University of Nebraska Press, 1975), 137.
7. "School Items," *The Morning Star*, March 1884, 3.
8. Kathy Mock, "From Ghoulies and Ghosties and Long-Leggety Beasties and Things That Go Bump in the Night," *Squaw Talk*, October 1974, 4.
9. Kendra Smith, "Lucy Prettyeagle," Carlisle Senior High School, February 27, 1978.
10. Elizabeth Ann Cromer, "Lucy Pretty Eagle," Lamberton Essay, 1985.
11. Barbara E. Stevens, "Carlisle's Gentle Ghost," *Army*, July 1990, 52.
12. U.S. Army, "Historic Carlisle Barracks," brochure of self-guided tour of the army post, n.d., 19.
13. Dan Miller, "Ghosts of Carlisle Barracks: Military Logic Suspended as Officers Live with Ghostly Lucy," *Sentinel*, January 2, 1996.
14. Review of Ann Rinaldi's *My Heart Is on the Ground: The Diary of Nannie Little Rose, a Sioux Girl*, http://www.oyate.org/books-to-avoid/myheart.html.

5. Loosening the Bonds

The Rapid City Indian School in the 1920s

Scott Riney

Scott Riney is known internationally for his work on the boarding school historically located in Rapid City, South Dakota. His book *The Rapid City Indian School, 1898 1933* garnered considerable attention within American Indian communities and from scholars worldwide. In this essay, Riney argues that from 1898 until the 1920s, federal officials operating the Rapid City Indian School strongly enforced assimilation. Riney compares the Rapid City school to Carlisle Indian Industrial School, focusing on the tight control the administration had on students. However, in the 1920s school officials liberated student life following a national investigation into American Indian affairs, led by Lewis Meriam, and subsequent administrative changes at the school.

In the 1920s, the Rapid City Boarding School became a public high school with a greater focus on Indian families and child welfare. After 1920, superintendents demonstrated a greater concern for student life, reservation conditions, and Native American society. They became more involved with Indian orphans, particularly those displaced from their people as a result of the Great Depression. Superintendents helped Indian families and encouraged children to watch comedy movies, participate in sports, join the YWCA, debate, play music, and enter school fairs. Superintendents allowed students greater freedom at the institution and changed the direction of the Rapid City Indian School, making it more student-friendly.

If a student from the Rapid City Indian School were to see today's Sherman Indian High School, he or she probably would not recognize Sherman as an Indian boarding school: the students are Indian, but they do not march to their classes, wear uniforms, or spend half of each day working in the kitchen, laundry, or dairy. Were it not for the Indian students and building names, Sherman would look like any other urban or suburban high school of the late twentieth or early twenty-first century, albeit one with an unusually large and beautiful campus.

That appearance of ordinariness is in itself extraordinary, for it shows just how much Indian education has changed since the Carlisle Indian Industrial School opened in Carlisle, Pennsylvania, in 1879. Carlisle established what might be termed the classic model of off-reservation instruction: students wore military-inspired uniforms, marched to and from their classes, and divided their time at school between academic and allegedly vocational instruction. Students enrolled for a period of several years, and for the period of their enlistment they were subjected to quasi-military discipline, including harsh punishment for running away from school. When the Rapid City Indian School opened in Rapid City, South Dakota, in 1898, it followed the Carlisle model.[1]

When it closed in 1933, Rapid City still followed the essential points of the Carlisle model. Yet despite the brevity of its history and the continuity in its basic mode of operation, significant changes occurred in how the school staff presented the school to students, reservation communities, and the Indian community in the Rapid City area. Correspondence from school staff, sports schedules, programs of athletic and literary events, and other documents from school archives show that in the 1920s the school evolved from being an institution that attempted to tightly control not only its students but Rapid City's Indian community to being an institution that more closely approximated a public high school, with a substantial role as a provider of child welfare services and relief for destitute families. While retaining the daily routines of marching and manual labor established at Carlisle, Rapid City began a cultural liberalization that brought it closer to non-Indian high schools of the period and to the Sherman Indian High School of today.

With the school curriculum set by the Office of Indian Affairs (hereafter referred to by its current name, the Bureau of Indian Affairs), students' after-school activities were the area open to negotiation and modification by school administrators. A Rapid City catalog for the 1916–17 academic year conveyed their ambivalent position on extracurricular activities. In the section titled "Athletics and Amusements," the catalog states that "amusements such as may be indulged in without injury to the individual and the institution are encouraged and it is desired that all cultivate a disposition to be happy and contented. However, the diversions which might result in injury to students are not permitted or encouraged by the school. These matters are given very careful study and attention. Whenever any pastime or pleasure appears to be operating against the best interests of the student it becomes necessary to prohibit it." If the catalog suggested a certain killjoy attitude, where *no* came quickly and *yes* reluctantly, if at all, it accurately reflected the cautious, disapproving nature of Rapid City's superintendent, Jesse F. House. Cast in the rigid, unyielding mold of nineteenth-century Protestantism, House banned public smoking and profanity by school staff and went so far as to ban card playing on Sundays in the sitting room of the employees' club.[2]

Superintendent House guarded the morals of the students in his care no less zealously. Although the school held student socials, for example, the socials did not include dancing. House banned not only traditional Indian dances (which the school never permitted) but also formal, ballroom dancing of the sort enjoyed (and no doubt dreaded) at public high schools. The sad affairs that resulted were so boring that later in 1917, Rapid City principal George E. Peters wrote Charles F. Peirce of the Flandreau Indian School, Flandreau, South Dakota, to ask if Peirce permitted dancing. If so, Peters wanted to know how often Peirce allowed dancing, how Flandreau conducted dances, and what effects dancing had on pupils. One wonders what effects, in Peters's and House's imagination, dancing could have had.[3]

If Superintendent House was restrained in his enthusiasm for student amusements, he was little more interested in promoting athletics. When House became superintendent of the Rapid City Indian School in 1904, athletics figured prominently at the school. Its teams met teams from the School of Mines, the Rapid City Athletic Club, Fort Meade, and nearby high schools in baseball, football, basketball, and track. Just getting to an "away" event could be an adventure: the last sixteen miles of a May 1905 trip to Spearfish, South Dakota, were by stage and were "the longest sixteen miles" student John Whipple had ever traveled. Tired as Whipple and his teammates might have been, they were hardly tired out. Given sleeping space in the high school gymnasium in Spearfish, the Indian school boys stayed up playing basketball nearly all night. The next morning they watched bronc-riding and steer-roping contests in town. When the track meet began that afternoon and the boys stepped out on the field, "the girls gave the yell. My! it sounded awful nice," remembered Whipple, "so we gave our yell, too."

Although the Indian school boys lost badly (too many cigarettes, Whipple thought), it was all good fun.[4]

Too much fun, perhaps, for mention of athletics at the Indian school soon disappeared from the local newspaper, the *Rapid City Daily Journal*. Rapid City was not so large a town that any news could be ignored, and the lack of coverage, while not conclusive, strongly suggests that the Indian school scaled back its participation in local athletic events. While lack of funds and staff time could have played a role in the decline of athletics at Rapid City, Whipple's account suggests that House may have found the exuberance of athletic contests (witness the students' yells) at odds with the sober, restrained educational environment he tried to cultivate.

Sobriety, literal as well as figurative, was certainly a priority with House. The school promoted sobriety among students with temperance clubs, and House used his position as superintendent to push for prohibition in Rapid City itself. Taking his case to city leaders in an address titled "The Indians and the Liquor Traffic," House cast alcohol as a threat to the civilizing mission of the school, to the progress of white and Indian education alike, and to the business interests of the city. Claiming intemperance was the greatest threat to Indian progress, House argued that "very much of the earnest effort of the government to bring these people into . . . the community, to make them good citizens, is either thwarted, or in a measure nullified by [the] degradation of the liquor traffic and its resultant vices." Threatening both body and mind, alcohol and the institution of the saloon worked against the development of the good in human nature which education sought to achieve. As such it threatened school interests, white and Indian, in Rapid City.[5]

House went on to contend that liquor prevented the full development of Rapid City's trade with the residents of nearby reservations. The Indian school brought at least $100,000 to the city. Its proximity to the Pine Ridge, Rosebud, and Cheyenne River reservations, "three of the largest Indian Reservations in the United States," made Rapid City a center for reservation residents, many of whom traveled to the city to visit their children at the school or to buy supplies or transact other business. "When superintendents of reservations become convinced that the Indians coming to Rapid City will not be in danger of coming under the influence of the saloon, getting drunk, losing their money and degrading themselves," House observed, the superintendents "will be much more willing to encourage them to come here, and consequently the interests of both Indians and legitimate business will be enhanced." House was sure the volume of Indian business done in the city could be doubled, to $200,000, and that contact with the city, if the city were dry, would be an uplifting experience for Indian visitors.[6]

Apparently, House believed that the legal traffic in liquor made enforcement of the prohibition against selling liquor to Indians more difficult to enforce, perhaps by increasing the volume of alcohol on the market and the number of outlets. "I am aware that many people who have not taken any decided stand against the saloon interests strongly condemn the selling or giving [of] intoxicants to Indians," he said, "but the fact remains that in many instances they get it and the traffic is responsible." House appealed to business interests, as fully half of his address concerned the economic benefits of prohibition, and his reference to "saloon interests" suggested a willingness to intervene in local politics, via the business community, on the liquor issue. Dated April 16, 1915, his address came only four days before an election in which Rapid City went dry on a forty-nine-vote majority.[7]

House had already shown a willingness to use the resources of his office to attack the illegal traffic in alcohol to Indians. In December 1910, at the request of an Indian, he wrote U.S. Attorney E. E. Wagner of Sioux Falls, South Dakota, to report an alcohol case at the school. There had been "considerable drunkenness on the part of Indians" in and around Rapid City, and an older, unallotted man, Two Arrows, complained to House and offered to help locate those selling the alcohol.[8]

Superintendent House sent Two Arrows, Henry Crow, and school employee Chauncey Yellow Robe to several Rapid City saloons to make what amounted to undercover buys. At one saloon the three succeeded in purchasing a quart of whiskey from a man who gave the appearance of being a saloon employee but was not the regular bartender. The three then gave the alcohol to House. Two Arrows, Crow, and Yellow Robe did not know the seller's name, but were sure they could identify the man by sight. On that basis, House wanted a John Doe warrant sworn out and a U.S. Marshal sent directly to the city to make the arrest. Otherwise, House feared that a preliminary hearing would give the seller time to flee the city, as had happened in a previous case. On learning that Wagner's office could not issue a John Doe warrant without at least a description that could be expected to lead to an identification, House succeeded, with some difficulty, in identifying the John Doe as one Charles Clark.[9]

Undercover buys of the sort ordered by House were common enough that Henry A. Larson, chief special officer of the United States Indian Service in charge of liquor enforcement, felt it necessary to issue guidelines in the form of a circular sent to all special officers and deputies. Larson warned against making too many cases, arguing that a few good cases that would stand up in court were more effective in suppressing the liquor traffic than a large number of poor cases. Larson also cautioned against improper use of "decoys," as he called Indian buyers, to prevent entrapment. Planned buys of alcohol were to be used only when officers had good reason to believe that criminal traffic in liquor existed and where evidence could not be secured by any other method. Furthermore, decoys were to be "of such a degree of Indian blood and racial appearance as to place the seller immediately on guard." Larson warned that "the use of light colored decoys will not be tolerated." Nor should the decoys be taken far from their home reservations.[10]

While House's use of planned buys appears to fall within Larson's guidelines, the procedure did not yield many convictions, in part due to a lack of cooperation from the office of the U.S. Attorney. While House kept no further correspondence on the case against Charles Clark, a case against one Tom Stevens went badly. House had Stevens arrested for supplying alcohol to students of the Indian school, and he gave his personal attention to the case. The U.S. Attorney for South Dakota knew of the case and promised assistance, but none arrived, and the case went to trial with the local State's Attorney prosecuting. The State's Attorney made a strong effort, but the defense presented an alibi that satisfied the jury, which acquitted Stevens. The case led House to remark in correspondence that he "very much dislike[d] any connection with such cases," which drew the ire of Assistant Commissioner of Indian Affairs E. B. Meritt, who demanded an explanation. When House explained that he preferred to leave such cases to those who specialized in them but that he would willingly participate when duty demanded he do so, Meritt let him off with a warning to be more careful in future correspondence.[11]

Despite the difficulties brought on by the Stevens case, House persisted in his efforts to control the liquor traffic in Rapid City. In December 1916, after the city had gone dry, he wrote Larson to request the authority and funding to hire his own deputies. In the fall and spring, depending on the work available, Rapid City attracted many seasonal laborers from near-by reservations. At these times, and whenever celebrations or other special occasions brought large numbers of Indians to the city, bootlegging flourished. Although Larson often supplied officers for these occasions, House did not think it was practical to ask for an officer each time. Furthermore, as special officers became known to the locals, their effectiveness diminished. Larson responded with very nearly the authority House requested: Larson applied with the Bureau of Indian Affairs to have House appointed a deputy special officer, with the authority to employ posse service for up to five days per month. While Larson did not place funds at House's disposal, as House had asked, the superintendent's commission allowed him to hire personnel subject to the regulations governing posse service, with vouchers to be submitted to Larson.[12]

House's efforts were not entirely successful, for in 1920 he once again requested assistance from Larson, asking that someone unknown in the Rapid City area be sent in to gather information on an Indian he suspected of bootlegging. By then the ratification of the Eighteenth Amendment and passage of the Volstead Act had made Prohibition the law of the land, and the Rapid City Indian School's crusade against liquor ended with House's departure in 1922. More broadly, with House's replacement by younger, less paternalistic administrators, the Indian school ceased being the platform for attempts to control Rapid City's Indian population.[13]

Instead, under Superintendents S. A. M. Young (1922–25, 1930–32) and Sharon R. Mote (1925–29), the Rapid City Indian School increasingly became a child-care provider of last resort for Indian families. Reservation officials applied varying degrees of suggestion and coercion to get children from financially strapped homes away from their families and enrolled at Rapid City. Superintendent C. H. Gensler of the Lower Brule Agency, South Dakota, sent two children of Mrs. Driving Hawk to Rapid City after the death of the father. Gensler knew Rapid City was filled to capacity, yet he asked Superintendent Young to take the children because there was no other way of caring for them. After the death of the children's father, Driving Hawk was left with "quite a large family." The nearest public school was some distance from the Driving Hawk home, and Driving Hawk could not, in Gensler's estimation, support the family and keep the children in school.

Young found Henry and Alvena Driving Hawk to be bright children, and apparently they were pleased to be enrolled at Rapid City. Despite the crowding at the school, Young promised to find "some nail on which to hang them" and was glad he could be of service to the children and their mother. Whether Gensler forced the children's enrollment at Rapid City or merely facilitated it is unclear.[14]

Whether extended families gave up their children willingly or under duress, boarding schools were common destinations for Indian children removed from their homes. In 1924, Superintendent Henry J. McQuigg of the Turtle Mountain Indian Agency, North Dakota, asked Young to enroll three orphans who had been staying with a married sister after the death of their parents. The sister lacked the resources to properly care for and educate the children, and a meeting of the Indian judges at Turtle Mountain agreed that McQuigg, acting for the government, should without delay seek the children's placement in a government school. Young, though noting that he "really should not take them, since we are more than full and there are children nearby without school facilities," again agreed to squeeze the children in.[15]

The Depression forced a number of families to enroll their children in the Rapid City Indian School. In July 1930, Rapid City resident Julia McGaa asked the Pine Ridge superintendent to permit the enrollment of her seven children in the Rapid City Indian School. Her husband, Hobert, could not find steady work, and the older children had not gone to public school the preceding year because the McGaas could not feed and clothe them properly. Clothes were also a problem for the Provost family. Josephine Provost sent her children, Grace and Harold, to a public school in Rapid City. The children, particularly Harold, did not like to go to school with white children, and they skipped school half the time. "I think it is because they cannot dress as they might," Provost said, "but I am the only one working in the family and I really cannot dress them & feed them as I should." Rapid City senior clerk George A. Day, investigating the Provost family's home conditions, learned that Provost's husband, disabled by a back injury and unable in the Depression to find suitable light work, received a pension of $40 per month for his service as an army scout. The Provosts paid $35 a month in rent for a house in Rapid City, plus $2.75 for electricity and $1 for water service. Money for food and clothing had to come from Josephine Provost's wages from occasional work as a maid at the Patton Hotel, and Day agreed that it would be better if the children were enrolled at Rapid City. Since the Provosts lived in town, sending the children to Rapid City would not mean sending them any distance away. Provost would not send her children away to school, for the last time she did so, "one came home so nearly dead he only lived four months after he came back."[16]

Paralleling Rapid City's emergence as a child-care provider of last resort was a significant change in the school's culture. Again, House's departure opened the way to liberalization. One had only to look at the school catalog to see the beginning, albeit superficial, of a generational change: where House had posed for his portrait in profile, wearing a mustache and beard that would have done a nineteenth-century patriarch proud, his obviously younger successor, S. A. M. Young, looked straight into the camera and wore only a small, neatly trimmed mustache. Sharon R. Mote, younger still, eschewed facial hair altogether and even smiled, albeit faintly, for the camera.[17]

While Young was largely a transitional figure in this area, Superintendent Mote, coming to Rapid City from a position at the Haskell Institute in Lawrence, Kansas, made substantial changes in life at the school. Under Mote, the Rapid City Indian School began to resemble city high schools of the era in many of its extracurricular activities. Movies alternated with student socials on a weekly basis. When ordering films, Mote wanted comedies but not slapstick. He would consider feature films, too, if they were not too expensive and were suitable for children. Films had to be "wholesome and uplifting in their nature but at the same time entertaining and instructive, if possible." The students liked outdoor pictures, and Mote put in special requests with agencies in Minneapolis and Denver for outdoor pictures and Westerns. Some of the films he ordered had such forgettable titles as *Great Main Robbery, Harvester, Freckles, Alex the Great,* and *When the Law Rides.* In the winter months the school offered basketball as an alternative to the movies, depending on the school's success in securing games with other teams.[18]

The socials enjoyed broad participation. Younger students had their socials from 6:30 to 7:30 on Saturday evenings, older students from 7:45 to 9:30. Various student organizations took charge of the socials, boys' and girls' organizations alternating. In October 1927 the Sons of Pahasapa, a student fraternal organization, sponsored the first social, the ywca sponsored the second, and Company A of the Boy's Battalion sponsored the third. In

November, Company A of the Girl's Battalion took the first social and Company B of the Boy's Battalion took the second. The school held a Halloween party, variously described as a social or a masquerade carnival. Committees composed of white and Indian staff and Indian students oversaw booths, stunts and prizes, refreshments, and decorating. Prizes included two first prizes, to be given to the "boy and girl wearing the most beautiful and original costume." Second prizes were to go to the boy and girl wearing the most comical costumes. Perhaps to make sure that nothing got out of hand, the committee in charge of stunts and prizes consisted of the principal, Carl Wilcox, disciplinarian Chauncey Yellow Robe, and matron Theresa Kaufman, the three highest-ranking employees in direct daily contact with students.[19]

The Student Activities Association had responsibility for all student activities, including the school store, student athletics, and the student band and orchestra. The association comprised the previous year's honor students, one boy and one girl elected from each of the three highest grades, and the student officers (students who held positions in the military organization of the student companies and battalions). A faculty advisory committee that included the superintendent, principal, disciplinarian, matron, and the athletic coaches oversaw the association's work. A pay social, a pay movie, and receipts from the school store funded it. From November 17 to December 15, 1925, the association earned $69.41 from the social, $16.35 from the movie, and $169.46 from the store. The store listed inventories of basic school supplies, including 133 pencils and 140 erasers, and an astonishing variety of snack food, including 91 Ding Dongs, 77 Fat Emmas, 7–1/6 dozen oranges, and 180 ice cream cones. Eva Enos remembered the store fondly, for purchases at the store tided her over between care packages from home. Although care packages might come once a month, or even less frequently, "at that little store we could buy a lot of things for maybe fifty cents."[20]

Oratory also enlivened the long winter and spring months at the Rapid City Indian School. Students read pieces that would not have been out of place at the city high school. For the 1926–27 school year, Principal Wilcox organized preliminary declamatory contests between the sixth and seventh grades to be held Wednesday evening, April 15, and a contest between the eighth and ninth grades to be held Thursday evening, April 16. Wilcox invited school employees and all others interested to the Saturday-evening finals, held in the school auditorium. The orchestra opened the evening with selected marches. Viola Hornbeck went first of the twelve contestants, reading "The Trouble with Rastus." Other pieces included "An Old Sweetheart of Mine," read by Lillian Swain; "The Red Man Eloquent," read by Godfrey Broken Rope; and the final piece, "The Necessity of War, March, 1775," read by Mortimer Hernandez. The contest ended with more music from the orchestra, and the classes performing their class songs and yells, before the judges rendered their decision. Hernandez took first. Albert McGaa came in second with his reading of "The Union Soldier," and Alvina Fallis third with "Jane-from Sixteen." Hernandez and McGaa won first and second, respectively, in a declamatory contest at the Pierre Indian School, a one-two punch for Rapid City students with patriotic speeches.[21]

As important as public speaking was to the Rapid City Indian School, though, it could not match the appeal of a revived athletics program. In *Education for Extinction,* David Adams shows the importance of football at the Carlisle Indian Industrial School. For Carlisle superintendent Richard Pratt, football was a powerful advertisement for the school, and for the possibilities of Indian achievement, in an era when upper-middle-class whites celebrated sport as the epitome of civilized virtues. Football was also an acculturating force, where Indian players learned "the value of precision, teamwork, order, discipline, obedience, efficiency, and how all these interconnected in the business of 'winning.' "[22]

The Bureau of Indian Affairs forced Pratt out by 1904, but football lived on at Carlisle. Under the legendary coach Glen "Pop" Warner, Carlisle fielded an outstanding team, one that made its reputation roughing up such early football powers as the University of Pennsylvania, the University of Chicago, Harvard University, and the University of Minnesota. The 1907 team had a 10–1 record, and the 1911–13 teams were nearly as successful. The Carlisle football team's national tours and the later successes of the Haskell Institute team and the incomparable Jim Thorpe indelibly linked Indian schools to football in the minds of American sports fans.[23]

Under Superintendent Mote, the Rapid City Indian School did its best to uphold the reputation of Indian athletics, but it was never the powerhouse that Carlisle and Haskell were in their heydays. Rapid City students were younger, rarely out of their teenage years, and Rapid City did not have the national recruiting base of Carlisle and Haskell. Nor did Mote inherit a viable athletic program. He brought to Rapid City a passion for football honed at Haskell, only to find that Superintendent Young had done no more to cultivate the pigskin talents of Rapid City students than had Superintendent House. For lack of uniforms and other equipment, for which the school had no funds in 1925, Mote could not even get up a good scrimmage. Remembering a box full of old football uniforms in storage at Haskell, Mote wrote his friend R. E. Hanley, Haskell's director of athletics, to get the uniforms shipped to Rapid City before Hanley threw them out. A determined Mote knew his team could not hope to challenge Haskell in their first year, but he promised Hanley a "Waterloo in South Dakota some day."[24]

Mote tried to secure membership for the Rapid City Indian School in the South Dakota High School Athletic Association. That organization's Board of Control rebuffed his application, with R. E. Rawlins, the association's secretary-treasurer, explaining that association rules limited membership to the public high schools of the state and the high school of the University of South Dakota, excluding the Indian school. Mote nonetheless scheduled full seasons for Rapid City Indian School basketball teams against a variety of opponents. In 1925–26 the boys' team played Holy Rosary Mission (Pine Ridge), Belle Fourche High School, Scenic High School, Nisland High School, Pine Ridge Boarding School, Pierre Indian School, and the local Methodists. The "midgets" team played the Nemo Bantams and the Rapid City Junior High team. The girls' team played the Whitewood, Scenic, Nisland, Nemo, and Deadwood high school teams. Only the midgets had a winning season. In 1927–28, Rapid City Indian School teams played the Sturgis, Nisland, New Underwood, Midland, Belle Fourche, Piedmont, Newell, Pringle, and Philip high school teams as well as the St. Francis Mission (Rosebud), Holy Rosary Mission, and Pine Ridge Boarding School. Many of the matches included both boys' and girls' teams. With the exception of Pierre Indian School, another off-reservation boarding school, Rapid City played teams in western South Dakota, avoiding long trips.[25]

Mote had less success with the football team. Winters were long in South Dakota, leaving the football season brief. Nearby high schools were unwilling to schedule games with the big boys from the Indian school, whom Mote described as husky but inexperienced, some never having played a game before. The Murdo, South Dakota, high school and the Sundance, Wyoming, high school both begged off, explaining that their weekends were already full. The soldiers at nearby Fort Meade (outside Sturgis) were willing to play, though, as were the young men of the Spearfish Normal School football team. Dan O. Root, director of physical education at Spearfish, guaranteed the entire travel expenses of the Rapid City team if they would play in Spearfish, an arrangement that was not unusual. Root also offered half the gate receipts, which he thought would be considerable, since football was popular in Spearfish and Indians were "always a great attraction athletically." Indian football was popular in Rapid City, too, even if the local teams would not play the older boys from the Indian school. For the Rapid City Indian School's first homecoming game, part of a celebration Mote elected to call "Indian Day," the Rapid City Indian School met the Pierre Indian School in downtown Rapid City, on the Rapid City High School's field. A flyer boldly advertised "football!" as the Pierre Indians met the Rapid City Indians, admission fifty cents.[26]

Basketball remained the most successful sport, probably because, as an indoor sport, it could be played through the long, harsh South Dakota winters. At the end of October 1928, the Rapid City Indian School had only two confirmed home football games scheduled for the season but at least ten basketball games, most of which were doubleheaders featuring both boys' and girls' teams. The girls' team was particularly strong. The previous season it had beaten all the local high school teams so soundly, often holding them to single-digit scores, that Mote tried unsuccessfully to set up an exhibition game with a college team that had overwhelmed the Flandreau Indian School girls' basketball team. To help finance such fine performances, the school sold season tickets, good for both football and basketball. Those who held two tickets could bring their entire family at no extra charge. Mote sent one of the $1.50 tickets to each school employee, with an accompanying memo all but ordering the recipient to accept the ticket and pay up. Through its faculty members, the Student Activities Association also sold tickets in town, mainly to local businesses. Such pillars of the Rapid City business community as the Pennington County Bank, First National Bank, the Rapid City Motor Co., and Henry Behrens, the undertaker, all bought tickets.[27]

In addition to its revenues from season tickets, the school store, and the pay movies and socials, the Student Activities Association used gate receipts to pay for uniforms, referees, and game expenses. The association apparently received fixed sums of money from host schools to pay the expenses of away games, collected gate receipts on home games, and paid fixed sums to visiting teams to cover their costs. Rapid City Indian School received twenty-five dollars per trip for basketball games at Pine Ridge Boarding School and Holy Rosary Mission, while St. Francis Mission at Rosebud paid thirty-five dollars and Sundance High School in Wyoming paid forty dollars. The Rapid City Indian School used employees' cars to transport the teams, minimizing expenses. Employees who owned cars might find themselves asked to "volunteer" when Mote was short of transportation.[28]

In January 1928, Superintendent Mote floated a proposal among the other Indian schools in South Dakota and northern Nebraska for a Northern Indian School Association. Mote modeled the association after the South Dakota State High School Athletic Association, which had refused to grant membership to Indian schools. The proposal went out to the Genoa Indian School in Nebraska, the Wahpeton Indian School in North Dakota, and the Pierre, Flandreau, Rosebud, and Pine Ridge Indian Schools and the St. Francis and Holy Rosary Missions in South Dakota. The proposal evoked mixed reactions, however, with several superintendents declining on grounds of cost or distance, and the idea ultimately died.[29]

Within a month, however, District Supervisor of Education James H. McGregor proposed an annual contest with athletic, public speaking, and group singing events for the mission and government Indian schools of South Dakota, with the option of forming a permanent association if the annual events went well. McGregor, whose invitation could not well be refused, arranged for the contest to be held at Pierre, the state capital, where South Dakota governor W. H. Bulow would be on hand to present the trophies. C. R. Whitlock, superintendent of the Pierre Indian School, hosted the two-day event. Although McGregor originally intended the meet to encompass only his district, he allowed C. B. Dickinson, superintendent of the Bismarck Indian School, North Dakota, to enter a Bismarck delegation, and he was willing to enter Wahpeton, Pipestone, and Genoa in subsequent years. Rapid City entered a strong contingent, with Albert McGaa trying his luck in the Boys' Orations with "I Am an American." The strongest contenders from the Rapid City contingent, though, were Alvina Fallis in the Girls' Dramatic category and Alberta Horne in Girls' Humorous, with near-perfect scores in a preliminary contest for their readings of "The

Soldier's Reprieve" and "The Football Fan," respectively.[30]

With McGregor's backing, Mote organized what he initially billed as a Tri-State Indian School Basketball tournament, to be held March 15–16, 1929. The states represented slipped to two, though, when the Pipestone Indian School in Minnesota declined to participate on account of bad weather. The snows were so deep that the twenty-five-mile road between Pipestone and Flandreau had been closed for two weeks, and Pipestone had disbanded its teams for the season. Fort Yates and Bismarck in North Dakota managed to send teams to Rapid City, the Bismarck Indian School students traveling six hundred miles round trip to spend one day at the tournament. The South Dakota School of Mines in Rapid City made all arrangements for the tournament, including officiating, and allowed its $100,000 gymnasium to be used for the finals.[31]

Bad weather held down attendance and revenues, but the tournament emerged as a success for the Rapid City Indian School. The Rapid City team of Cecelia Janis, Julia Black Fox, Alice DeMarshe, Mildred McGaa, Eloise LaPlante, Agnes Marin, Margaret Two Bulls, Nellie Craven, Agnes Clifford, and Mabel Newman defeated the favored Bismarck team, 23–16, buoyed by the cheering crowd. The Flandreau boys' team, confident from wins in the eastern part of South Dakota, fell to the Rapid City team of Edward Quick Bear, Raymond Picotte, Jacob Two Bulls, David Spotted Horse, William Lends His Horse, Max One Feather, Bert Afraid of Hawk, Dominic Day Eagle, and Ambrose Day Eagle by the score of 25–14. The Holy Rosary Mission boys' team picked up the Class B cup (for younger boys) after defeating Pine Ridge, and the trophy for most sportsmanlike conduct went to the Bismarck girls.[32]

Spring brought better weather and a successful trip to the Pierre Declamatory Contest, Track Meet, and Music Contest. Principal Kirk K. Newport held a general school assembly in the auditorium the evening of May 10, 1929, to celebrate the successes of Rapid City students. Roy McLeod reported on the trip to Pierre, Alberta Horne on the declamatory contest, Albert McGaa on the track meet, and Agnes Clifford on the music contest. McLeod and Sam LaPointe presented the Class A (older students) cup, Agnes Clifford receiving it on behalf of the Class A girls. Rose Swimmer presented the Class B (younger students) cup, James Gayton receiving. Mote offered concluding remarks.[33]

Mote left the Rapid City Indian School in 1929, when the Bureau of Indian Affairs brought in Dr. Ira C. Nelson to supervise the school's short-
lived transition to a sanatorium school for tubercular students. When the
bureau abandoned the sanatorium school concept after only a single year,
S. A. M. Young returned as superintendent. By then, however, student life
at Rapid City had been badly disrupted, and extracurricular activities never recovered the diversity or importance they had enjoyed under Mote. The
school's welfare work continued, however, and as the Depression took its
toll on Indian families living in the Rapid City area, emergencies frequently
required the intervention of the Rapid City Indian School. The school both
administered relief to destitute Indians and forwarded requests for funds
to their reservations. In January 1932, Superintendent W. O. Roberts of the
Rosebud Agency wrote Young to ask for his assistance in disbursing Red
Cross funds. Agency offices had Red Cross money on hand for the use of
reservation residents. Roberts observed that while the money was primarily for the more needy on the reservation, "we find it necessary in some instances to give help also to the able-bodied Indians who are not able to obtain any productive work. We are requiring this class of Indian to supply
labor in lieu of a handout."[34]

While Roberts did not know how many people on Rosebud rolls were
in Rapid City, he hoped Young would be able to put some of them to work,
thus making them eligible for relief. Roberts proposed that able-bodied Indians in Rapid City be given two days of work per week through January,
crediting them $1.50 per person per day. They would be paid not in cash but
rather in purchase orders for groceries issued through the Rosebud offices. Roberts suggested that Young contact Joseph Pawnee, who might need
work and who would likely know the names of others in need of employment. Roberts cautioned Young that he did not intend "to give unlimited
assistance to these Indians as we do not have enough allowance to take care
of these needy cases on the reservation," and he urged Young to be conser-
vative in his assistance of Indians in Rapid City.[35]

Young sent out letters to several men in the Rapid City area, explaining
the conditions of Roberts's offer and asking the men to report to the school
for duty if they wished to work. Young employed four men under this arrangement in January, giving each four days of work, allowing them to earn
six dollars per person for the month. As Young noted to Roberts, four days

of work was all he could give each man, since Roberts's letter did not reach him until January 14. Still, Young found a way to stretch his authority. Taking Roberts's letter as immediate authorization for employment, he gave each man employed two days per calendar week left in the month, thus fitting in four days of work in a week's time. Young wanted to know if the arrangement would be continued, for Roberts's letter only authorized work through January, and Young thought there would be continuing demand for this form of relief.[36]

Roberts authorized additional work, but only under conditions that placed a considerable administrative burden on Young. Since Roberts had only seventy-five dollars on hand for Indians living in towns off the reservation, he would not authorize relief for anyone who had family members with funds on account at Rosebud. Nor would Roberts issue more than one purchase order per family or living group. Roberts wanted Young to investigate each case and be sure that the applicant had dependents to support and was in genuine need. Those without dependents were on their own. "There are many young, single, able-bodied Indians who have no responsibility and who have always got along in some way," Roberts wrote. "It is not our purpose to maintain and support that class from relief funds." He wanted the money to go only to responsible heads of households, and he trusted that Young's long experience in the Indian Service would enable him to distinguish between "the worthy cases" and those less deserving of assistance. Young was to fill the role of a welfare case officer, dispensing money according to both material and moral criteria.[37]

Young and his successor at the Rapid City Indian School, Raymond E. Staley, also acted as intermediaries for people left destitute by the depression, writing reservation offices on behalf of enrolled tribal members living in the vicinity of the city. Young prefaced one such letter to W. F. Dickens, superintendent of the Cheyenne River Agency, with the explanation that members of a family had called on him and asked him to write in their favor and that he did not presume "to interfere in any way with [Dickens's] regular course of business."

The care with which Young distanced himself from the requests of the Rousseau family may have been due to his lack of familiarity with their cases. Ellen Beatrice Vosburg, a member of the family who claimed to be one-fourth Indian and a widow, asked for her pro rata share of the Chey-

enne Three Per Cent Fund and asked that she be allowed twenty-five dollars a month for the support of herself and her five-year-old son, Vance La-
Verne Vosburg. She also asked that Dickens look into enrolling her son at
Cheyenne River, and she wanted it known that her last interest check had
failed to arrive. Maggie Powell Rousseau and Edward and Dan Rousseau
also complained about missing interest checks. Hazel Rousseau Magstadt
had applied for her pro rata share and wanted to know if any action had been
taken on her request. Although disclaiming any knowledge of the regulations concerning the Rousseaus' requests, Young recommended that they
be allowed to withdraw their money, since he thought them "to all intents
and purposes white people" and therefore not truly the responsibility of the
Bureau of Indian Affairs.[38]

Young appeared more sympathetic to Sylvester Garreau, a 1931 graduate
of the Rapid City Indian School on tribal rolls at the Cheyenne River reservation. Garreau had married another graduate not long after the close of
school, and the young couple soon had a child. Young wrote Dickens that
Garreau had "been willing to work at all times," but like so many other people during the depression, he had been unable to find employment. The couple needed money to pay the doctor and other expenses related to their son's
birth. Young passed along Garreau's request that Dickens send Garreau any
money he might have to his credit, in whatever amount Dickens saw fit.[39]

Superintendent Staley found the role of letter writer to be both tiring and
embarrassing. In December 1932 he wrote to Dickens detailing the plight of
Mrs. Joseph Crane Pretty Voice, who was at one of the semi-permanent Indian encampments near Rapid City. The family, with seven children, lived
in a tent. County authorities had provided a small amount of short-term
relief in the form of food and fuel, but the family was again destitute, and
Crane Pretty Voice wanted money which she believed was due her husband.
Staley wrote to Dickens that "you will think that I am a professional beggar
since it seems that about every other letter I write you it is about somebody's
claim or money due them," and explained that the role was one thrust on
him by people who "come after me and make all kinds of reports as to the
amount of money due, how long it has been due, how long they have written
you and all like that." Assuring Dickens that he knew just how annoying his
letters must be, Staley asked Dickens to understand that he helped the Indians with their inquiries only because they begged him to do so.[40]

Despite the limited relief funds available to the Bureau of Indian Affairs, local officials tried to hide cases of extreme poverty from the general public. In April 1933, Superintendent McGregor of the Pine Ridge Agency wrote Superintendent Staley, asking him to look for a woman named Nellie Swimmer, who McGregor had heard was begging on the streets of Rapid City. According to McGregor, Swimmer presented the following typewritten note to those from whom she sought aid:

To Whom it may concern:
I am Nellie Swimmer with a Family of eight children to take care of. I cant see to sew, also I have been sick for the past twenty years.
I want food and clothing.
Yours very truly,
P.S. Nellie wants a Dollar.

McGregor hoped to find out where she lived, though there were Swimmers on a number of the reservations, and he asked Staley to look into the case should she appear again. McGregor thought it unnecessary for Swimmer to be on the street, "as [Indians] can be taken care of in our reservations without begging," and he hoped to discourage the practice. Making inquiries, Staley heard that Swimmer had gone on to Scenic. Staley asked Rapid City police and welfare workers to notify him if Swimmer returned to Rapid City, and he promised McGregor that he would also ask the Indian community at a camp near the city to watch for her. Staley's ready cooperation suggests that he shared McGregor's abhorrence of begging. Staley's role as an outreach worker was short-lived, however, for the Rapid City Indian School closed for good later that year.[41]

The liberalization of student life at the Rapid City Indian School in the 1920s showed the adaptability of the boarding school model. Under Superintendent House the school tried to impose on students strict, late-nineteenth-century standards of Protestant propriety, exemplified by school temperance societies and House's strict oversight of student activities. By the end of the decade, under Superintendent Mote, Rapid City had acquired the extracurricular trappings of a public high school. Students enjoyed movies, socials with dancing, speech contests with other schools, and, above all, sports, particularly basketball. Throughout these changes, Rapid City re-

tained the marching, drill, half-and-half schedule, and quasi-military organization of the classic off-reservation boarding school.

Adaptable as it was, however, Rapid City Indian School was overtaken
by the changing needs of the people it was intended to serve. Superintendent House thought he knew what Indians needed: a basic education, the
inculcation of Christian values, and protection from alcohol. His succes-
sors backed away from the social-control agenda implicit in House's crusade against alcohol and found themselves serving more and more as social workers, whether their clients were children taken from their homes or
destitute families in the Rapid City area. The wrenching poverty and social
dislocation of the depression and the devastating spread of tuberculosis on
northern plains reservations further shifted the focus of the Bureau of Indian Affairs from the forcible assimilation of Indians to the provision of
health and welfare services to reservation communities. Under these conditions, Rapid City Indian School could not compete with larger, better-
established off-reservation boarding schools at Pierre, Bismarck, and else-
where. The liberalization of Indian education continued, but not at Rapid
City. The school closed in 1933, and its grounds later became the site of Sioux
Sanatorium, the notorious "Sioux San."

Notes

1. For a comprehensive discussion of the origins and routines of Indian boarding
   schools in the late nineteenth and early twentieth century, see David Wallace Adams, *Education for Extinction: American Indians and the Boarding School Experience, 1875–1928* (Lawrence: University Press of Kansas, 1995).
2. "Catalog and Synopsis of Courses, United States Indian School, Rapid City, South
   Dakota, 1916–17," p. 10, Superintendents Subject Correspondence Files [SSCF] Box
   9, School Annuals, Graduate Programs, School Paper file; Jesse F. House, Superintendent, Rapid City Indian School, "General Order No. 2, 1919–1920, Profanity & Smoking," August 29, 1919, General Correspondence Files [GCF] Box 3, Decimal Classification [DC] 112 Circulars file; House, "To Members of School Club and
   Others Interested," December 20, 1920, GCF Box 3, DC 112 Circulars file; all in Records of the Rapid City Indian School, Record Group [RG] 75, National Archives
   Central Plains Region, Kansas City, Missouri [NACPR].
3. George E. Peters, Principal, Rapid City Indian School, to Charles F. Peirce, Superintendent, Flandreau Indian School, October 10, 1917, GCF Box 87, DC 842 Flandreau
   Indian School file, Records of the Rapid City Indian School, RG 75, NACPR.
4. "The Spearfish Trip," *Rapid City Daily Journal*, May 27, 1905.
5. "The Indians and the Liquor Traffic," Superintendent Jesse F. House, April 16, 1915,
   SSCF Box 10, Policy & Liquor Control 1909–1921 file, Records of the Rapid City Indian School, RG 75, NACPR.

6. "The Indians and the Liquor Traffic."
7. "The Indians and the Liquor Traffic"; House to Henry A. Larson, Chief Special Officer, United States Indian Service, Denver, Colorado, April 21, 1915, SSCF Box 10, Policy & Liquor Control 1909–1921 file, Records of the Rapid City Indian School, RG 75, NACPR.
8. Correspondence between House and E. E. Wagner, U.S. Attorney, Sioux Falls, South Dakota, December 14, 1910, through January 11, 1911, in SSCF Box 10, Policy & Liquor Control 1909–1921 file, Records of the Rapid City Indian School, RG 75, NACPR.
9. Correspondence between House and Wagner, December 14, 1910, through January 11, 1911.
10. "Circular #4. Operations," Larson, October 17, 1912, SSCF Box 10, Policy & Liquor Control 1909–1921 file, Records of the Rapid City Indian School, RG 75, NACPR.
11. House to Larson, November 19, 1914, and correspondence between House and E. B. Meritt, Assistant Commissioner of Indian Affairs, January 14, 1915, through February 23, 1915, all in SSCF Box 10, Policy & Liquor Control 1909–1921 file, Records of the Rapid City Indian School, RG 75, NACPR.
12. House to Larson, December 5, 1916, and Larson to House, December 15, 1916, both in SSCF Box 10, Policy & Liquor Control 1909–1921 file, Records of the Rapid City Indian School, RG 75, NACPR.
13. House to Larson, November 24, 1920, SSCF Box 10, Policy & Liquor Control 1909–1921 file, Records of the Rapid City Indian School, RG 75, NACPR.
14. C. H. Gensler, Superintendent, Lower Brule Agency, to S. A. M. Young, Superintendent, Rapid City Indian School, November 2, 1922, and Young to Gensler, January 16, 1923, both in GCF Box 88, DC 842 Lower Brule Agency file, Records of the Rapid City Indian School, RG 75, NACPR.
15. Henry J. McQuigg, Superintendent, Turtle Mountain Indian Agency, to Young, December 26, 1924, and Young to McQuigg, December 29, 1924, both in GCF Box 30, DC 840.2 Enrollment and Attendance—1924 file, Records of the Rapid City Indian School, RG 75, NACPR.
16. Julia McGaa to Superintendent, Pine Ridge Agency, July 28, 1930, Josephine Provost to Day School Inspector, August 16, 1930, and George A. Day, Senior Clerk and Special Disbursing Agent, Rapid City Indian School, to C. P. Detwiler, Acting Superintendent, Pine Ridge Agency, August 25, 1930, all in Pine Ridge Agency General Records, Main Decimal Files Box 687, 806.26 Rapid City 1 of 3 file, Records of the Pine Ridge Agency, RG 75, NACPR.
17. "Catalog and Synopsis of Courses, United States Indian School, Rapid City, South Dakota, 1916–17," and "The School of the Hills, Rapid City, South Dakota, 1922," both in SSCF Box 9, School Annuals, Graduate Programs, School Paper file, Records of the Rapid City Indian School, RG 75, NACPR; "The School of the Black Hills, Rapid City Indian School, Rapid City, South Dakota, President's Number, Catalogue 1928," Records of the Cheyenne River Agency Box 443 (518431), Misc. Correspondence Rapid City School 1923–1928 file, RG 75, NACPR.
18. Sharon R. Mote, Superintendent, Rapid City Indian School, to Pathe Exchange, Inc., July 16, 1929, Mote to Ludwig Film Exchanges, January 9, 1926, and "License for F. B. O. Pictures (Standard Exhibition Contract)," September 18, 1928, all in

GCF Box 25, DC 751 Amusements and Athletics, Moving Pictures, Supplies, etc. file, Records of the Rapid City Indian School, RG 75, NACPR.

19. "Annual Calendar, 1927–1928, U.S. Indian Boarding School, Rapid City, South Dakota," SSCF Box 9, School Annuals, Graduate Programs, School Paper file; "Committees for Hallowe'en Social, Saturday evening, Oct. 30," n.d., GCF Box 85, DC 826.1 Student Activities file; both in Records of the Rapid City Indian School, RG 75, NACPR.

20. "Annual Calendar, 1927–1928, U.S. Indian Boarding School, Rapid City, South Dakota"; "Statement of the Students' Activities Association, 15 December 1925" and "Inventory of the Store, 15 December 1925," both in GCF Box 85, DC 826.1 Student Activities Association file, Records of the Rapid City Indian School, RG 75, NACPR; oral history of Eva Enos, p. 33, Warm Valley Historical Project, Shoshone Episcopal Mission, Fort Washakie, Wyoming.

21. Carl E. Wilcox, Principal, Rapid City Indian School, "To those concerned," April 12, 1927, and "Declamation Contest," April 18, 1927, both in GCF Box 91, DC 864 Inspection Reports 1925–1928 file; "Annual Banquet, Rapid City Indian School," May 14, 1927, GCF Box 26, DC 781 Menus file; all in Records of the Rapid City Indian School, RG 75, NACPR.

22. Adams, *Education for Extinction*, 185.

23. Adams, *Education for Extinction*, 181–90.

24. Mote to R. E. Hanley, Director of Athletics, Haskell Institute, September 29, 1925, GCF Box 88, DC 842 Haskell Institute 1923–1925 file, Records of the Rapid City Indian School, RG 75, NACPR.

25. Mote to R. E. Rawlins, Superintendent of Schools, Pierre, South Dakota, September 2, 1926, GCF Box 25, DC 752 Football file; R. E. Rawlins, Secretary-Treasurer, South Dakota High School Athletic Association, Board of Control, September 13, 1926, GCF Box 25, DC 750 Amusements and Athletics file; "Basket Ball Schedule for season of 1925–1926" and "Basket Ball Schedule, 1927," handwritten, GCF Box 25, DC 754 Basketball file; all in Records of the Rapid City Indian School, RG 75, NACPR.

26. Mote to Superintendent, Murdo High School, September 22, 1927, handwritten reply by name illegible in the margin; Mote to Superintendent, Sundance High School, September 22, 1927, handwritten reply by L. G. Crouch, Superintendent, Sundance High School, in the margin; Mote to Lieutenant Greeg, Manager, Football Team, Fort Meade, October 24, 1926; Dan O. Root, Director of Physical Education, Spearfish Normal School, September 29, 1926; Mote to Euclid Cobb, Football Coach, Rapid City High School, October 7, 1927; "Indian Day Homecoming Football!" flyer; all GCF Box 25, DC 752 Football file, Records of the Rapid City Indian School, RG 75, NACPR.

27. Fred C. Basler, Faculty Secretary-Treasurer, Student Activities Association, form letter to season ticket buyers, October 27, 1928; Mote, "Memorandum to All Employees," October 31, 1928; and Basler, handwritten list of season ticket purchasers, November 23, 1928; all in GCF Box 26, DC 758 Season Tickets file; Mote to O. C. Upchurch, District Superintendent, Flandreau Indian School, January 31, 1927, GCF Box 15, DC 161 (T-Z) Gen. Supt. O. C. Upchurch file; all in Records of the Rapid City Indian School, RG 75, NACPR.

28. "Statement of Student Activities Association, April 1, 1928," GCF Box 25, DC 750

Amusements and Athletics file; Mote, memorandum, "To Any Employee who has a car," January 20, 1928, GCF Box 25, DC 754.6 Basketball Tournament file; both in Records of the Rapid City Indian School, RG 75, NACPR.

29. Mote to R. W. Skinner, Principal, Rapid City High School, May 5, 1927, GCF Box 26, DC 755.0 Track Meet file, Records of the Rapid City Indian School, RG 75, NACPR; Mote to C. R. Whitlock, Superintendent, Pierre Indian School, January 18, 1928, J. W. Balmer, Superintendent, Pipestone Indian School, to Mote, January 27, 1928, Principal [name illegible], Rosebud School, to C. M. Ziebach, Superintendent, Rosebud Agency, February 7, 1928, Carl Stevens, Superintendent, Wahpeton Indian School, to Mote, February 11, 1928, and W. J. Birmingham, S.J., St. Francis Mission, to Mote, February 12, 1928, all in GCF Box 25, DC 750 Amusements and Athletics file, Records of the Rapid City Indian School, RG 75, NACPR.

30. James H. McGregor, District Superintendent, to the Heads of Mission and Government Indian Schools, February 25, 1928, and C. R. Whitlock, Superintendent, Pierre Indian School, to C. B. Dickinson, Superintendent, Bismarck Indian School, April 29, 1928, both in GCF Box 26, DC 755.0 Track Meet file; "Declamatory and Oratorical Contest, Rapid City Indian School," April 30, 1928, and "Indian School Meet, May 11–12, 1928, Program," both in GCF Box 26, DC 757 School Plays, Entertainment, etc. file; all in Records of the Rapid City Indian School, RG 75, NACPR.

31. Mote, unaddressed letter, December 10, 1928, and McGregor to Mote, December 14, 1928, both in GCF Box 25, DC 754 Basketball file; Mote to Dickinson, February 21, 1929, Balmer to Mote, February 25, 1929, and Mote to Dr. C. C. O'Harra, President, South Dakota School of Mines, March 19, 1929, both in GCF Box 25, DC 754.6 Basketball Tournament file; all in Records of the Rapid City Indian School, RG 75, NACPR.

32. "Inter-Indian School Tournament, Rapid City, S.D. March 15 & 16, 1929," entry sheets, girls' and boys' teams; Mote to O'Harra, March 19, 1929; McGregor to Commissioner of Indian Affairs, March 30, 1929; all in GCF Box 25, DC 754.6 Basketball Tournament file, Records of the Rapid City Indian School, RG 75, NACPR.

33. K. K. Newport, Principal, Rapid City Indian School, to Mote, May 10, 1929, GCF Box 26, DC 757 School Plays, Entertainments, ect [*sic*] file, Records of the Rapid City Indian School, RG 75, NACPR.

34. W. O. Roberts, Superintendent, Rosebud Agency, to Young, January 8, 1932, GCF Box 90, DC 842 Rosebud Agency 1932–1933 file, Records of the Rapid City Indian School, RG 75, NACPR.

35. Roberts to Young, January 8, 1932.

36. Young to Mitchell Desersa, January 14, 1932, Young to Joseph Pawnee, January 14, 1932, and Young to Roberts, January 26, 1932, all in GCF Box 90, DC 842 Rosebud Agency 1932–1933 file, Records of the Rapid City Indian School, RG 75, NACPR.

37. Roberts to Young, January 27, 1932, GCF Box 90, DC 842 Rosebud Agency 1932–1933 file, Records of the Rapid City Indian School, RG 75, NACPR.

38. Young to W. F. Dickens, Superintendent, Cheyenne River Agency, March 9, 1932, GCF Box 86, DC 842 Cheyenne River Agency 1930–1933 file, Records of the Rapid City Indian School, RG 75, NACPR.

39. Young to Dickens, March 14, 1932, GCF Box 86, DC 842 Cheyenne River Agency 1930–1933 file, Records of the Rapid City Indian School, RG 75, NACPR.

40. Raymond E. Staley, Superintendent, Rapid City Indian School, to Dickens, December 15, 1932, GCF Box 8, DC 842 Cheyenne River Agency 1930–1933 file, Records of the Rapid City Indian School, RG 75, NACPR.

41. James H. McGregor, Superintendent, Pine Ridge Agency, to Staley, April 12, 1933, and Staley to McGregor, April 17, 1933, both in GCF Box 89, DC 842 Pine Ridge Agency 1930–1933 file, Records of the Rapid City Indian School, RG 75, NACPR.

Richard Henry Pratt, 1899, the architect of the federal American Indian boarding school. Courtesy Cumberland County, Historical Society, Carlisle, Pennsylvania.

Boy students at most off-reservation American Indian boarding schools wore military dress, marching everywhere, and saluting officers like the young man on the far right. Courtesy Sherman Indian Museum, Riverside, California.

In 1919, the girls at Sherman Institute wore dress uniforms in front of the Minnehaha Dormitory. Students and staff referred to them as Minnehaha Girls. Courtesy Sherman Indian Museum, Riverside, California.

Girls' reading room at Haskell Institute, Lawrence, Kansas. Administrators at American Indian boarding schools believed in separate spheres for boys and girls, keeping them apart through the creation of such gender-specific spaces. Courtesy National Archives and Records Administration.

These boys lived at the farm at Sherman Institute. Each day they gathered dozens of eggs that were consumed by fellow students. Courtesy Sherman Indian Museum, Riverside, California.

Girls attending St. Boniface Indian School worked in orchards on and off their campus in Banning, California. Here the girls load wooden trays of apricots into a dryer. Courtesy Tanya Rathbun.

Girl students at Carlisle dressed in their uniforms in front of the bandstand. Captain Henry Pratt is seated to the far right in the bandstand. Courtesy Cumberland County Historical Society, Carlisle, Pennsylvania.

Group photograph of teachers at Carlisle Indian School: Mary Hyde, Emma A. Cutter, Anne S. Ely, Marianna Burgess, and Miss Spencer. Courtesy Cumberland County Historical Society, Carlisle, Pennsylvania.

Off-reservation boarding schools supported athletic teams. Carlisle Indian School had a successful baseball program. Courtesy National Archives and Records Administration.

Boy and girl students at American Indian boarding schools did the laundry for the entire school. Note the ironing boards on the far left. Courtesy Sherman Indian Museum, Riverside, California.

American Indian students at boarding schools spent part of their day attending classes. These students are in science class. Note the specimens in the glass case. Courtesy Sherman Indian Museum, Riverside, California.

Instructors at Sherman Institute during the 1910s. Mary Israel (*top left*) directed a successful and exclusive nursing program for Native American girls. Courtesy Sherman Indian Museum, Riverside, California.

A classroom setting during World War II at Sherman Institute with an American Indian teacher and teacher's aide. Courtesy Sherman Indian Museum, Riverside, California.

Older Native American students studied Mary Furlong Moore's *The Baby Sitter's Guide*. These girls are studying to be hired as babysitters and nannies. Courtesy Sherman Indian Museum, Riverside, California.

In the 1930s, Sherman Institute had a mixed male and female choir that sang at events on and off campus. Students often enjoyed singing, but the choir also represented the school as civilizing Indians and promoted the American Indian boarding school system. Courtesy Sherman Indian Museum, Riverside, California.

Sherman Institute boasted a winning football team that beat the University of Southern California many times in the early twentieth century. Courtesy Sherman Indian Museum, Riverside, California.

Boys and girls took classes in typing to learn to become secretaries and office managers. Courtesy Sherman Indian Museum, Riverside, California.

These girl students prepared the dining room for an evening meal at Crow Agency Boarding School. Courtesy National Archives and Records Administration.

In 1900, the boys at Phoenix Indian School constructed small projects in wood shop. Courtesy National Archives and Records Administration.

This photograph depicts the many disciplines taught at American Indian boarding schools, including reading, writing, and spelling as well as painting, and ironing. Courtesy Sherman Indian Museum, Riverside, California.

Around 1940, girls and boys at St. Boniface Indian School in Banning, California, dressed for confirmation. Superintendents, priests, and teaching nuns expected every student to excel in Catholic education. Courtesy Tanya Rathbun.

In the 1950s, Sherman Institute sponsored the Navajo Program to educate students from the largest Indian tribe in the United States. Here children learn about George Washington and Abraham Lincoln and read several books. Note the Navajo scene in the picture of sandstone buttes and a herd of sheep. Also see the poster, "How to Catch a Cold," to the far left. Courtesy Sherman Indian Museum, Riverside, California.

Older American Indian girls at Indian boarding schools often learned to bake. Note the wood-burning stove on the far right and electrified lights on the ceiling. Courtesy Sherman Indian Museum, Riverside, California.

Sherman All Star Basketball Team, 1903 (*left to right*): George Magee, Alex Tortez, Alex Magee (holding the ball), John Pugh, and John Ward. Courtesy Sherman Indian Museum, Riverside, California.

For girls, American Indian boarding schools emphasized a curriculum of domestic science (home economics). Here students learn to use a measuring cup. Note the instructional posters behind the Native American teacher depicting how to cut sewing patterns. Courtesy Sherman Indian Museum, Riverside, California.

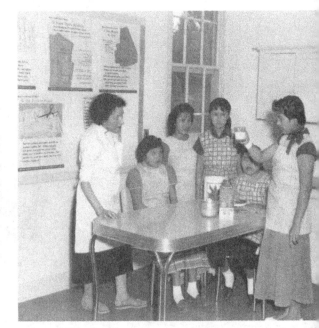

Girls learned sewing as a vocation at Indian boarding schools. These students are working on treadle sewing machines. Note "Lesson 3" written on the blackboard behind the instructor on the left. Courtesy Sherman Indian Museum, Riverside, California.

Richard Henry Pratt began the "outing" program at Carlisle Indian School. In the 1950s, four Indian girls trained to be maids at the Mission Court Motel. Courtesy Sherman Indian Museum, Riverside, California.

American Indian girls learned to be nannies and governesses at a nursery located on the grounds of Sherman Institute. Courtesy Sherman Indian Museum, Riverside, California.

We LEARN to WORK and EARN MONEY

The federal Indian school curriculum emphasized job training so students could "LEARN to WORK and EARN MONEY." Bureau of Indian Affairs educators wanted to make Indian students "useful" and ignored the fact that Indian people had worked and been useful for thousands of years. Courtesy Sherman Indian Museum, Riverside, California.

Teachers at federal American Indian boarding schools taught boys about agriculture. Here students receive a lesson on dairy farming. Courtesy Sherman Indian Museum, Riverside, California.

Some American Indian students trained to be firefighters with the United States Forest Service. Note the painted symbol for the Dalton Hot Shots, which incorporates a Navajo lightning design, the Hopi face of Tawa (Sun), and a crowned dancer. Courtesy Sherman Indian Museum, Riverside, California.

6. Hail Mary

The Catholic Experience at
St. Boniface Indian School

Tanya L. Rathbun

Tanya L. Rathbun is the foremost scholar of St. Boniface Indian School, established by the Roman Catholic Church in Banning, California, in 1890.
Unlike other boarding schools discussed in this volume, St. Boniface was
a Catholic boarding school. Trained at the University of California, Riverside, in Historic Preservation, Rathbun is the first scholar to provide a
scholarly essay on St. Boniface, and her essay is part of a larger research
project that will result in a book on this school. Rathbun argues that the
priests and nuns who ran St. Boniface put religion first in their academic work and extracurricular activities, making Christianity the school's
dominant theme. She maintains that some students adjusted to the strict
Catholic emphasis, while others rebelled. Using records of the St. Boniface
school and oral histories, she weaves an interpretive analysis surrounding
the significance of Catholic dogma in the school's everyday operation.

Rathbun compares St. Boniface Indian School to the Spanish missions
of colonial California, when Christian schools emerged to uplift and convert "heathen" Indians. Priests and nuns at St. Boniface viewed Indians as
backward "savages" who lusted after each other and had to be saved from
Satan. Mother Katharine Drexel personally paid for the site and school
north of Banning, a site situated in the shadow of one sacred mountain
and in view of another. The Office of Indian Affairs augmented St. Boniface's budget in the 1890s, but school officials remained suspicious of involvement by the federal government, believing it was too secular. However, as at other boarding schools, priests emphasized hard work, believing
that idle hands were "the Devil's workshop."

"A student was selected to give the commands," explained a former student
of St. Boniface Indian School, who had attending during the 1940s. The nuns
pointed students toward "a cross mounted in an archway, between the classrooms." Then, "after a short prayer to the cross, the command was given
to face the American flag." At a signal, a student sounded bugles and "the

flag was raised up the flag pole, with the students saluting the flag."[1] Nuns and priests at St. Boniface demanded that the allegiance of students at the school focused first and foremost on God and only secondarily on the United States. Thus, children attending this Catholic off-reservation boarding school participated in this and several other genuflections every day, because the church established the school with indoctrination into Christianity as its overriding objective as an educational institution. Students prayed upon awaking, before breakfast, during classes, and at lunch and dinner. As the sun set each night over the mountains and hills to the west, nuns forced students to remain silent in observance of the bells for St. Angelus. Before bed each night, a priest offered a final prayer, and students reportedly went to bed in the arms of the Christian savior. Every activity within the school resonated with religious themes and rituals. St. Boniface's administrative structure created an outward atmosphere of piety and fostered a unique experience among all the students, one that they would never forget.

Its association with Catholic religious education separated St. Boniface from nearby Perris Indian School and, later, Sherman Institute as well as most other nonsectarian off-reservation boarding schools. St. Boniface, like other Catholic boarding schools for American Indian children, highly emphasized Christianity. While other schools included elements of Christian teaching in their philosophy, St. Boniface forced students to follow a strict religious curriculum and church authority. This was the intent of the school's founders. From the founding of St. Boniface Indian School in 1890 until its closure in 1952, Catholic clergy and their Christian ideology dominated the school. A nun founded and initially funded the school. Catholic missionary periodicals promoted the institution. Priests and nuns from the Midwest came to California to locate the site of St. Boniface with the intention of furthering the Christian faith among the Indian people of southern California and civilizing their "heathen" charges.

Nun and heiress Mother Katharine Drexel created the St. Boniface school through her personal donation of large sums of money. Her intention was to establish an institution to Christianize and civilize young Native Americans to benefit them in this life and the next. Drexel's goals coincided with those of the U.S. government, which contracted with the Catholic school to take Indian students. At least from 1890 to 1900, the Office of Indian Affairs used the Indian Appropriation Bill to allocate St. Boniface $125 per student each year.[2] The difference in the two types of off-reservation boarding schools centered around the fact that St. Boniface focused strongly on Catholic education and the teaching of Christian beliefs.

In 1890, Drexel bought 258 acres of land in Banning, which is about seventy miles east of Los Angeles in the foothills of the San Bernardino Mountains. Drexel paid for the land and construction of the buildings at St. Boniface, and not long after the construction of the physical plant she donated an additional $40,000 for the purchase of school furniture, beds, and farming equipment. By 1904 she had contributed over a million dollars for the building of several Catholic Indian schools and had committed herself to providing St. Boniface school with $100,000 per year to keep it running.[3] No doubt Drexel had a major hand in determining the direction of the Catholic boarding school.

Drexel committed herself to Indian education more than any other Catholic in the nineteenth and twentieth centuries. During her lifetime she supported nearly sixty schools and missions for Native American and African American people. The Vatican considers her largest contribution to be the establishment of Xavier University of Louisiana in 1925, the only predominantly African American Catholic institution of higher learning in the United States. Drexel also founded the Sisters of the Blessed Sacrament, a multiracial organization of nuns who have staffed Native American and African American schools from 1891 to the present day. In 2000, Pope John Paul II declared Katharine Drexel a saint.[4]

St. Boniface was one of many Indian mission schools supported by the Bureau for Catholic Indian Missions (bcim), an agency founded in 1874 by church officials in the United States. The bcim founded Indian missions across the country and maintained review powers over them on behalf of the Roman Catholic Church. Beginning in 1893 the bureau published the *Indian Sentinel* to raise money for these missions.[5] Although the bcim did not found St. Boniface, it supported the off-reservation boarding school. For example, the bureau twice dedicated an issue of the *Indian Sentinel* to the school, full of glowing articles intended to persuade Catholic donors to support St. Boniface with cash donations. Furthermore, after 1900 the bcim gave St. Boniface one hundred dollars per annually student to offset the loss of federal dollars. This made it possible for the St. Boniface school to continue to offer education to Native American students who were unable to provide tuition.[6]

Between 1890 and 1950, St. Boniface received support from Mother Drexel's estate, the BCIM, and government foster-care funds. Although the school received some contract funds from the Office of Indian Affairs, the Catholic administrators of St. Boniface were suspicious of the federal government and its secular approach to Indian education. In fact, the BCIM recorded in the *Indian Sentinel* a general Catholic suspicion of the federal government, stating in some of the articles that some mission administrators viewed the nonsectarian off-reservation boarding schools as godless, unclean, and unsanitary institutions, particularly when compared with "that exquisitely neat and motherly school of the Loretto Sisters at Bernalillo."[7] In part, the BCIM supported St. Boniface because it was a Catholic institution that stood in marked contrast to the federal Indian boarding schools, which generally ignored Christianity as a major focus and did not teach Native students to sing, pray, and worship God. The BCIM strengthened its relationship with St. Boniface in the 1890s in part to help counter the government's secular approach to boarding schools.

In 1890, Mother Drexel worked with the Jesuit order to establish the school. The Jesuits appointed Father George Willard the first superintendent of the school. However, Father Willard led the school only a short time, dying in 1890 before the first school year began.[8] Father Florian Hahn took Father Willard's place, and the new superintendent demonstrated his nature and direction from the outset. The hard-driving, determined German priest threw himself into the work, exhibiting a tremendous work ethic which he hoped students would emulate. In addition to administering the school, he took on several other responsibilities. Hahn led the school band, raising funds for purchasing instruments and teaching music to Indian children. He scheduled music recitals and sporting events. He also chronicled the early history of the institution through his correspondence and through the school newspaper, the *Mission Indian*, which he established in 1890. His account of the Christmas Earthquake of 1899 is one of the few sources of daily life at St. Boniface at the turn of the century.[9] Equally important, Hahn wrote several articles for the BCIM in the *Indian Sentinel* and in his own newsletter, the *Mission Indian*, that popularized St. Boniface and encouraged Catholic donors to give to the schools in order to save and uplift California's Indian children. Hahn's legacy lived on long past his tenure as superintendent.[10] He infused Catholicism into nearly all of the activities at the school, both sacred and mundane, and expected children to leave the institution with Christian and capitalistic values firmly ingrained. His emphasis on hard work and Catholic instruction established the foundation for which the school became known from the 1890s until it closed in 1952.[11]

St. Boniface reflected the traditions of the Spanish mission system in that it embraced a concentration of Native Americans on one site. The priests and nuns carried on some educational and Christian traditions of Father Junipero Serra, the founder of the mission system of Alta California. Father Justin Deutsch carried on Serra's legacy, writing with reverence about "continuing the great works of Father Serra."[12] The missionaries who established the latter-day mission school of St. Boniface emulated the California mission system by assuming (incorrectly) that Indian people were not "clean hardworking Catholics."[13] The officials who operated St. Boniface still viewed California's Native people as primitive Christians with heathen or unorthodox beliefs and practices. The Catholic administration of St. Boniface believed that California Indians needed their help, just as infants and children require the firm hand and direction of their parents.

Priests and nuns at St. Boniface saw themselves as parents and counselors, but they also themselves to be holy agents of Christian civilization, God's disciples on earth charged by the Almighty to act on his behalf. School administrators believed themselves to be an extension of Jesus Christ and believed that they had a holy obligation to bring the wayward sheep into the one true fold. They came to St. Boniface to bring civilization, education, and Christianity to "ignorant" Indians whose lives had been directed, in southern California, by Indian nets, puls, and a host of non-Christian medicine people who stood in the way of the "light."[14] Like Father Serra before them, the priests and nuns believed they were on a mission from God, and in this crusade they differed from administrators and teachers working at nonsectarian, off-reservation boarding schools. The priests and nuns at St. Boniface zealously strove to convert Indian children to Christianity and force them to honor and obey the church dogma. Although priests and nuns did not forcefully remove Indian children from their homes or invade Native villages to establish missions in the heart of Indian communities, they did establish the school in close proximity to the Morongo, San Manuel, Soboba, Agua Caliente, Cabazon, Torres-Martinez, and Twenty-nine Palms reservations.

Like the founders of the Spanish mission system, the founders of St. Boniface carefully selected the site for the school. They built the institution in the Banning Pass near a major automobile highway and railroad, in the heart of Indian country. As at the Spanish missions, school administrators and teachers provided students with a heavy dose of Catholicism, and they forced students to work so that idle hands would not become "the Devil's workshop." They had students work in the laundry, kitchen, orchards, and gardens. Students mixed mortar, hauled rocks, laid bricks, and constructed outbuildings. They painted buildings, cleaned rooms, and stoked furnaces. Essentially, students did the vast majority of the manual labor, and school administrators intended the students to be laborers.

Priests and nuns at St. Boniface followed the pattern found at other off-reservation boarding schools by using students to do most of the hard labor, and like their nonsectarian counterparts, policy makers justified the use of child labor by arguing that this was part of the educational curriculum and would make the children "useful."[15] However, unlike many nonsectarian Indian boarding schools, St. Boniface did not offer a curriculum rich in the industrial arts such as carpentry, mechanics, printing, masonry, animal husbandry, or agriculture. Instead, children learned how to launder clothing, pick fruit, build stone fences and retaining walls, mop, dust, and sweep. Based on the school's curriculum, the boys could learn to work in farm labor or masonry, and girls could become maids or laundresses. Perhaps Father Hahn and other superintendents intended this to be the case, because religion, not trades, was the primary focus for children attending the school.

Most federal off-reservation boarding schools, such as nearby Sherman Institute in Riverside, California, had chapels on campus where Protestant and Catholic officials offered students religious services on Sundays and religious holidays. In contrast, the priests at St. Boniface performed mass every morning before breakfast, seven days a week. Children had to line up in front of the church and await the priest's invitation to enter. Once inside, nuns forced boys and girls to sit on separate sides of the church.[16] Former student Donald Kolchakis reported that he anticipated mass every day, less for the religious experience than for the chance to see a certain girl with whom he was enamored. "As I helped serve communion by holding the wafer plate," Don remembered, "I'd gently bump the plate against that special someone's chin, just to get her reaction."[17] Some students enjoyed the religious rigor and atmosphere at St. Boniface. August Martinez recalled that some of his friends embraced Catholicism and planned to become priests and nuns. One former student, Marceline Mamake, became a loyal lay leader of the Roman Catholic Church in Los Angeles. Marceline was born into a leadership family on the Tohono O'odham Reservation of Arizona and was slated to become a chief among his people. After graduation from St. Boniface, however, he attended St. Mary's Academy in Los Angeles, run by the Corondelet nuns. He did not return to Arizona to become a tribal leader but entered the church's administration. Marceline ultimately became an engineer and worked for St. Mary's physical plant.[18]

Other students disliked mass and the layers of religious education at St. Boniface. Some resisted the priests and their emphasis on Catholicism. Chemehuevi elder Joe Benitez remembers being unimpressed by the Catholic rituals and hating the strict discipline forced on the children. In fact, Benitez expressed regret that he ever had to attend St. Boniface, and most of his memories of his school days remain negative.[19] Donald Kolchakis did not appreciate the school's emphasis on Catholicism, and today neither he nor Benitez is Catholic, attributing their views of the church somewhat to their experiences at St. Boniface. Other children rebelled against Catholic discipline at the school. Serrano-Cahuilla elders Frances Morongo de los Reyes and Martha Manuel Chacon of the San Manuel Reservation often resisted the religious and secular training of the nuns of St. Boniface. The nuns slapped Martha for refusing to wash the underwear of other students at the school, so Martha slapped a nun. A priest then whipped her, but she refused to wash any clothing in the school's laundry. The nuns also hit Frances. When the two girls received permission from the school to visit their parents, they reported the punishments to their elders. The girls told their parents that they would not return to St. Boniface, so their parents consented to permitting them to remain at home on the San Manuel Indian Reservation. As young girls, Martha and Frances found the atmosphere of the school alien, unfriendly, and oppressive. Both had been raised by nurturing parents of the leadership class, and neither had been abused as a child. They had learned the traditions and laws of their tribes, but the church had not had a strong presence on the San Manuel Reservation. When the girls entered the St. Boniface school, their parents had agreed to their enrollment so that they could cope better with an ever-changing society dominated by non-Indians. Furthermore, their parents expected them to be future leaders of the tribe and felt that training at an off-reservation boarding school would better prepare them for tribal responsibilities. However, both girls reacted negatively to the strict policies of the nuns and priests at St. Boniface, and both quit the school to pursue their education at other institutions. As adults, Chacon and Morongo de los Reyes reported their disdain for St. Boniface.[20] In fact, many former students at St. Boniface disliked the institution because of the religious instruction and because their Catholic supervisors expected a great deal of the children in the classroom and the workplace.

Priests and nuns who operated St. Boniface expected children attending the school to progress successfully through their classes and participate in confirmation ceremonies. Because St. Boniface went up to the eighth grade, confirmation often coincided with the students' graduation. The diocese considered confirmation extremely important. In 1942 priests from throughout southern California attended the confirmation and graduation ceremonies. The presiding bishop, Charles F. Buddy, conducted the confirmation exam himself. As a result of this ceremony and the attention provided by Bishop Buddy, St. Boniface expanded its influence within the Catholic world. On a local level, the church used the ceremony to win over students and parents to Catholic education and religion. Of course, the priests and nuns diligently sought the same objective in the school's everyday operations.[21]

Male students could serve the church officially as altar boys and acolytes, but girls could not serve in either capacity, a circumstance that mirrored the gender gap found within the Roman Catholic Church worldwide. Priests required altar boys and acolytes to learn all the prayers and words of the mass in Latin. August Martinez recalled that altar boys always had some task in the chapel, suggesting that perhaps they were exempt from most of the manual labor outdoors expected of other boys and girls. A boy might not have chosen to become an altar boy for spiritual purposes alone but to avoid work as an act of resistance to the boarding school system. The priests entrusted many boys with religious ceremonies as well as the sacramental wine, and some of the boys took advantage of the opportunity to sample the alcohol. Don Kolchakis stated that he enjoyed "sampling the wine, just to see how good it was."[22]

In addition to religious services, catechism, and religion classes, students taking secular or academic classes experienced a variety of religious elements embedded in the curriculum. Many extracurricular activities sponsored by St. Boniface priests served a purpose for the church. Students progressed through secular course work that included Bible history class and Catholic philosophy. The holistic missionary approach taken at St. Boniface suggests that the nuns continued to indoctrinate students through the three R's. The nuns brought religion into the curriculum whenever they could, incorporating Catholic dogma and ideals into everyday schoolwork.

The Sisters of St. Joseph composed the teaching faculty at St. Boniface for more than sixty years. They had entered southern California with some knowledge of Native Americans but little accurate information about Indian tribes of California. Originating in St. Louis, Missouri, they believed themselves to be "cultured, religious women" who originally "came from St. Louis to convert Indians."[23] They came from the American Midwest armed with experience with Indian tribes gained from the St. Joseph Indian School in Indiana but with no experience with southern California tribes. As a result, they accepted many stereotypes made by former missionaries of California's Indian people, including calling them "Mission Indians," an inaccurate designation. The Indian tribes in southern California distinguished themselves from each other and did not refer to themselves as "Mission Indians," although the Office of Indian Affairs used this designation for all Indians living in southern California. The nuns incorrectly thought that all Indians in the region had been a part of the Spanish mission system, but only a few select tribes had participated in the Spanish missions during the eighteenth and nineteenth centuries.

When new priests and nuns began working at St. Boniface they often believed the false information that circulated at the time about Indians of southern California. The educators believed that the so-called Mission Indians had been somewhat "tamed" by the Spanish mission system and were a docile, unintelligent, and "dirty" lot that ate snakes, lizards, and spiders as well as a host of plants they dug from the ground. Priests and nuns assigned to southern California undoubtedly learned that some people had labeled the Native Americans of the region "Digger Indians," a derogatory term used by non-Indians to liken California's first peoples to African Americans, or in the pejorative word of the time, "Niggers." Clearly, non-Indians did not have to stretch their minds too far to connect "Digger" with "Nigger," and they did so purposely to denigrate people of a different culture and race. Indian people in southern California included Cahuillas, Serranos, Cupeños, Kumeyaay, Quechans, Mojaves, Acjachemen, Luiseños, Tongva-Gabrielenos, and Chemehuevis. Priests and nuns instructing students at St. Boniface quickly learned that their charges demonstrated little resemblance to their stereotypes, although many Indian children kept their own religious beliefs and clung tenaciously to their cultures, particularly their languages. Students accepted elements of Christianity, but they did not abandon their Native religions. Nevertheless, the fact that students held onto their own spiritual beliefs encouraged nuns and priests to destroy that which these non-Natives perceived as heathen ways.

Nuns at St. Boniface often incorporated conversion into reading and writing lessons. The priests and nuns asked students to discuss the nature of God, and they asked children to explore this issue on formal written examinations. Of course, the priests and nuns wanted children to regurgitate what they had learned in catechism. Donald Kolchakis remembered his bewilderment over one question dealing with the comparison of a circle with God.

> The words "circle" and "circus" gave me problems. In a test, the question asked was "How is a circle compared to God?" Answer: A circle had no beginning and no end. Circus was the closest word I could relate to circle, so I answered, "The circle has lots of people doing tricks and animals going around the ring." The teacher called me up and drew a circle. "What is this?" she asked. I called it a zero. She said a large zero could be called a circle. Only then did I understand the question from the test.[24]

A question like this in a reading class suggests that students had to apply Christian principles learned in catechism to their secular subjects as well. St. Boniface students had little time in any of their classes to contemplate any subject in depth apart from Catholicism. A teacher for a similar class at a federal boarding schools such as Sherman Institute would have rejected so much religious content, especially the Catholic elements. Such an emphasis on religion separated St. Boniface and other Catholic boarding schools from federal off-reservation schools. Indeed, according to August Martinez, the only lessons in science taught to students were lessons in proper hygiene and bacteria. Nuns at St. Boniface failed to teach basic lessons in science that some federal boarding schools would have considered necessary to a Western scientific understanding of the world. The nuns likely felt that understanding religious doctrine held greater importance than scientific principles, with the exception of personal cleanliness, which they felt the Indians sorely needed.[25]

Several extracurricular activities also had religious uses. Father Hahn started the school's first band before the turn of the century. The band received complimentary reviews from local newspapers and from Catholic publications such as the *Indian Sentinel* and *The Tidings*, but some students felt coerced into joining. Donald Kolchakis resisted joining the band when he was eight years old, and as a result he was whipped by Father Justin for impudence.[26] St. Boniface also boasted a large student choir. In addition to teaching instrumental music, Father Hahn taught the students Gregorian chants. The *Indian Sentinel* edition of 1905–6 suggests that the choir sang every morning at mass and that the "sweet melodious voices of the well-trained choir inspire[d] even the least devout with reverence."[27] The later Franciscan administration held mass with less frequency, but nevertheless the program at St. Boniface included a large dose of religious music through instruments and voices. Thus, extracurricular activities such as music included Catholic themes, a situation not found in most federal off-reservation Indian boarding schools. The priests sponsored extracurricular activities because they augmented traditional Catholic activities. Although these activities composed only a short time of the student's day, the priests used religious content to ensure that the children were completely inundated with Catholicism. The priests' continual indoctrination of students was characteristic of the California mission system, and the priests also adopted the principle of work to train Indian students to be civilized and useful.

The Catholic missionary system greatly affected the students' workload at St. Boniface. The priests and nuns treated students like neophytes at a Spanish mission. In a mission, neophytes did all of the daily work to maintain the mission's population and also made improvements to maintain the mission's stature as a "showplace for God." Indians provided all of the labor and much of the skill to perform carpentry, tile work, masonry, farm-

ing, and ranching. Indians did all of the heavy lifting at missions. Father
Justin openly embraced this model for St. Boniface and described his role as
continuing the work of Father Serra. Thus, priests expected students to follow a rotating cycle of chores to maintain the school's population, including cleaning of dormitories, washing clothing and dishes, picking fruits
and vegetables, milking cows, and processing fruit and milk. They also participated in school improvement projects, such as leveling the ground for
a baseball field and pouring cement for the foundation of new buildings.
Some of the male alumni remember making cinder blocks for a retaining
wall along the west side of the school. Such manual labor cut costs for the
school and provided concrete lessons for students. Priests found projects
for students commensurate to their age. As an eight-year-old, Don Kolchakis cleared dishes and helped wash them.[28] Luiseño elder Gloria Wright remembers sweeping the dormitory stairs every day while she was in the third
grade.[29] August Martinez worked in the dairies as an older boy. Regardless
of age, St. Boniface students worked for the maintenance of St. Boniface as
a mission school.

In addition to maintenance and improvement work, students provided the labor for most of the school's fund-raising activities. Just as monks
produced surplus products to support a monastery, St. Boniface students
worked in orchards and canneries picking and processing fruit for St. Boniface. For some of these jobs, priests gave students a little incentive. Gloria
Wright remembered receiving two pennies for each can she filled with olives.[30] School officials put some of the money students earned into an account for each student so that he or she could learn the value of saving
money. Still, Indian students generally had little money, so they spent their
small earnings every Sunday on soda pop, candy, and trinkets. They also
sent money home to their parents. For the most part, however, the Catholic
administration at St. Boniface did not compensate their students and constantly forced them into manual labor.

When students found themselves in trouble, the priest often gave them
extra work as penance. August Martinez remembered that the priest forced
him to perform extra work in so many "loads" of dirt. For coming to class
late, talking back, or smoking, the priest forced students to move a prescribed number of wheelbarrow-loads of dirt from the hillside near Indian
School Lane to the area planned for new basketball courts.[31] Gloria Wright

remembered that girls would often have to pick more fruit or clean unde-
sirable loads of laundry.[32] In a story told by her daughter, Pauline Ormego
Murillo, and cousin, Frances Morongo de los Reyes, one of the nuns made
Serrano elder Martha Manuel Chacon clean underwear all of the time, pos-
sibly as punishment for something the nuns found objectionable. Martha
rebelled in a small way, washing jeans instead of underwear. When the nun
discovered what Martha was doing, she told her to stop. When Martha continued to clean the jeans, the nun slapped her. In response, Martha slapped
the nun in the face. The nun protested, telling Martha that she had sinned
by striking God's agent. Martha responded that if it was a sin for her to slap
a nun, it was a sin for a nun to slap an Indian. The nun ran off to protest
to a priest, who whipped Martha. When Martha went home for a holiday,
she refused to return to St. Boniface, and her parents enrolled her in public
school in San Bernardino. According to her contemporary relatives, Martha used to say that her experience at St. Boniface was "tantamount to slavery," a description that matched Indian perceptions of the California mission system.[33]

Although few records have been uncovered about St. Boniface's outing
program. Father Gerard's first report to the BCIM included a small description of a "follow-up system" he had begun in cooperation with St. Mary's
Academy in Los Angeles. "There are at this time about 50 Indian girls doing ordinary house-work and even cooking etc. in some of the better Catholic families. This is done to give the Indian girl an idea of what a Catholic home should be like. . . . After the girls remain there about three or four
years, they usually come back to their respective homes and . . . are much
better equipped to find better Catholic homes on the reservation."[34] Some
former students describe St. Boniface's outing program as a loosely struc-
tured program similar to those instituted at federal boarding schools.[35] The
Corondelet nuns at St. Mary's Academy supervised the girls and the "follow-up" program. Every three weeks the girls gathered at the academy for a
Sunday brunch to visit with each other. The ideology behind girls' outings
at St. Boniface took on a different flavor from that of federal off-reservation
boarding schools. St. Boniface girls worked only in Catholic households as
a continuation of the church's influence and as an extension of their religious education. The St. Boniface notion of religious reinforcement through
modeling Catholic homes was little different from federal boarding school

girls modeling civilized homes as a societal reinforcement. This shows a confluence of cultural assimilations and religious conversion by St. Boniface priests, much in the same way that Franciscan missionaries converted California Indians within the missions to become Christians and to work in a civilized manner.

However, unlike the outing programs at federal off-reservation schools, the program at St. Boniface did not include older boys and manual labor. In a report, Father Gerard explained the lack of an outing program for boys. The boys suffered from the lack of camaraderie with their friends, he wrote, and because the employers of the boys typically took little interest in the boys' welfare, they often fell in with the wrong crowd. August Martinez recalled that he and other boys, instead of going to Los Angeles, sometimes made extra money working at off-campus farms, ranches, and orchards, such as picking olives at the neighboring Gilman Ranch. However, the priests did not organize many of these jobs; the boys generally secured paid, off-campus labor on their own. The absence of an outing program for boys suggests that the priests may have wanted to keep the boys on campus for work that would directly benefit the school.[36] St. Boniface priests preferred to work male students for the betterment of St. Boniface, imitating the pattern set by Serra's California mission system.

Another imitation of the California mission system occurred at St. Boniface in the absolute separation of boys from girls. While federal boarding schools generally created separate spheres in which male and female students operated, the separation of the sexes at St. Boniface was far more pronounced. Priests wanted to maintain virtue between boys and girls, even though the children at St. Boniface were of primary school age. Still, the church had long been concerned that sexual relations between the sexes be strictly prohibited. In the Spanish missions in California, priests and nuns had separated young neophytes, placing girls between the ages of twelve and eighteen in a dormitory called a *monjario*. The church forced Native girls from their homes, "protecting" them from males until they were married. Unfortunately, the monjarios were dark, dirty, and depressing structures that served as wonderful hosts for a variety of deadly bacteria, viruses, and molds that took the lives of hundreds of Native girls. The administrators of St. Boniface also created separate living areas for female students, including a separate dormitory building and a play area surrounded by a concrete wall where they were constantly watched by nuns. The administrators separated the sexes in much the same manner as the mission fathers six decades before them. Yet in spite of these efforts, girls and boys developed crushes on each other. Priests and nuns were as worried about improper contact between the sexes as the mission fathers, believing that such infatuations might lead children into the sin of premarital sex and separate them from God.

Administrators at St. Boniface forced male and female students to occupy separate worlds. The separation was so pronounced that the male alumni who have been interviewed could not be certain that they could accurately describe any of the girls' activities.[37] With the exception of some classes, mass, and meals, boys and girls rarely saw each other. Priests and nuns forced the physical separation of the sexes during those limited times when boys and girls congregated together. A 1927 photograph of one of the school's classrooms shows suited boys on one side of the room and befrocked girls sitting on the other side.[38] School officials re-created this pattern in the dining room and at mass. Joe Benitez recalled that students could go to the movies in Banning twice a month, but the nuns kept watch over the boys and girls, separating them as they walked to the movies and sat in the seats.[39]

The Sisters of St. Joseph dominated the entire world of females at St. Boniface. While it seems that boys spent a good portion of their free time unsupervised, the nuns always hovered over the girls. Male alumni provide numerous stories about clandestine activities such as running into town to smoke cigarettes and digging secret caves, but the females have few comparable stories. The boys resisted school rules in these ways, but they had opportunities to defy the system, whereas girls spent almost all of their time under the nuns' supervision. They played in a separate playground behind a block wall, sometimes trying to sing loud enough for the boys to hear.[40] Their chores kept them in the kitchen, sewing room, or laundry. Nuns continually corrected the improprieties of the girls. It was difficult, but sometimes the girls managed to slip away. Frances Morongo de los Reyes remembered a time when the girls of St. Boniface went on an outing to a fair in Riverside: "Girls would go to the fair, get on the street car to Fairmont Park. We all had to wear the same things, all white. Girls would wear clothes underneath, take it off and leave the other clothes somewhere, in the bathroom or some place and would run away from school."[41] Whether this behavior is the reason why the nuns generally kept the girls close or a result of constraining the girls too closely is open to disagreement, but Frances leaves little doubt that Indian girls defied the nuns. She attended both St. Boniface and Sherman Institute, and while she attended Sherman she ran away. She recalled that she once became ill, and school officials confined her to the school hospital. Her bed was on the second floor of the hospital and faced north. From her bed she saw the imprint of the arrowhead on the south side of the San Bernardino Mountains, a landmark located just above her reservation at San Manuel village. Frances was determined to go home, so under cover of darkness she escaped from Sherman and walked nearly twenty miles to her home. Girls and boys attending all of the off-reservation boarding schools resisted captivity and formal education by running away, and as a result, church officials began to take in other children in order to boost enrollments and accrue county, state, and federal funding through other child services.

Toward the end of the 1930s, Father Gerard began to take in a growing number of orphaned children or children from broken homes. These incoming students came from a variety of cultural backgrounds: Latinos, African Americans, American Indians, and Japanese Americans. In addition, Gerard increased the number of day students to blunt growing complaints from parishioners regarding the lack of a Catholic day school. These influences decreased the importance of St. Boniface as an Indian boarding school. In fact, by the end of the 1940s local journalists often called St. Boniface an orphanage rather than an Indian school, in spite of the fact that Native children still boarded at St. Boniface, albeit with a diverse student population.[42] An increase in the number of day students also reflects the influence of the Catholic administration. The superintendent priest at St. Boniface also served as the priest for the local Precious Blood Parish. In a letter to the Los Angeles Diocese, Father Justin Deutsch complained of pressure from his parishioners to establish a Catholic day school for the Banning Pass area, so Deutsch used St. Boniface to accommodate the parishioners' children rather than establishing a separate Catholic day school. Essentially, Deutsch turned the Indian school into a Catholic day school to accommodate the wishes of his parishioners.[43]

St. Boniface's shifting identity from an off-reservation Indian boarding school to a mission orphanage and day school is different from that of nearby federal boarding schools in Riverside and Phoenix. The change came as a direct result of the Catholic influences at St. Boniface. While some federal schools, such as Sherman Institute, developed a strong Indian identity over time, St. Boniface did not, in large part because of the school's Catholic focus. Indians and non-Indians who attended St. Boniface tended not to appreciate the central theme of the school to root out and threaten children with sin and damnation. After the 1940s, St. Boniface focused on at-risk Catholic youth, not necessarily Indian children. Because priests ran St. Boniface like a missionary institution rather than a secular institution, they had an ideology in place that encouraged charity cases from any cultural background, regardless of the school's official status as an Indian mission. By the 1940s, St. Boniface was a Catholic mission school first and an Indian boarding school second. This distinction is important to make when comparing real-life experiences at the school to the overall concept of life at federal boarding schools. Like students attending other off-reservation boarding schools, students at St. Boniface attended class and learned some basic educational and vocational skills, but they received a constant dose of Catholicism through many different venues of curricular and extracurricular activities at St. Boniface. Former students describe a wide variety of interests and memories, but the common thread is the huge role Catholicism played in their varied experiences. Children often offered Hail Marys at school, and many alumni give divine thanks that their educational experiences at St. Boniface are over and that time has separated them from their school days at the Catholic institution.

Notes

1. Donald Kolchakis, interview by Tanya Rathbun, February 13, 2002, Chula Vista, California.

2. Clifford Trafzer alerted me to the existence of files on St. Boniface in the 1920s kept by the Office of Indian Affairs in the National Archives. He suggested that the records indicate that the federal government resumed funding the school after the Meriam Report of 1928 by contracting with the school to educate Indians. The issue of federal funding will become clearer as more records from the Bureau for Catholic Indian Missions become available.

3. Bruce Harley, *St. Boniface Indian School*, Readings in Diocesan Heritage 8 (San Bernardino CA: Diocese of San Bernardino Archives, 1994), 3. On pages 2–5 Harley describes early school funding. The shifts between supporting agencies is more complex than I have described here.

4. Consuela Marie Duffy, *Katharine Drexel: A Biography* (Philadelphia: P. Reilly, 1966). Also see the official Vatican website, http://www.vatican.va, and the website for the Sisters of the Blessed Sacrament, http://www.katharinedrexel.org/pope.

5. A complete forty-volume collection of the *Indian Sentinel* is now in University of California, Riverside, Special Collections.

6. My findings demonstrate that the involvement of the Bureau of Indian Affairs spans only through the turn of the century, but other scholars believe I will find a federal connection sometime later in the twentieth century once I go through the BCIM records.

7. "A Friend in Need," *Indian Sentinel*, 1902, 11. For further comparison of Catholic and secular boarding schools, see *Indian Sentinel*, 1904, 24, and "Can the Faith Be Kept in a Government School?" *Indian Sentinel*, 1930, which features St. Boniface.

8. Father Willard was the first person to be buried in the St. Boniface school cemetery. St. Boniface priests buried approximately seventy-five people in the school cemetery between 1870 and 1940, and about half of them were school-age children who probably died while attending St. Boniface. Overgrown by weeds, this cemetery is the only recognizable part of the St. Boniface campus remaining. The Roman Catholic Church abandoned the St. Boniface cemetery in the 1970s.

9. Father Hahn's narrative is in Harley, *Readings in Diocesan Heritage*, 24.

10. Father Hahn retired in 1912.

11. The majority of former students I interviewed attended St. Boniface between 1937 and 1951 (one exception is Florence Lyons, who attended in the 1920s), during the Franciscan era. Finding former students from before this era who are still alive is extremely difficult.

12. *Indian Sentinel—St. Boniface Edition* (Marquette WI: BCIM Press, 1930), 1. The introduction cited here was written by Father Justin Deutsch.

13. *Mission Indian*, 1890, 4.

14. A net is a Cahuilla leader of the Big House. A pul is a medicine man or woman. See Lowell John Bean, *Mukat's People* (Los Angeles: University of California Press, 1972), 104–8.

15. As part of her dissertation at the University of California, Riverside, Leleua Loupe is currently researching the theme of "usefulness" as applied to student labor and education at Sherman Institute from 1902 to 1912.

16. August Martinez, interview by Tanya Rathbun, December 2001, Banning, California.

17. Kolchakis, interview, February 13, 2002. Donald was painfully aware of the boy-girl separation. Not only did he miss his "special someone," but he was only allowed to talk to his older sister once a week on Sunday.

18. Obituary for Marceline Mamake originally in a Roman Catholic Church publication named *The Tidings*, reprinted in the *Serran Newsletter* 8, no. 9 (1987): 3–4.

19. Joe Benitez, interview by Tanya Rathbun, March 2002, Cabazon Reservation.

20. Frances Morongo de los Reyes, interview by Clifford Trafzer and Leleua Loupe, October 9, 2001, San Manuel Indian Reservation, California. Frances made no mention of Catholic rituals such as mass, but she described several times when she and Martha Manuel Chacon encountered problems with the nuns due to their

strict Catholic ideology.

21. "Bishop Buddy Conducts Confirmation, Graduation," *Banning Record Gazette*, May 31, 1942.

22. Kolchakis, interview, April 17, 2002; Martinez, interview, December 2001.

23. Bruce Harley, "The Founding of St. Boniface Indian School, 1888–1890," *Southern California Quarterly* 81, no. 4 (1994): 3.

24. Kolchakis, interview, February 13, 2002. I asked both Donald Kolchakis and August Martinez about what was read in class, wondering if they used the Bible as a reader. Both responded no, but they read the Bible in Bible history class every day.

25. Martinez, interview, December 2001.

26. Kolchakis, interview, April 17, 2002.

27. *Indian Sentinel*, 1905–6, 1–4, described a complete school day for St. Boniface students. At 6:15 all students lined up for mass, where the choir sang.

28. Martinez, interview, December 2001; Kolchakis, interview, April 17, 2002. Both alumni remember making cinder blocks.

29. Gloria Wright, interview by Tanya Rathbun, May 7, 2002, Soboba Reservation, San Jacinto, California.

30. Wright, interview, May 7, 2002.

31. Martinez, interview, December 2001.

32. Wright, interview, May 7, 2002.

33. Morongo de los Reyes, interview, October 9, 2001.

34. Father Gerard's report is in Harley, *Readings in Diocesan Heritage*, 45–46.

35. Donald Kolchakis's sister, Delphina, participated in this program.

36. Martinez, interview, December 2001.

37. August Martinez's mother actually worked for St. Boniface in the kitchen, but he never saw her at school because the kitchen was off limits to him. Martinez, interview, December 2001. Similarly, when I asked Donald Kolchakis about his sister's time at St. Boniface, he replied that he needed time to go ask her. Kolchakis, interview, April 17, 2002.

38. Photograph in Harley, *Readings in Diocesan Heritage*, 40. The date of this photograph is in dispute. While Harley and the *Press Enterprise* date it at 1916, the girl standing in the picture has been identified by some people as Margaret Pina Cash, a student who attended St. Boniface in the 1920s.

39. Benitez, interview, March 2002.

40. Kolchakis, interview, April 17, 2002.

41. Morongo de los Reyes, interview, October 9, 2001.

42. "130 Boarders Register at St. Boniface Mission," *Banning Record*, September 25, 1947. For references regarding St. Boniface as an orphanage see *Banning Record*, December 18, 1947, as well as the *Banning Live Wire* and the *Riverside Press-Enterprise*.

43. Father Marcian Bucher, Father Gerard's successor, to Monsignor Daniels of the San Diego Diocese, November 7, 1951, San Bernardino Diocesan Archives, San Bernardino, California. In his letter to Daniels, Bucher explains that his parish wants him to open St. Boniface to day students.

7. Learning Gender

Female Students at the
Sherman Institute, 1907–1925

Katrina A. Paxton

Katrina A. Paxton is completing her graduate work at the University of Washington, Seattle, but she works in Manuscripts and Archives at the Washington State University Library, Pullman. In her contribution to this volume, Paxton uses the phrase "gender assimilation." In 1902, the Office of Indian Affairs located the Sherman Institute in Riverside, California, where school officials established a gendered campus and curriculum based on Carlisle Indian Industrial School. Like Richard H. Pratt, Sherman superintendent Harwood Hall separated boys and girls, while female and male teachers encouraged Native American girls to accept the place of women within the dominant society. They did not want Indian girls to develop into professional women, becoming doctors, lawyers, professors, concert pianists, actresses, or ballet dancers. They wanted Indian girls to achieve the Victorian ideal and become housewives, housekeepers, seamstresses, and domestics. The school curriculum provided opportunities for girls to become dressmakers, cooks, and servants. Sherman girls became trained in the domestic sciences and had far fewer opportunities than boys.

Paxton argues that in addition to the cultural assault on students, officials at Sherman tried to force the Protestant ideal of "true womanhood" on Indian girls. Superintendents and teachers tried to make the girls pious, pure, obedient, selfless, meek, and clean. They emphasized that girls had a God-given role to become mothers and to care for their families, thus reinforcing the general non-Native belief that a woman's place was in the home. School officials encouraged the YWCA to offer talks to young women so that they could learn about righteous living, temperance, pure thoughts, and servitude. Life for girls at Sherman encouraged a transformation, one that did not stick to many Indian girls who came from leadership families or sought greater gender freedom after leaving the institute.

Female students at Sherman Institute faced an educational system that included, among other goals, gender assimilation. Two influential organizations that many female students encountered at Sherman Institute were the Young Women's Christian Association (YWCA) and the outing system. Both of these were essential in teaching female students what "being female" meant in Euro-American terms. Using the school newspaper (the *Sherman Bulletin*), superintendent ledgers, and the outing system records, I explore in this essay how the YWCA and the outing system "instructed" young female students in the "arts of homemaking." It is important to note that the voices of individual Native women were underrepresented in the research materials used for this chapter. Historical data originated from on-site research at the Sherman Indian Museum, where personal letters, diaries, or other first-person accounts from the schoolgirls were either not present or unidentified. Nonetheless, the primary sources used here do provide an understanding, although not inclusive, of the overall structure of gender indoctrination. What follows is an account and analysis of how two unique programs, the YWCA and the outing system, worked in combination to indoctrinate young Native women into specific Protestant domestic and gender ideals.

In the late nineteenth century, the U.S. government implemented a program to ameliorate the nation's "Indian problem." This solution was to relocate of thousands of Native American children to one of the approximately 150 government-run boarding schools. The government established these schools in order to reeducate the young Native population in the "ways of the whites." Under the pretense of instruction, Native American female students found themselves indoctrinated into white Protestant gender and domestic ideals. The YWCA and the outing system became the tools of such overt gender assimilation. Both assisted in the creation of the Native American domestic worker, trained in Euro-American "homemaking" and prime for employment in white, middle-class homes.

In 1879, U.S. Army captain Richard Henry Pratt established the first boarding school for Native American children, in Carlisle, Pennsylvania.[1] Pratt viewed the boarding school as a space where Euro-American culture would replace indigenous beliefs, cultural practices, values, and mores. However, convincing distrusting communities to relinquish their children to whites proved challenging. Although some families voluntarily put their children in boarding schools, many resisted further governmental meddling. As a result, on March 3, 1891, Congress passed legislation that made education compulsory for Native American children. In order to enforce compulsory governmental education, police, Indian agents, and soldiers threatened parents with various forms of retribution—ranging from a stop of rations to imprisonment—for keeping children out of the governmental educational system.[2] Family members' and communities' fears of surrendering their children for reeducation were well founded; the goals of government-run Indian boarding schools were explicit: "Kill the Indian in him and save the man."[3]

Like many other states, California had several Indian boarding schools. In southern California, the Bureau of Indian Affairs (BIA) opened the doors of Sherman Institute to Native American boys and girls in 1902. In 1900 Congress had allocated $75,000 to relocate the Perris Indian School (1890–1902), originally situated about ten miles south of Riverside, California. In 1901 the government had begun construction of the first building of Sherman Institute. Between 1902 and 1916 the institute provided education for Native American children ranging from grade one to grade eight, and in 1916 its offerings expanded to include children through grade ten.[4]

Nationwide, young girls at Indian boarding schools experienced instruction regarding "proper" housekeeping, or more specifically, culturally specific domestic ideals. Initially, the government included a domestic curriculum for female children in order to decrease operational costs. The early domestic curriculum in boarding schools focused on day-to-day operations, such as dusting furniture or darning socks. Shortly after the government established most of its boarding schools, local YWCA chapters were established at schools, including Sherman Institute. Staying true to the Victorian domestic ethos, the YWCA instructed girls at Indian boarding schools that domesticity did not stop at dusting furniture. The extracurricular instruction that the YWCA provided became a quiet indoctrination of hundreds of young women into Protestant domestic and gender ideals.

During the era from 1902 to 1925, the faculty, administration, and staff of Sherman Institute engaged in gendered cultural assimilation of the female student body, interfusing major academic instruction, vocational training, and private social programs.

Creating Sherman Ladies

Indian boarding schools provided space and opportunity for whites and young Native people to meet and interact.[5] From 1907 to 1925 a particular relationship flourished between young, local white women involved in the YWCA and young female students. Indeed, boarding schools supplied white, middle-class women with a captive audience for two of the Victorian era's most prominent domestic gender ideologies: the "cult of true womanhood" and "separate spheres." With historic roots dating back to Martin Luther, the "cult of true womanhood" defined good women vis-à-vis characteristic traits of purity, piety, obedience, domesticity, selflessness, sacrifice, personal cleanliness, meekness, reverence of motherhood, and dedication to family.[6] Over the years, American society had developed "separate spheres," or distinct sites where women and men should be found. Within American society of the late nineteenth and early twentieth centuries, men were expected to work, receive an education, participate in politics, and act as the heads of families. Women were to keep house, bear and care for children, and be seen, not heard. Many white women embraced their separate sphere, while others challenged the "place" of women in society. For many American Indians, the boundaries between men and women were more open and less confining. As a result, the separate spheres of white America sometimes confused and confounded Native American children and created problems for them when they returned to their people.

The American Indian perspective regarding womanhood or gender spheres was of no concern to women who volunteered to teach Indian girls through the YWCA. Local white women involved with the YWCA instructed female Indian students in both "moral" and domestic ideologies at the school as well as off campus. The addition of private social organizations such as the YWCA marks a subtle yet significant change in the earlier domestic training of female boarding school students. The earlier domestic education model found at Sherman Institute, and arguably other boarding schools, was geared toward maintaining the day-to-day operations of a large organization, but with the introduction of the YWCA the domestic curriculum expanded to include ideological instruction.

Influential in establishing and reinforcing notions of Euro-American gender ideology, the YWCA became an institutional fixture at Sherman Institute. It found support due to women such as Miss Vera Wight, a local YWCA

directress at Sherman Institute. Wight and other local white women directed weekly meetings, selected predetermined topics, and chose student dis-
cussants for the YWCA meetings held on campus.[7]

In order to attract more female students at Sherman Institute to become
involved in the YWCA, the school newspaper published glowing articles that
presented the YWCA as a way to become more social and to gain help and
support in schoolwork. Girls involved with the YWCA would learn how to
perform "good, earnest, faithful work," and regardless of personal interest
in the YWCA, membership would both aid and complement school studies
and work.[8] Since the school newspaper was directed, operated, authored,
and edited by school authorities, such reports and articles appear as pseu-
do-organizational approval of the YWCA and its ideology. Indeed, the YWCA
at Sherman Institute knew that much of the training that female students
received at school was directing them as domestic workers.

To continue to increase this awareness and attract new members, the
school newspaper faithfully published upcoming YWCA meeting topics. Re-
flecting the "cult of true womanhood," meeting topics included "Living for
Others,"[9] "How Young Women Could Work for the Temperance Cause,"[10]
"Things We Should Remember and Things We Should Forget,"[11] "Righteous
Living," "Pure Thoughts Make a Pure Life,"[12] and "Help Somebody."[13] Furthermore, the YWCA identified purity, piety, selflessness, domesticity, obedience, and meekness as unique to the female gender. As a dialectic to these
qualities, "assertive" characteristics were viewed as "unfeminine" and "un-
desirable." Indeed, it was the goal of the YWCA meetings to aid female students to develop appropriate female "faculties."[14]

"Experts" on such feminine characteristics frequently lectured female
students at Sherman Institute on Sundays, instructing the young wom-
en in a path toward "the development of true womanhood."[15] Instructors
stressed the importance for students to physically *display* "ladylike" characteristics regardless of environment, for it was promoted that "a true lady
will keep herself sweet and attractive at all times, for by that is the soul expressed."[16] Furthermore, instructors encouraged female Native students to
refrain from loud voices and aggressive/assertive language. Rather, YWCA
instructors expected young Native women to speak in a soft and low voice,
an outward sign of submission, for it was promoted to students that a "soft
voice is the mark of a lady."[17] The primary goal of the YWCA talks was to en-

courage the girls to accept a "higher call" through fostering loving, kind, true relationships with family members, friends, and others close to them. The YWCA's institutional discourse further supported Sherman's outside employment program, the "outing" system.[18]

Gender and Vocational Training

As defined in 1925, the ultimate goal of female education was to train students as homemakers in areas such as cooking, cleaning, health, and consumerism.[19] Male students were accorded many more vocational options than female students. As reported in the first issue of the school newspaper, boys were trained in blacksmithing, harness making, and carpentry, while girls were taught sewing and laundry.[20] Not until the late twentieth century did the Office of Indian Affairs expand vocational training for both boys and girls.[21]

The BIA educational system tracked the majority of students into institutionalized vocational training that stressed and valued the Native American student as worker and servant, regardless of gender. Estelle Reel, superintendent of education for the BIA, put this idea into words in 1901 in the "Uniform Course of Study for the Indian Schools of the United States." Reel declared that Indian girls should "become proficient in cooking, sewing and laundry work before allowing them to spend hours in useless practice upon an expensive instrument [piano] which in all probability they will never own."[22] She believed that the student's time in school had to be devoted to training as a worker, not a thinker. Male vocations were to lead to wage work in the public sphere—outside the home—whereas the female training, also to lead to wage work, remained within the private sphere—inside the home of white employers or in their homes as mother.

For a girl being trained in sewing or laundry, a typical day revolved around a division of schoolwork and vocational training. Depending on their age, girls in the sewing department learned how to operate a sewing machine, cut and fit skirts and shirts, and make "fancy dresses." Female students were acquiring skills that could help them provided for their families, since dressmaking had the potential for future employment. Instruction began early in female students' educational career, as even "tots," the youngest students, were included in vocational training.[23] The administration also expected female students to prepare meals for fellow students.[24]

Table 1. Vocational Training Options as Recorded
from Published Industrial Examination Topics

Boys	Girls
Landscape gardening	Dressmaking
Agriculture	Sewing
Stock raising	Regular cooking
Vegetable gardening	Nursing
Poultry	Dining room service
Dairying	Laundry
Steam cooking	Housekeeping
Printing	Farm housework
Shoemaking	Farm cooking
Harness making	Art needlework
Baking	
Laundry	
Cleaning	
Tailoring	
Care of horses	
Carpentry	
Blacksmithing	
Engineering	

Source: *Sherman Bulletin*, March 25, 1907, 2, 4.

Without the labor and products that children produced, boarding schools would have not been able to sustain themselves economically.[25]

In order to demonstrate proficiency in the areas of domestic knowledge, the school required female students to take "Industrial Exams." Areas of testing for girls included laundry, housekeeping, dressmaking, primary sewing, intermediate sewing, art needlework, domestic science (cooking), nursing, farm housekeeping, and farm cooking.[26] With the exception of nursing, the outcome of these domestic examinations tracked students into domestic work.

Some of the female students viewed their time at Sherman as a way for them to acquire a skill that could help their family when they returned to their homes. Female students frequently adapted the institutional curriculum in a manner that would help their families and communities. For example, Lena Smith, a student enrolled in Sherman's intermediate sewing classes in 1908, asked to remain in the garment-fitting training so that she would "be well equipped to help her mother when she returns home this summer."[27] Agnes Aguilar, who graduated in 1908, received both academic training and dressmaking diplomas, hoping to take her newly acquired skills in both academics and vocation and open her own dress shop.[28]

School administrators and educators reinforced the importance to students of acquiring domestic skills for their usefulness not within their own homes but for employment opportunities. In this context, Sherman faculty promoted domestic science classes as useful in training young women for future "work in the real well-kept homes . . . while furthering your knowledge . . . [and] receiving good pay."[29] However, encouraging young women to work outside the home directly diverged from the ideologies of "separate spheres" and the "cult of true womanhood," which restricted women to their own homes. The outcome of ideological gender training combined with domestic training and instruction was that many female students entered wage work with the entire Indian educational system supporting them.

The Outing Program

While at Sherman and similar boarding schools, young women received training in order to become both good housewives and adept live-in domestic workers.[30] Captain Pratt founded the first outing program at the Carlisle school in Pennsylvania. The outing system put young women and men to work in the surrounding white community. Schoolteachers and administrators believed that accelerated acculturation of the Native students could be brought about by complete immersion in white society.

Prior to the move to Riverside, the Perris Indian School provided a supply of young students to work as domestics and helpmates in local middle-class homes. Superintendent Hall told many prospective employers how Perris female students were "superior to white girls [who work as domestics] of the same age, owing to their methodical and painstaking ways as well as reliability."[31] Meanwhile, once Perris had relocated to Riverside and become Sherman Institute, the outing system grew and flourished. Over summer breaks, Sherman Institute sent out young boys and girls to local families, business owners, and farmers to work as inexpensive manual laborers. Indeed, potential employers overwhelmed Sherman Institute with requests both state- and nationwide for student laborers; at one time it became so problematic that the school's staff struggled to convince community members that the institute was not an "employment agency."[32]

Regardless of whether participants in the outing system were categorized as "students" or "employees," employers paid students in return for their labor. For example, in 1900, female outing students earned between $1.00 and $10.00 per month, depending on age and experience.[33] In comparison, according to the 1900 U.S. Census for Riverside County, California, on average a child under the age of sixteen earned roughly $4.39 per month, and women age sixteen and older earned approximately $13.04 per month.[34] Accordingly, the young women who participated as wage earners in the outing system earned below the average pay for Riverside County. While students' earnings were below regional averages, school officials maintained that the outing program was an opportunity for students to earn some extra money and practice their learned vocational skills.[35] Furthermore, student wages were routinely docked for transportation costs to and from their place of employment. Supporting such action, the superintendent openly wrote to tell employers to dock wages of students in order to offset transportation costs that were incurred procuring a domestic worker from the Sherman Institute.

The superintendent instructed employers to pay wages directly to the student.[36] Justification for low wages frequently came from the superintendent, who advised employers that the pay was only secondary and that the primary value was "the civilization [the outing system students] gain by working in our typical American Homes. Yet we feel that small wages must be given to the girl in order to stimulate her to better work and be an encouragement."[37] Although school administrators encouraged students and employers participating in the outing system to develop a mentor/apprentice relationship, school officials also envisioned the outing system as an opportunity to further train young female students as domestic wage workers.[38] In a letter to the commissioner of Indian Affairs in 1902, Superintendent Hall articulated the goals of the outing system in frank terms:

> [A heavy portion of female instruction] will be devoted entirely to training the girls to be competent to accept and fill positions in the better homes of California. To succeed in such homes the pupils must not only know the practical plan of caring for the homes and furnishings, but come in direct contact with the articles of furniture, etc. and know the meaning

and uses of same, and to arrange a home of their own and receive practical instruction as will fit them to make a small home attractive. . . . They will thus learn what home means, and the method of making and keeping one. The instruction of the girls at the domestic science building together with that given at the farm home will be the means of fitting them for excellent domestics or wives.[39]

School officials attempted to regulate overall behavior for those students engaged with the outing system. For example, young women received advice on how to conduct themselves in order to best represent the school. In 1908, school administrators admonished students in this way:

"Outing Girls, Read Carefully"

1. Never say you don't know how to do a task that you know but your employer wants done differently.
2. Adapt to [your] lady's way.
3. Keep your room clean and picked up.
4. Keep your door open to relieve odor.[40]

The guidelines for Sherman outing students to be polite, clean, attentive, and agreeable reflect the larger Victorian gender ethos of the "cult of true womanhood" and "separate spheres." In 1901, Victorian gender ideologies emerged in an official government publication regarding the goals of the outing system. While living in a white, middle-class home, young Native women received hands-on instruction in the "habits of order, of personal cleanliness and neatness, and of industry and thrift, which displace the old habits of aimless living, unambition [*sic*], and shiftlessness."[41]

Defining Success for Sherman Graduates

If reality meant for most students a struggle to find employment, the idealism envisioned by school administrators and educators was personified in the honor student. The honorary female academic student occasionally graced the school newspaper. High-achieving female students were idolized as models of female potential, as indigenous Horatio Algers who "pulled themselves up by their bootstraps." However, the "success" stories were few and far between, and most students faced relatively few employment opportunities, racism, and economically depressed government reservations. The few young women who became "successful" went on to distinguish themselves in public high schools, postsecondary schools for Native Americans, and colleges. For instance, Sherman Institute graduate Edna Hill received a scholarship to attend the Immaculate College in Hollywood, California. Ellen Norris worked to pay her tuition at the University of California, Berkeley. Norris recounted how she worked as a domestic to pay her tuition: "It was hard, doing housework all the time in order to get an education, but that was my only means of one. And I believe that all the worthwhile things are worth working for."[42] Many students had to "pull themselves up by their bootstraps," working long hours as domestic workers.

In effect, the boarding school system of the early twentieth century trained young women in "feminine domestic skills." However, skills such as decorative handiwork, housekeeping, care for draperies and upholsteries, proper arrangement of pictures, color schemes, and elements of decorated parlors and private rooms were frequently proved useless for economic and cultural survival.[43] Educating young women in proper color schemes neglected the fact that many students would return to socioeconomically depressed government reservations.

In conclusion, the YWCA weekly meeting carefully indoctrinated young Native women into the philosophy of Euro-American gender ideologies. The ideologies of the "cult of true womanhood" and "separate spheres" supported female passivity and subjugation to authority figures. These concepts were echoed and further fostered within the school curriculum. The YWCA and the outing system both worked to reshape the gender ideologies of the young women who attended both Perris Indian School and Sherman Institute.

Notes

1. Clifford E. Trafzer, *As Long as the Grass Shall Grow and Rivers Flow: A History of Native Americans* (Fort Worth: Harcourt College Publishers, 2000), 288.
2. Trafzer, *As Long as the Grass Shall Grow*, 289; David Wallace Adams, *Education for Extinction: American Indians and the Boarding School Experience, 1875–1928* (Lawrence: University Press of Kansas, 1995), 63.
3. Richard H. Pratt, "The Advantages of Mingling Indians with Whites," *Proceedings of the National Conference of Charities and Corrections*, 1892, 46.
4. "A Brief History of the Sherman Institute," unpublished typescript, Sherman Indian Museum, 1969.

5. Although interaction occurred between Native American girls and white, middle-class, Protestant women in a variety of places, this study focuses solely on the boarding school.

6. Kathryn DuPont-Cullen, *The Encyclopedia of Women's History in America* (New York: Facts on File, 1996), 47.

7. YWCA curriculum and student participants, Miss Vera Wight Collection, Sherman Indian Museum, Riverside, California.

8. *Sherman Bulletin*, September 11, 1907, 3.

9. *Sherman Bulletin*, March 13, 1907, 3.

10. *Sherman Bulletin*, March 27, 1907, 4.

11. *Sherman Bulletin*, October 16, 1907, 2.

12. *Sherman Bulletin*, April 8, 1908, 3.

13. *Sherman Bulletin*, May 27, 1908, 2.

14. *Sherman Bulletin*, April 1, 1908, 3.

15. *Sherman Bulletin*, February 26, 1908, 2.

16. *Sherman Bulletin*, September 29, 1909, 1.

17. *Sherman Bulletin*, September 29, 1909, 1.

18. Laura Klure, *Let's Be Doers: A History of the YWCA of Riverside, California, 1906–1992* (Riverside CA: YWCA, 1992), 51.

19. *Sherman Bulletin*, October 23, 1925, 1, 4.

20. *Sherman Bulletin*, March 6, 1907, 1, 3; Margaret L. Archuleta, Brenda J. Child, and K. Tsianina Lomawaima, eds., *Away from Home: American Indian Boarding School Experiences, 1879–2000* (Phoenix: Heard Museum, 2000), 34.

21. *Sherman Bulletin*, March 25, 1908, 2, 4.

22. Estelle Reel to Commissioner of Indian Affairs, December 28, 1906, Box 8, Records of the Office of Indian Affairs, Record Group 75, National Archives, Washington DC.

22. Archuleta, Child, and Lomawaima, *Away from Home*, 31, 32.

23. *Sherman Bulletin*, December 18, 1907, 3.

24. *Sherman Bulletin*, October 28, 1908, 4.

25. Adams, *Education for Extinction*, 149.

26. *Sherman Bulletin*, May 29, 1907, 3.

27. *Sherman Bulletin*, April 1, 1908, 4.

28. *Sherman Bulletin*, September 20, 1907, 4.

29. *Sherman Bulletin*, June 1, 1910, 1.

30. *Sherman Bulletin*, January 17, 1912, 1.

31. Superintendent Ledger, Outing System, February 15, 1900, p. 34, Sherman Indian Museum.

32. Adams, *Education for Extinction*, 162.

33. Superintendent Ledger, Outing System, 1900, Sherman Indian Museum.

34. Inter-University Consortium for Political and Social Research, *Study* 00003: *Historical Demographic, Economic, and Social Data: U.S., 1790–1970* (Ann Arbor: ICPSR, n.d.).

35. *Sherman Bulletin*, September 1, 1909, 1; April 17, 1907, 3; May 16, 1907, 4.

36. Sherman Institute Ledger, Outing System, February 1900–August 1901, Sherman Indian Museum.

37. Superintendent Ledger, Outing System, February 20, 1900, pp. 50–51, Sherman Indian Museum.

38. Superintendent Ledger, Outing System, February 10, 1900, p. 6, Sherman Indian Museum.

39. Superintendent Ledger, No. 6, March 31, 1902, p. 260, Sherman Indian Museum.

40. *Sherman Bulletin*, May 27, 1908, 1.

41. *Course of Study for the Indian Schools of the United States: Industrial and Literacy* (Washington DC: Government Printing Office, 1901), 189.

42. *Sherman Bulletin*, April 17, 1907, 1; February 2, 1923, 3.

43. *Sherman Bulletin*, March 13, 1907, 1; March 27, 1907, 1; April 10, 1907, 1; October 30, 1907, 2.

8. Through a Wide-Angle Lens

Acquiring and Maintaining Power, Position,
and Knowledge through Boarding Schools

Margaret Connell Szasz

Margaret Connell Szasz emerged in the 1970s as a leading scholar of American Indian history. She was one of the first scholars to examine American Indian boarding schools and other aspects of Native American education when she published her classic study, *Education and the American Indian: The Road to Self-Determination*, now in its third edition. In the present essay, Connell Szasz, a senior professor of history at the University of New Mexico, draws on her extensive research to provide a comparative approach to the Native American boarding school experience.

Employing a wide-angle lens to contrast the history of boarding schools among Europeans and Native Americans, Connell Szasz argues that in England and Scotland only the privileged attended boarding schools, which served as training grounds for leadership positions. Similarly, she maintains that the Cherokee Nation created a two-tiered school system in Indian Territory to educate its elite in the Cherokee Female Seminary and Cherokee Male Seminary. Members of the Choctaw, Muskogee, and Chickasaw nations also established schools, and Connell Szasz argues that, like the Cherokees, these tribes used their educational institutions to enhance tribal sovereignty, self-determination, and Indian identity. She points out that attendance of Indian students at federal boarding schools often relied on kinship relationships with other students. As in other parts of the world, leading families often wanted their youth to receive an education, and sometimes Indian people viewed boarding schools a means to gain knowledge and position, a universality that crosses cultural boundaries.

Boarding schools go against the grain of the human experience. By substituting an institutional setting for the traditional family, they intervene in the educational nurturing historically provided by home, kin group, and community. Yet their apparent drawbacks have not prevented some cultures from embracing these institutions and retaining them into the twenty-first century.

In Indian country, the subject of boarding schools always evokes an emotional response. Of all the issues that whirl around Native American education history, none is more driven by raw emotion and painful memory than this institution. Within this context, most critics target the boarding schools run by the Bureau of Indian Affairs (BIA), which still looms as the symbol of assimilation. Whenever and wherever someone introduces the topic of Indian education and its checkered past, the discussion invariably turns to this much-maligned institution.

Despite its high profile in American Indian history, the BIA boarding school is not unique. Beyond Indian country, a number of other indigenous societies, such as the tribal people in African nations, the Irish, and the First Nations of Canada, have expressed similar fears and concerns toward boarding schools.[1] In still other societies, such as the Scottish and the English, generations of families have viewed boarding schools as an expected and altogether normal aspect of their children's education.

The diversity of attitudes toward these institutions challenges us to expand our focus beyond the historical confines of the BIA boarding school. By placing the early decades (1880s–1940s) of the BIA into a comparative framework, we may discern some larger patterns in this form of schooling. Since the education of children—viewed in the broadest sense of teaching youth the knowledge they need to become mature adults—remains a universal human experience, we may discern a comparative role for the boarding school in our efforts to understand how different societies have educated their children.

In this essay I will address some of the common themes linking nineteenth- and early-twentieth-century boarding schools. Initially, I will introduce the schools that retained a positive profile within their respective societies. In this context, I will describe the role of the Scottish and English boarding schools. I will then turn to Indian country to look at the prominent seminaries and academies of the Southeast Indian nations who removed to Indian Territory during the 1830s. Finally, I will give a brief nod to the institutions that lie at the core of the debate, the BIA boarding schools. Although the examples may appear to be unrelated, they will share some universal themes.

A reminder: this essay is a preliminary exploration. I have chosen to broaden the focus because of the insights that can be drawn from comparative history. Comparison may engender new perspectives on Native American schooling. On occasion, it may offer some surprises.[2]

In the nineteenth century, England remained a class society. By contrast, historians of Scotland argue that the Scots had fashioned a much more democratic culture than their neighbor to the south. Unlike the English, from the seventeenth century forward most Scots who lived in the Lowlands— as opposed to the rugged Highlands—had access to basic learning.[3] Still, while the Lowland Scot was better educated than his or her English counterpart, in both countries education beyond primary school continued to split along lines determined by class and wealth. This restriction applied to secondary education, and especially to university.

Within both of these societies, middle- and upper-class families sent their children to elite schools that were comparable to private schools in the United States. In Britain, however, these institutions were commonly known as "public schools." The English or Scottish public school was designed for upper classes and the royalty. Whether a youth enrolled in Eton, the well-known English institution; or in St. Margaret's School for Girls, located in Aberdeen, Scotland; or in Gordonstoun Academy, situated north of Aberdeen, in Morayshire, where the current Duke of Edinburgh sent his son, Charles, Prince of Wales, suggesting that Charles might suffer the same privations that his father had known—all of these students found themselves immersed in an environment that was exclusive and expensive, and in some cases, quite harsh.[4]

Expensive or no, these institutions targeted the privileged. Upper-class families deemed them an imperative training ground for the future leaders of Scottish and English societies. Within these sturdy walls, the students forged the personal connections and honed the intellectual skills that their status demanded. The politicians, the solicitors (lawyers), the university lecturers, those selected for positions at the Foreign Office, the Civil Service, or the merchant banks, the ecclesiastical leadership, the military officers, and the prominent figures of literature and the arts—virtually all of these figures had attended public school before moving on to universities. In Scotland they enrolled in the universities of Edinburgh, Glasgow, Aberdeen, and St. Andrews. In England they flocked to Oxford or Cambridge.[5] During the nineteenth century, the Duke of Wellington and Prime Minister William

Gladstone attended Eton, where they gained the humanities knowledge considered essential for an educated Englishman and cemented the long-lasting friendships among those who mattered. Wellington allegedly remarked that (the Battle of) "Waterloo was won on the playing fields of Eton."[6]

Language also defined class in these societies. Like other public schools in Scotland, Merchiston Castle School in Edinburgh reminded its Scottish student that, along with his humanities learning, he was to eradicate the "Scots" dialect of the Lowlands, replacing it with an upper-class English accent. The hallmark of the educated Scot was an accent that could not be traced. The hallmark of the educated Englishman was the "public school accent."[7]

Some of these private schools, such as Eton, were located in rural environs, requiring students to board; even those located in urban areas like Glasgow drew in students from outlying communities, who were also forced to board. Hence the public school, which often served as a boarding school (more so in England than Scotland), educated the elite, the wealthy, and the future leadership of these two societies. Even though individual students might initially find the pressures overwhelming, all of them eventually learned that conformity bore a certain persuasive logic. Even Harry Potter knew he ought to abide by the peculiar set of standards imposed at Hogwarts. Since the public schools served distinctly as the purveyors of leadership, the elite retained these institutions as a distinctive element of the Scottish and English educational systems.

The large Native nations of the southeastern United States held a unique position in Indian country during the early nineteenth century. Like the Iroquois (Hodenosaunee), many of them had fought against the Americans during the War for Independence, but unlike the Iroquois, they could not remove to a southern equivalent of Quebec because British Florida had been returned to Spanish control in 1783. Hence their homelands remained directly in the path of American expansionists. Comparable to or exceeding the Hodenosaunee in population, these nations—Cherokee, Creek, Choctaw, Chickasaw, and Seminole—remained contending powers in the Southeast until Congress passed the Indian Removal Act in 1830.

The two generations of leaders who reforged these Native nations between the Revolution and removal bore the cultural legacy of their ancestors' decisions to marry outsiders. During earlier centuries, when their grandparents had engaged in the international trade in deerskins, some of their grandmothers had married Scottish and English traders who had come to live in their towns, and from these liaisons had come a small but significant number of mixed-blood families who exerted their influence within the nations.[8] This influence would play a role in the nations' education decisions. The story of each Southeast nation is unique, but the brevity of this essay limits the description of each nation's schooling to a brief overview.

By the 1820s and 1830s, two forces—the mixed-bloods and the missionaries—had prompted the opening of boarding schools in the traditional homelands of these people. The mixed-bloods, who had often received a European or an American education, sought a similar opportunity for their children. John Ross, the prominent Cherokee leader of this era who was primarily of Scottish background with only one-eighth degree of Cherokee blood, absorbed an education that drew on both strains of his ancestry. During the 1830s his adherence to this dual heritage garnered the strong support of the full-bloods.[9]

Often, the mixed-bloods sought schooling for their young children within the borders of their Native lands. Hence, the missionaries. In the early nineteenth century, well before the removal era, Protestant missionaries representing various denominations had received a mixed reception among the Cherokee, Choctaw, and Chickasaw nations. Some of these missionaries had opened schools in conjunction with their denominations, while others, such as the well-known Baptists, Evan Jones and his son John B. Jones, had lived their commitment by traveling alongside the seventeen thousand Cherokees who walked the Trail of Tears to Indian Territory.[10]

Although the Cherokees granted missionaries permission to open boarding schools in their old homelands, after the people settled within their new lands west of the Mississippi River they anticipated full sovereignty in education. The survivors of the Trail of Tears envisioned self-determination in education as the first line of defense against further attacks on their land, their nation, and their culture. Each of the Southeast nations responded differently to the need for schools. Hence, their choices in the realm of educational sovereignty served as a barometer measuring their expressions of independence.

The Cherokee Nation saw school sovereignty as essential. After their prolonged pre-removal struggle to reconfirm their status as an independent nation—acknowledged by the U.S. Supreme Court but not by the U.S. president—they moved quickly toward educational control. Within three years
of their arrival in Indian Territory in 1841, they had established a national
school system that operated exclusive of the Protestant missionaries who
had opened the schools in the Southeast. Although the Cherokee Nation
permitted the missionaries to construct schools, these institutions remained
private and were separate from the nation's school system. Like the Choctaws, the Cherokees secured funding through the education clause in their
contested treaty of removal—the Treaty of New Echota—and through mon-
ies derived from direct land sales.[11]

A decade after the nation established the common schools, the national council moved to a two-tiered education system by opening two boarding schools near the capital at Tahlequah. The Cherokee Female Seminary
and the Cherokee Male Seminary, alongside the common schools, achieved
a significant degree of independence. Unlike the Choctaw, Chickasaw, and
Creek nations, the Cherokees chose to exercise full control over their own
schools.[12]

However, this choice did not preclude all eastern influence. One could
suggest that the Cherokee Female Seminary shifted the nation's earlier connection with missionaries to a connection with an eastern institution, since
it relied on Mount Holyoke College (Massachusetts) for filling its positions
of principal and staff, as well as its curriculum. Following suit, the Cherokee Male Seminary attracted two graduates of eastern colleges as its first
instructors.[13]

In 1842, some ten years after most members of the Choctaw Nation removed from Mississippi, the Choctaw Council expanded funding for a national education system by appropriating almost twenty thousand dollars to
maintain the nation's schools. This additional money came from annuities
that had previously been distributed as per capita payments. With common
schools already in place and a decade of living on their new lands behind
them, the Choctaw Nation saw the need to add secondary schools.[14]

This decision served as a declaration of schooling sovereignty. During the
previous fifteen years or so, the small number of Choctaw youth seeking
higher education had found it necessary to travel outside the nation to Blue

Springs, Kentucky, where they attended the famous Choctaw Academy, an intertribal school opened in 1825 by U.S. senator (later vice president) Richard M. Johnson. The Choctaw Academy thrived for about a decade, but educational self-determination dogged its final years. When the Southeast nations, who furnished many of the 100 to 165 students at the academy, began to expand their own national school systems in Indian Territory to include secondary schools, they drifted away from this outside institution. In 1841, Peter Pitchlynn, the prominent Choctaw mixed-blood who was current superintendent of Choctaw Academy, allied with the Choctaw full-bloods to persuade the council to sever the nation's relationship with the school.[15] Pitchlynn's integral role in the demise of Choctaw Academy probably sprang from his eagerness to open a national academy within the nation itself.

The following year the council acted accordingly, passing ambitious education legislation. Through this measure it established two male academies and four female seminaries. Although the council placed all but one, the national school, or Spencer Academy, under the direction of missionaries, it assumed control of Spencer itself. Within three years, however, the council asked the American Board of Commissioners for Foreign Missions (Congregational and Presbyterian) to direct Spencer. Hence all Choctaw boarding schools came under missionary guidance.[16]

The Chickasaw academies in Indian Territory began with yet another twist. In 1838, when the Chickasaws arrived from their removal journey, they settled on a portion of the Choctaw land established through the Treaty of Doaksville, negotiated in 1837. In that year, smallpox spread through much of the old southeastern Indian country, and the Chickasaws brought with them the disease they had contracted during their travels. This epidemic led to the death of more than five hundred Chickasaws and Choctaws.[17]

The two nations remained a single administrative unit for well over fifteen years. In 1855, however, they signed the Chickasaw-Choctaw Treaty, which permitted the Chickasaws to organize a separate government. As the Chickasaws gained political independence, they, too, began to open boarding schools. The four institutions they founded in the 1850s came under the direction of the Methodists and the Presbyterians. These initial schools included the Bloomfield Academy for Chickasaw Females, established in 1852 by the Methodists. Toward the end of the decade the Chickasaw Council, established under the Constitution of 1856, approved a fifth school, the Burney Academy, but it had not begun classes when the American Civil War engulfed Indian Territory, forcing closure of virtually all of the Indian nations' schools. Devastated by the war, the nations reopened the schools as they could, but some of the institutions did not resume classes until the 1870s.[18]

A different story unfolded for the Southeast Native people who battled the federal troops ordered to remove them from their homelands. Members of the Seminole Nation faced brutal guerrilla warfare within their lands in Florida. After removal, the federal government moved the Seminoles about in Indian Territory both before and after the Civil War. Decades of trauma meant the Seminoles could not open schools there until some time later.

The Creek or Muskogee Nation's school system bore the brunt of the violence that shattered many Creek lives in the early nineteenth century. Bitterness engendered by the Creek Civil War (1812–14) and the horrors of the second Creek removal, from Alabama to Indian Territory, led the traditionally antagonistic Lower Towns and Upper Towns to agree in 1836, when the members of the Upper Towns reached the new lands, that the Creeks would expel all missionaries from the nation's lands in Indian Territory.[19]

The Creek Nation's missionary expulsion held for about a dozen years. Before it was revoked in 1848, however, the chiefs of the Lower Towns, traditionally more receptive to Christianity, had permitted a Presbyterian boarding school to open within their district, at Coweta. Shortly thereafter, when the Creek Council authorized the opening of missionary schools in each district, the Lower Towns hosted a second Presbyterian school, the famous Tullahassee Manual Labor School. Similarly, the Upper Towns concurred with the council's decision to contract with the Methodists for the operation of Asbury Manual Labor School. After the Civil War, the Baptists joined these denominations by contracting to direct several Creek boarding schools.[20]

Creek control of their schooling expanded in 1856 when funds acquired from the sale of a portion of their lands to the Seminoles enabled them to assume full financial control of their national schools. They opened day schools under the direction of Native superintendents, and in the postwar years they exerted some authority over the contract boarding schools by relying on Creek trustees for each school. As mission school graduates, these trustees gained the responsibility for selecting new students. Although the Creek education system, like the Choctaw and Chickasaw, still relied on missionary contracts, the Baptists and Methodists who served at these schools were increasingly Creek themselves.[21]

Beyond the question of missionary direction of the schools, which each nation resolved in a different fashion, lay the issue of elitism. Each nation envisioned the boarding schools as selective institutions, as training grounds for future leaders. At the same time, the related issue of full-blood versus mixed-blood compounded the presence of elitism. The Cherokee Council supervised a national school system that divided the two types of schools by student profile. The Cherokee Female Seminary student was almost exclusively a mixed-blood, English-speaking pupil who, while a strong Cherokee nationalist, simultaneously studied an eastern college curriculum and favored American culture. By contrast, the Cherokee common school student was almost invariably a full-blood, or traditional Cherokee who spoke the language, studied the three R's, and remained immersed in Cherokee culture. While the Cherokees respected their nation's schools, their education system maintained the cultural divisions introduced during the deerskin trade of the eighteenth century.[22]

The federal government's involvement in Indian boarding schools began in the early 1800s, when Congress accepted limited responsibility for Indian education through its acknowledgment of the educational clauses in the treaties negotiated with Indian nations and its passage of the Indian Civilization Fund Act of 1819, a measure that provided for the government's moral support and modest financial aid for Indian education.[23] During this era, however, the government depended heavily on missionary organizations for personnel and funding, and, more importantly, on Native nations themselves for much of the monetary support for their children's schooling.

About a decade after the Civil War, the federal government shifted tactics, stepping directly into the business of schooling in Indian country, with the singular exception of the Indian nations' sovereign schooling programs in Indian Territory. Enter government bureaucracy. Within a short time the Office of Indian Affairs had assumed the role of school accountant, builder, bureaucrat, teacher, disciplinarian, and assimilationist policy maker, thereby embedding its powerful stamp of authority on these institutions.

Between the 1870s and the 1950s, as many as four generations of Native people engaged in a prolonged encounter with the federal Indian schools, institutions generally intent on remolding Indian children. David Wallace Adams, Tsianina K. Lomawaima, Sally Hyer, Brenda Child, Clyde Ellis, Jacqueline Fear-Segal, Michael C. Coleman, Scott Riney, and other scholars in this field have shown us the convoluted layers of this encounter.[24] In their studies they have punctured some of the old stereotypes, especially the assumptions that all Native students, and their communities, hated the schools; that all students were taken from their homes by force; and that none readjusted with any ease on their return. The research of these scholars has highlighted unexpected complexities, including the rise of pan-Indianism; the use of English as a lingua franca; the strength of student influence within individual schools; and the growth of pride in those schools adopted by Native nations who had sent generations of children there. At the same time, the misunderstandings and losses; the physical, psychological, and cultural suffering; and the alienation—all of these wrenching aspects of the schooling environment have held their own as another dimension of the stories. The federal boarding schools, alongside the Residential Schools of Canada, left a decidedly mixed legacy, one that remains alive in Native communities across North America.

In the stories related above, the concept of elitism runs as a common thread. Within each educational environment, the boarding schools taught their students to absorb the knowledge and cultural values that would enable them to achieve distinctive positions, either among their people or within the foreign culture that the school adopted. The institutional course of studies and cultural focus retained an elite character because only these students were privy to this instruction. Other youth in their respective societies who did not attend these institutions had little access to this unique learning.

Boarding schools among the Scots and the English, as well as the five Southeast nations, targeted their students for positions of leadership within their societies. Most Native students who attended federal boarding schools in the late nineteenth century found positions as cultural intermediaries, bridging the gap between the old ways and the changes taught at school. As Wilbert Ahern has demonstrated, by 1899, Indian employees composed about 45 percent of the Indian School Service staff. This trend declined early in the twentieth century, when new federal administrators restricted Indian Service job opportunities for the former students.[25]

During the same era, the Society of American Indians, the first pan-Indian organization of the twentieth-century, illustrated how a small but significant number of Native graduates, including Gertrude Bonnin, Alexander Eastman (Ohiyesa), and Carlos Montezuma, could assume leadership positions, largely outside their homelands, where they remained for most of their lives. These intermediaries moved toward prominence in the mainstream culture or found themselves serving within the uneasy space that lies between cultures. By the 1920s and 1930s, however, the returned students began to earn some recognition among their own people, where they proved to be shrewd negotiators with the federal government and other outsiders.[26]

Graduates of the Scottish public schools roughly duplicated this pattern. When the "public school Scots" graduated from university and immigrated to England or the distant lands of the British Empire, where they earned prominent positions, they seldom returned home. The absence of a Scottish Parliament for almost three hundred years (1707–1999) bore echoes in the United States' denial of sovereignty to the five Southeast nations from 1907 to the 1970s. Both events affected the shape of political leadership within Scotland and the Southeast nations. For the Scottish public school graduates, the lack of opportunity in their homeland ensured a diaspora of political leadership to Westminster. Only the recent reopening of the Scottish Parliament suggested an opportunity for a political power shift to the north. Likewise in Indian Territory. When Oklahoma became a state, the federal government closed the five nations' schools, thereby cutting off the flow of leadership from their seminaries and academies. In the last third of the twentieth century, when the federal government, once again, recognized the nations' sovereignty, the question of whether leadership emanated from the seminaries and academies was a moot point. The institutions had been closed for over half a century.

Closely related to the issue of elitism is the issue of identity: the mixed-blood versus the full-blood, a dichotomy sometimes cast as the progressive versus the traditional. Both of these categories are complex, but for the sake of brevity we shall rely on them. Once again, the strongest parallels can be drawn between the Scots' public schools and the boarding schools of the Southeast nations. Although it appears that the boarding schools of the Southeast nations enrolled largely mixed-blood students, at this stage in my research it is not possible to draw distinct parallels because of insufficient data, especially for the Scots. In the late twentieth century, however, Scots continued to exhibit a strong anti-English bias that stretched well beyond the popular image of Mel Gibson's film *Braveheart.* This deeply rooted attitude led to some antagonism toward Scots mixed-bloods (Scottish and English) or even Scots who spoke with the English accent they had learned in public school.

By the early nineteenth century, the public school was an accepted part of the educational systems of Scotland and England. Its position in the educational hierarchy of these nations contrasts sharply with the position of the Southeast nations' boarding schools and the federal government schools. In Indian country the parallel has little value until the Indian nations had opened their schools in Indian Territory and the federal boarding school had become a well-recognized institution. In Indian Territory the nations' boarding schools probably gained this stature by the last third of the nineteenth century, only a few years before the federal government closed the schools. For the federal boarding schools, I would estimate that Native communities did not perceive these foreign institutions as an integral part of their culture until the second generation of students had enrolled, perhaps by the turn of the century. Only when a relative within one's kinship group—whether a parent, an uncle, a sibling, or a cousin—had attended Carlisle or Haskell or Sherman or Albuquerque Indian School did the schools lose some of their foreign flavor and begin to find a secure place within Native communities. In Indian country the family connection remained crucial.

When members of the family drew the boarding school into their world, they altered their attitudes toward the institution. After they had heard stories of the school, well, then, they too might decide to go to the school. Whether they had kind or harsh thoughts toward the boarding school, it had entered their culture. And eventually it became "their school," a status that characterizes the relationship between the Yakama Nation and Chemawa Indian School in Salem, Oregon.

In each of these nations and on both sides of the water, the students who enrolled in a boarding school in the nineteenth and early twentieth century may have had more in common than we have imagined. Although they were reared in very different cultures, all of them met an institutional environment when they stepped into the space dominated by the boarding school and its staff. The harsh reality of living away from home and family could have propelled any student—in Scotland or England or in Indian country—onto a dizzying ride in a foreign culture. Enforced language change, especially in Scotland and throughout Native America, diminished one's birthright and one's sense of identity. Still, some of these students enjoyed a shared satisfaction in knowing that they were being educated to serve in leadership positions among their people. Surely any returned student would have struggled with the common difficulties of reentry, and long after returning home to one's community a student might have felt more comfortable among peers from the school than with anyone else in the society.

Perhaps the boarding school experience, admittedly unique within each environment and perhaps for each student, retained a degree of universality. Among the students themselves, whether in seminaries and academies in the Southeast nations, the public schools of Scotland and England, or the federal boarding schools scattered across Indian country, the shared encounters of this separate environment within an institution often located at some distance from their families might well have struck a common chord.

Notes

1. See, e.g., Jean Barman, Yvonne Hebert, and Don McCaskill, *Indian Education in Canada*, vol. 1, *The Legacy* (Vancouver: University of British Columbia Press, 1986), 1–22; Maggie Hodgson, "Rebuilding Community after the Residential School Experience," in *Nation to Nation: Aboriginal Sovereignty and the Future of Canada*, ed. Diane Engelstad and John Bird (Concord, Ontario: House of Ansi Press, Limited, 1992), 101–12; Roger L. Nichols, *Indians in the United States and Canada* (Lincoln: University of Nebraska Press, 1998), 225–32; Michael C. Coleman, "The Responses of American Indian and Irish Children to the School, 1850s–1920s," *American Indian Quarterly* 23 (summer and fall 1999): 83–112; and Coleman, "Western Education, American Indian and African Children: A Comparative Study of Pupil Motivation through Published Reminiscences, 1860s–1960s," *Canadian and International Education-Education Canadienne et Internationale* 18 (1989): 36–53.
2. The author would like to thank Donald E. Meek, Michael Coleman, and Jacqueline Fear-Segal for their analyses of comparative education among indigenous people.
3. In Scotland, geography, culture, and language also played a role. Especially before the Education Act of 1872, which made school attendance compulsory from ages five to thirteen, children in the Highlands and Islands (largely Gaelic speaking) had the least access to school, notwithstanding the schooling efforts of the Kirk

of Scotland and the Society in Scotland for the Propagation of Christian Knowledge. T. C. Smout, *A Century of the Scottish People, 1830–1950* (New Haven: Yale
University Press, 1986), 95–216.

4. Oral history, anonymous, July 27, 2000, Aberdeen, Scotland.

5. Smout, *Century of the Scottish People*, 221–23; T. M. Devine, *The Scottish Nation,
1700–2000* (London: Allan Lane, The Penguin Press, 1999), 402–3; Iain Finlayson, *The Scots: A Portrait of the Scottish Soul at Home and Abroad* (New York: Atheneum, 1988), 88–89; Donald J. Withrington, "Education and Society in the Eighteenth Century," in *Scotland in the Age of Improvement: Essays in Scottish History
in the Eighteenth Century*, ed. N. T. Phillipson and Rosalind Mitcheson (Edinburgh: Edinburgh University Press, 1996), 183; Linda Colley, *Britons: Forging the
Nation, 1707–1837* (New Haven: Yale University Press, 1992), 167–70, 191–93; Antho-
ny Sampson, *Anatomy of Britain* (New York: Harper and Row, 1962), 174–82.

6. See Colley's comment on this statement in *Britons*, 191–92.

7. Finlayson, *The Scots*, 86; Sampson, *Anatomy of Britain*, 182.

8. See, e.g., J. Leitch Wright Jr., *Creeks and Seminoles: Destruction and Regeneration of
the Muscogulge People* (Lincoln: University of Nebraska Press, 1986), 60–62, 166–
68; William McLoughlin, *Cherokee Renascence and Renewal in the New Republic* (Princeton: Princeton University Press, 1986), 67–72; Duane Champagne, *Social Order and Political Change: Constitutional Governments among the Cherokee,
Choctaw, Chickasaw, and Creek* (Stanford: Stanford University Press, 1992), 52–
54. For a case study see Ronald Eugene Craig, "The Colberts in Chickasaw History, 1783–1818: A Study in Internal Tribal Dynamics" (Ph.D. diss., University of
New Mexico, 1998), 112–24.

9. Gary E. Moulton, *John Ross, Cherokee Chief* (Athens: University of Georgia Press,
1978), 1–14.

10. William G. McLoughlin, *Cherokees and Missionaries, 1789–1939* (New Haven: Yale
University Press, 1984, 158–62, 197–99. For a brief overview, consult McLoughlin's
"An Alternative Missionary Style: Evan Jones and John B. Jones among the Cherokees," in *Between Indian and White Worlds: The Cultural Broker*, ed. Margaret Connell Szasz (Norman: University of Oklahoma Press, 2001), 98–121.

11. Article 10, Treaty of New Echota, in *The Cherokee Removal: A Brief History with
Documents*, ed. Theda Perdue and Michael D. Green (Boston: Bedford St. Mar-
tins, 1995), 142. Also see Robert H. Skelton, "A History of the Educational System
of the Cherokee Nation, 1801–1910" (Ed.D. diss., University of Arkansas, 1967),
100–102.

12. Skelton, "History," 104–5; Devon Mihesuah, *Cultivating the Rosebuds* (Urbana:
University of Illinois Press, 1993), 20–23.

13. Mihesuah, *Cultivating the Rosebuds*, 27–28; Skelton, "History," 105–6.

14. Article 20, Treaty of Dancing Rabbit Creek, September 15, 1830, in Arthur H. DeR-
osier Jr., *The Removal of the Choctaw Indians* (Knoxville: University of Tennessee
Press, 1970), 181, appendix B; W. David Baird, *Peter Pitchlynn, Chief of the Choctaws* (Norman: University of Oklahoma Press, 1986), 64.

15. Baird, *Peter Pitchlynn*, 23–31, 57–61; Grant Foreman, *The Five Civilized Tribes* (Norman: University of Oklahoma Press, 1970), 33, 35–36, 57; Carolyn Thomas Fore-

man, "The Choctaw Academy," *Chronicles of Oklahoma* 6 (December 1928): 453–80; Foreman, "The Choctaw Academy," *Chronicles of Oklahoma* 9 (December 1931): 382–411; Foreman, "The Choctaw Academy," *Chronicles of Oklahoma* 10 (March 1932): 77–114.

16. Baird, *Peter Pitchlynn*, 64–66; G. Foreman, *The Five Civilized Tribes*, 57–64; Angie Debo, *The Rise and Fall of the Choctaw Republic* (Norman: University of Oklahoma Press, 1961), 60–65.

17. G. Foreman, *The Five Civilized Tribes*, 49.

18. On the 1855 Chickasaw-Choctaw Treaty see Champagne, *Social Order and Political Change*, 196–98. On their schools, see G. Foreman, *The Five Civilized Tribes*, 125–27; and Amanda J. Cobb, *Listening to Our Grandmothers' Stories: The Bloomfield Academy for Chickasaw Females, 1852–1949* (Lincoln: University of Nebraska Press, 2000).

19. Angie Debo, *The Road to Disappearance: A History of the Creek Indians* (Norman: University of Oklahoma Press, 1941), 117–20; Mary Jane Warde, *George Washington Grayson and the Creek Nation, 1843–1920* (Norman: University of Oklahoma Press, 1999), 39–40.

20. Warde, *George Washington Grayson*, 41–45; Althea Bass, *The Story of Tullahassee* (Oklahoma City: Semco Color Press, 1956).

21. Debo, *The Road to Disappearance*, 120–21.

22. Mihesuah, *Cultivating the Rosebuds*, 30, 80–84.

23. Yumiko Mizuno, "Indian Civilization and Thomas L. McKenney," unpublished essay in author's collection.

24. David Wallace Adams, *Education for Extinction: American Indians and the Boarding School Experience, 1875–1928* (Lawrence: University Press of Kansas, 1995); Tsianina K. Lomawaima, *They Called It Prairie Light: The Story of Chilocco Indian School* (Lincoln: University of Nebraska Press, 1994); Scott Riney, *The Rapid City Indian School, 1898–1933* (Norman: University of Oklahoma Press, 1999); Sally Hyer, *One House, One Voice, One Heart: Native American Education at the Santa Fe Indian School* (Santa Fe: Museum of New Mexico Press, 1993); Brenda Child, *Boarding School Seasons: American Indian Families, 1900–1940* (Lincoln: University of Nebraska Press, 2000); Clyde Ellis, *To Change Them Forever: Rainy Mountain Boarding School, 1893–1920* (Norman: University of Oklahoma Press, 1996); Jacqueline Fear-Segal, "Nineteenth-Century Indian Education: Universalism versus Evolutionism," *Journal of American Studies* 33 (1999): 323–41; Michael C. Coleman, *American Indian Children at School, 1850–1930* (Jackson: University Press of Mississippi, 1993).

25. Wilbert H. Ahern, "An Experiment Aborted: Returned Indian Students in the Indian School Service, 1881–1908," *Ethnohistory* 44 (spring 1997): 271–72, 280–81, 288, 292.

26. Donald J. Berthrong, "Jessie Rowlodge: Southern Arapaho as Political Intermediary," in Connell Szasz, *Between Indian and White Worlds*, 223–39.

9. Indian Boarding Schools in Comparative Perspective

The Removal of Indigenous Children in the
United States and Australia, 1880–1940

Margaret D. Jacobs

Margaret D. Jacobs, a professor of history at the University of Nebraska, Lincoln, is known for her innovative comparative research about race and gender. Her book *Engendered Encounters: Feminism and Pueblo Cultures, 1879–1934* is a remarkable study of women in the West. In the present essay she compares the forced removal of American Indian and Aboriginal children in the nineteenth and twentieth centuries, arguing that governments intentionally removed indigenous children to institutions as acts of colonial control, not assimilation. Since colonial governments in the United States and Australia did not value traditional cultures of American Indians and Aborigines, they sought to destroy them.

Jacobs argues that non-Natives purposely removed indigenous children to make them "useful" to non-Natives. As a result, indigenous children's institutions taught a curriculum designed to be of benefit to employers who could exploit Native labor. Every state in Australia had a policy of removing children of lighter skin, the mixed-bloods or half-castes that white people feared might threaten the racial and social order. Government officials in both countries created myths about the removal of Native children, saying they acted out of concern, kindness, and Christian duty. In reality, governments actively and aggressively destroyed families, clans, kinships, and cultures as acts of colonialism.

This is a history that must live now for us.

MARJORIE WOODROW

When she was growing up, Rose recalls, "the agents were sending out police on horseback to locate children to enroll [in school]. The stories we heard frightened us; I guess some children were snatched up and hauled over there because the policemen came across them while they were out herding, hauling water, or doing other things for the family. So we started to hide ourselves in different places whenever we saw strangers coming toward where we were living."[1] Iris remembers a similar situation in her community: "[A Sister] would visit the mission every month or so in a shiny black car with two other officials and always leave with one or two of the fairer-skinned children. . . . [W]e wised up! Each time that car pulled into the mission, our aunties, uncles and grandparents would warn the older children and they grabbed the little ones and ran into the scrub."[2] Although adults in Rose's and Iris's communities tried to hide the children, the authorities eventually found many of them and spirited them away to schools, missions, or other institutions. "I shed tears when I remember how those children were ripped from their families, shoved into that car and driven away," Iris writes. "The distraught mothers would be powerless and screaming, 'Don't take my baby!' "[3]

Although these two stories sound remarkably and disturbingly similar, they took place in almost opposite corners of the world in the early twentieth century. Rose Mitchell, or Tall Woman, a Navajo (Diné) girl, grew up in northeastern Arizona, while Iris Burgoyne, a Mirning-Kokatha woman, came of age in South Australia. Despite being poles apart, Rose and Iris, as well as their indigenous communities, shared a common experience at the hands of white governmental authorities and the missionaries and local police forces that carried out their bidding. In the late nineteenth and early twentieth centuries in both the United States and Australia, state officials developed and carried out policies of indigenous child removal. In Australia, authorities claimed that removing children of part-Aboriginal descent from their families and communities would lead to their gradual absorption into white Australia. In the United States, officials promoted assimilation for Indian children through separating them from their communities and educating them at distant boarding schools.[4]

The subject of these boarding schools has long attracted attention from many American Indian scholars, authors, and activists as well as non-indigenous scholars. Early studies examined the origins of the government's assimilation policy and its boarding school system, largely portraying it as a well-intentioned but misguided effort.[5] Another generation of scholars emphasized the oppressive nature of the schools, exemplified best in David Wallace Adams's *Education for Extinction*.[6] Of late, scholars have focused on the unintended and seemingly positive consequences of the boarding schools—the fostering of a strong peer culture and the accompanying emergence of a pan-Indian identity. All-Indian organizations designed to confront and challenge discriminatory government practices, scholars have argued, partly grew out of the boarding school experience. Other scholars have focused on the way in which Indian communities began to embrace and use some of the boarding schools for their own benefit and purpose.[7] This scholarship has had a significant impact in moving the field away from seeing Indian peoples as simply passive and reactive victims of government policy. We know that not all Indian children's journeys to the boarding schools were forced like the children Rose described, and that not all children's experiences within the schools were tales of unrelenting oppression. Rose relates in her autobiography, in fact, that she begged her parents to let her attend school, and she describes in later chapters her willingness to allow some of her own children to attend boarding schools.[8] Many Indian authors also recount their Indian school days with a degree of nostalgia and fondness for certain aspects of their experience.[9]

Yet the fact that some Indian children and parents adapted to a coercive government policy and seized and reshaped it to meet their needs should not lead scholars to neglect an analysis of that policy or to conclude that it was benign. At its heart, U.S. assimilation policy and its promotion of boarding schools demanded the removal of Indian children from their families during crucial periods of their development and socialization. By examining the boarding schools per se, scholars have often overlooked this central element of their purpose. Studying the boarding schools in relation to other practices of indigenous child removal in Australia helps bring into focus the ways in which governments removed indigenous children not simply as a means to assimilate them but also as an official strategy of colonial control and subjugation.

In Australia, policies of indigenous child removal originated in the late 1860s, when Australian colonies began to appoint official Aborigines Protection Boards and Chief Protectors of Aborigines to oversee indigenous affairs. These entities almost immediately began to make distinctions between "full-blood" Aboriginals and "half-castes." Most white Australians believed that "full-blood" Aboriginals were doomed to extinction and that the government could but ease their inevitable passing on isolated reserves.[10] On the other hand, popular Australian discourse portrayed "half-castes," who were actually increasing in numbers, to be a threat to the racial and social order. Neither Aboriginal nor white in Australian officials' minds, such children represented a racial anomaly and a threat to their vision of a "White Australia."[11] Government officials recommended that "half-castes" could be gradually absorbed into the white population by removing such children from Aboriginal communities. By 1911 every Australian state (except Tasmania, which claimed it had no Aboriginal population and therefore no "problem") had adopted special legislation enabling the forcible removal of Aboriginal children to homes and missions. Authorities in Australia did not target every Aboriginal child for removal, but primarily those who were lighter-skinned. They also intended removal to be a permanent separation of a child from its family and community. Up until World War II, most Australian states removed Aboriginal children to institutions. Thereafter, state governments turned instead to placing them in foster or adoptive families. Since the 1980s, many Aboriginal people who were separated from their families, often calling themselves "the Stolen Generations," have bitterly condemned this policy and sought reparations, government services to help reunite and rebuild Aboriginal families, or at the very least, an official apology.[12]

Beginning about 1880, the U.S. government began to promote boarding schools for American Indian children, modeled on Colonel Richard Henry Pratt's Carlisle Indian Industrial School in Pennsylvania, as a primary means to assimilate Indian children.[13] By 1902, according to David Wallace Adams, the government was operating 154 boarding schools (including 25 off-reservation schools) as well as 154 day schools for about 21,500 Native American children.[14] Officials sought to remove every Indian child ("mixed-blood" and "full-blood" alike) to a boarding school for a period of at least three years. Assimilation policy, including the policy of removing children to boarding schools, fell out of favor for a brief time period from 1934 to 1945 under Commissioner of Indian Affairs John Collier, but it was revived under a new name—termination and relocation—after World War II. Although many boarding schools remained in operation after the 1930s, Indian child removal after World War II followed the same model as Australian policy. Up until the Indian Child Welfare Act of 1978, it more often manifested itself in the form of social workers who removed Indian children from families they deemed unfit, to be raised in foster homes or adoptive families.[15]

Although both nations developed similar policies toward indigenous children, there is little evidence of any direct influence of one administration upon the other or of contact between officials. U.S. administrators did not cite other countries as examples or models for their policy. Australian authorities appear to have been generally aware of American Indian policy, but they demonstrated no direct knowledge of specific U.S. policies such as the boarding schools. Perhaps, most tellingly, when Australian officials did refer to racial policy in other colonial contexts, they commonly cited South Africa and U.S. experience with African Americans. This may help to explain their eugenic orientation, their fixation with questions of blood, and their use of terms such as "half-castes," "quadroons," and "octoroons" to refer to Aboriginals.[16]

Both the United States and Australia developed powerful national myths regarding their policies of indigenous child removal. Government authorities in both countries represented the removal as a kind and benevolent policy designed to rescue and protect indigenous children. A member of the Aborigines Protection Board in New South Wales asserted, for example, "These black children must be rescued from danger to themselves."[17] Commissioner of Indian Affairs Thomas J. Morgan characterized the boarding schools as "rescuing the children and youth from barbarism or savagery."[18]

This myth of rescue rested on a discourse in both countries that equated indigeneity with backwardness, poverty, immorality, and parental neglect. In 1911, for example, the agent to the Hopis, Leo Crane, removed fifty-one girls and eighteen boys from the Hopi village of Hotevilla on Third Mesa. Of the children taken, Crane wrote, "nearly all had trachoma. It was winter, and not one of those children had clothing above rags; some were nude."[19] Crane deemed the children's diseased and bedraggled condition as proof of parental neglect and Hopi pathology; therefore he claimed his actions of removing the children from their families to be a necessary and humane act of rescue. Crane seemed unaware of the role that colonialism played in bringing disease, poverty, and starvation to the Hopi villages.

White authorities on both sides of the Pacific used a surprisingly common vocabulary to create an association between indigeneity and neglect. As Jan McKinley Wilson has observed, authorities in New South Wales constantly invoked the specter of Aboriginal "camps" as places of iniquity and backwardness that did not provide a proper atmosphere for indigenous children.[20] Interestingly, one finds similar rhetoric regarding Indian "camps" among the writings of American officials and reformers. For example, the missionary John C. Lowrie argued that civilization "can only be effectually accomplished by taking them [Indian children] away from the demoralizing & enervating atmosphere of camp life & Res[ervation] surroundings & Concomitants."[21] Consider one of the most common other uses of the term in the nineteenth century: mining camps. In this case, the word signified a temporary, makeshift, ramshackle community full of lawlessness and immorality. By representing indigenous communities as "camps," white observers pathologized them as impermanent, unstable, and disorderly.

Furthermore, white officials made careful distinctions between white "towns" and indigenous "camps." Donna Meehan, an Aboriginal woman, remembers the train ride on which she and her brothers were taken away from her mother and community. "We were on that train for a very long time," she recalls. "I had run out of tears to cry. The flat country from home that was covered with warm red dirt was now very hilly and layered with trees, and the camps which were situated alongside the train track became more frequent and visible. The white woman corrected Barry [Donna's brother] as she overheard him telling . . . me that they were the camps of the white man, and said: 'They are called towns.' "[22] This incident further illustrates the ways in which both official and popular discourse demonized indigeneity by contrasting it unfavorably with "civilization."

In addition to portraying the removal of indigenous children as "rescue," American officials and some Australian authorities created national myths that such removal served a noble goal of providing education and opportunity. For example, the famed nineteenth-century author of *Uncle Tom's Cabin*, Harriet Beecher Stowe, declared, "We have tried fighting and killing the Indians, and gained little by it. We have tried feeding them as paupers in their savage state, and the result has been dishonest contractors, and invitation and provocation to war. Suppose we try education? . . . Might not the money now constantly spent on armies, forts and frontiers be better invested in educating young men who shall return and teach their people to live like civilized beings?"[23] Like the myth of rescue, this notion characterizes the removal of indigenous children as an act of kindness toward the children.

Yet it was a particular kind of education that white officials promoted, for indigenous peoples already possessed their own complex systems of transmitting knowledge. Despite their unique cultures and perspectives, indigenous communities seemed to share in common an emphasis on communal child rearing and education through example. In her novel *Waterlily*, Dakota anthropologist Ella Cara Deloria conveys the importance of extended family: "Any family could maintain itself adequately as long as the father was a good hunter and the mother an industrious woman. But socially that was not enough; ideally it must be part of a larger family, constituted of related households, called a *tiyospaye* ('group of tipis')." Deloria explains, "In the atmosphere of that larger group, all adults were responsible for the safety and happiness of their collective children. The effect on the growing child was a feeling of security and self-assurance, and that was all to the good. . . . To be cast out from one's relatives was literally to be lost. To return to them was to recover one's rightful haven."[24] Within such a community, all members played a role in the education and upbringing of children. Many Native authors single out the role of grandmothers in instructing children. For example, Lame Deer, a Lakota, noted, "As with most Indian children, much of my upbringing was done by my grandparents. . . . Among our people the relationship to one's grandparents is as strong as to one's own father and mother."[25]

Within indigenous communities, education did not take place within fixed spaces and at fixed times but constituted an ongoing process of learning by example and through modeling. As Deloria writes, Waterlily's grandmother "did not lecture" the little girl "all the time. Instead she stated the rules of behavior toward one another and pointed out examples."[26] Buludga, a Mungari person of the Northern Territory in Australia, explained that "it is during . . . games . . . when we are children, that we black people are taught many things which are useful to us when we grow up and which we must know in order to live in this land. What we learn from our play white children learn from books."[27] Such indigenous systems of education prepared indigenous children to take their place within their own societies.

Yet, by the late nineteenth century, both the U.S. government and Australian state governments regarded the persistence of indigenous communities as problematic and in need of transformation. Authorities failed to acknowledge indigenous educational systems and considered indigenous "curricula" incapable of preparing indigenous children for their new roles in the colonial system. Thus government officials in both countries sought to replace indigenous education with formal institutional systems of colonial education as well as to supplant teachers within indigenous communities with government employees.

Although reformers such as Stowe portrayed education as a benevolent policy designed for the good of indigenous children, the ubiquitous rhetoric of government officials regarding the need to make indigenous people "useful" reveals a more practical motivation for "education." In a typical comment, one official in South Australia declared, "There are not only black children of a school-going age but half-castes and quadroons that should be taken from the camps and taught to become useful members of society."[28] The concept of "usefulness" functioned in a similar way to the use of the term "camps." It suggested that, if left unreformed by a colonial education, indigenous children were *useless*, lacking a purpose in the colonial regime. Few reformers recognized an inherent value in the existence of indigenous people and their cultures. And the idea of supposedly primitive peoples living independently in the midst of industrializing, modern nations who needed cheap sources of labor seemed to pose an affront to white Americans and Australians.

In the new institutions to which indigenous children were sent, they would be trained to become "useful" members of white society, that is, primarily domestic servants in white households and laborers on farm and ranches. Missions and homes in Australia routinely apprenticed their Aboriginal inmates out to white families, most of their earnings deposited in trust funds that more often than not mysteriously disappeared.[29] Similarly in the United States, many boarding schools adopted Pratt's "outing" program, placing Indian children as field hands and servants among white American families for part of each school day and in the summers. As in Australia, many Indian children received only a fraction of their earnings; the rest was collected and controlled by their agents and superintendents.[30]

One does not have to look far below the rhetoric of benevolent rescue to find base economic motives lurking. Sir Baldwin Spencer concluded that

Aboriginals would disappear if not completely segregated from whites, and "that was regrettable, as without them, it would be difficult to work the land."[31] With this desire to "fit them for that station of life in which they are to live," institutions for indigenous children became virtual labor recruiters for local white families who sought cheap laborers.[32] According to Pratt, "so great is the demand [by local white families] for the Indian boys and girls that more than twice as many applications for pupils as can be supplied are received." This led the Carlisle Indian School newspaper to rhapsodize, "Think of the splendid opportunity these girls have to become good housekeepers."[33] Indigenous children were thus trained to become menial "useful" laborers, not educated to assume equal status and citizenship with the white colonists of their countries.

Even if the major goal of each government was to educate indigenous people to become useful to their new conquerors, however, such education could have taken place within indigenous communities. After all, within the United States, white reformers, missionaries, and officials routinely established schools among the people they deemed in need of colonial education—African Americans, Mexican Americans, and prior to this era, Native Americans. Some missionaries and reformers within Australia had also founded schools among Aboriginal communities.

Despite the fact that such education conflicted with their own systems of teaching their children, Indian communities often welcomed such endeavors, especially when faced with the alternative of removing their children. In one particularly poignant plea, the Kiowa man Kicking Bird explained his point of view to Thomas Battey, a Quaker teacher who taught among the Caddos on a neighboring reservation in Indian Territory. Battey wrote that Kicking Bird and his wife informed him that "they had come to ask me to be a father to their little girl. I told them that if they would bring her here, and leave her with me, I would be a father to her, and treat her as I would one of my own children. Kicking Bird said, 'We cannot leave her; we have lost five children; she is all we have; we cannot leave her here; but we want you to be a father to her, as you are to these children here.' " Battey then asked the Kiowa leader if he wanted Battey to come live among the Kiowa and to teach their children. Kicking Bird replied "yes."[34]

Some Native leaders tried to convince the government to establish schools on the reservation rather than shipping their children away from them. John

Grass, a Lakota leader, explained, "It will not cost so much to give us schools at home on our own lands, and it will be better for our children and our people, too. You now educate our children in the East, and fit them for your life full of civilization, and then send them back to us, who have no civilization. You spend a great deal of money, and make our people very unhappy."³⁵ Some tribes consented to or even promoted on-reservation boarding schools, especially on reservations where the great distances between settlements made day schools impractical. For example, the Pit River Indians in northern California asked the government "to establish an Indian boarding school at or near [the] village (Fall River Mills), it being a common centre to which they could all, within a circuit of fifty miles, send their children. If such a school cannot be had they earnestly desire two district schools about fourteen miles apart."³⁶ The Navajos, according to Women's National Indian Association president Amelia Stone Quinton, favored on-reservation boarding schools, where they "can see their children when hungry for the sight of their faces, . . . while the plan of taking the children off the reservation meets their utter disapproval and bitter hostility."³⁷ In fact, when Quinton spoke with Navajo soldiers at Fort Wingate in 1891, they were cordial with her until she brought up the education of their children. This "revealed the angry fear of a non-reservation school, or the suspicion that I had come to steal their children for one of the latter."³⁸

Thus if education were the primary goal of U.S. and Australian authorities, even for such a limited program of "usefulness," removal of indigenous children would not have been necessary. Clearly, deeper and more sinister motivations played a role in the decisions of administrators to take the drastic step of separating indigenous children from their families and communities. In the United States, government desires to squelch Indian resistance on a large, collective scale played a major role in adopting child removal as policy. For example, white authorities in the United States often remarked on the inverse connection between child removal to boarding schools and wars with the Indians. The Women's National Indian Association newsletter, *The Indian's Friend*, cleverly asserted, "The Indians at Carlisle and Hampton [Institute] are rising; and the more they rise there, the less uprising there will be on the Plains." General Thomas Morgan, commissioner of Indian Affairs in the late 1800s, concurred. "It is cheaper to educate a man and to raise him to self-support," he asserted, "than to raise another generation of savages and fight them."[39]

White authorities also perceived that removing Indian children rendered the children's parents more docile. This strategy can be seen particularly in the story of Geronimo and the Chiricahua Apaches. In April 1886 the U.S. government arrested 77 Chiricahua Apaches for breaking the terms of their surrender. Late in August 1886, military officials rounded up 383 more Chiricahua and Warm Springs Apaches and boarded them on a train bound for prison at Fort Marion, Florida. In the meantime, General Nelson A. Miles had also defeated the Apache leader Geronimo and sent him and his followers into exile near Fort Marion at Fort Pickens.[40] Among the POWs at Fort Marion and Fort Pickens there were more than 165 Apache children.[41]

Originally, white authorities believed the entire group of POWs should be educated and rehabilitated to prevent them from ever returning to the warpath. Colonel Loomis Langdon, commander at Fort Marion, filed a report in August 1886 that promoted this solution: " 'What is to be done with the prisoners?' In the nature of things they cannot remain prisoners here till they all die. This is as good a time as any to make a permanent disposition for them. . . . Nor can they very well always remain at Fort Marion without necessitating the constant retention at this post of a battalion of troops." Therefore, Langdon recommended that the "*whole* party of prisoners be sent as soon as possible to Carlisle, Pa." Langdon proposed this solution because he asserted that the Apache prisoners had been promised that they would never be separated from their children. "A breach of faith in this respect—a separation—is what they constantly dread."[42]

Yet the government did just that. Although a local order of nuns, the Sisters of St. Joseph, started to voluntarily teach some of the children and promoted the opening of an industrial school for the Indians in the vicinity of Fort Marion, government officials decided instead to remove most of the Apache children from their imprisoned parents. In October 1886 officials identified thirty-two boys and twelve girls to be sent to Carlisle.[43] A year later Pratt boasted that the forty-four Apache children had arrived "as wild, untrained, filthy savages" but had been transformed into peaceable scholars by Carlisle's "civilizing atmosphere."[44]

Later in the spring of 1887, Pratt "recruited" sixty-four more students for Carlisle from among the exiled Apaches. Jason Betzinez was one of those "recruited" when Pratt lined up all the younger Apache POWs. "No one volunteered," Betzinez remembered, but when Pratt came to Betzinez, "he stopped, looked me up and down, and smiled. Then he seized my hand, held it up to show that I volunteered. I only scowled; I didn't want to go at all."[45] The remaining Apache prisoners were slated to be removed to Mount Vernon, Alabama. The prisoners protested both the taking of their children and their own removal to yet another location by holding nightly dances atop the fort. Nevertheless, the U.S. government carried out its plans to take their children and to remove the Apache adults yet again.[46] Government officials, missionaries, and reformers all conceived of the removal of children for the stated purposes of education as a means to fully pacify the POWs. The fact that the government broke its promise to the Apaches and went ahead and separated the children from their families and tribes suggests that the government used the tactic to compel obedience and docility, as a powerful means of control. The Apache children were essentially kidnapped; in order to ever hope to see their children again, their families had to pay ransom through their compliance with government wishes.

In another instance, the purpose of Pratt's scheme becomes clear as well. In a letter to the editor of the *New York Daily Tribune,* Episcopal bishop Henry Benjamin Whipple observed that Pratt's prisoners at Fort Marion had "learned by heart life's first lesson, 'to obey.' " He further asserted, "Here were men who had committed murder upon helpless women and children sitting like docile children at the feet of women learning to read."[47] Reformers and government officials conceived of institutions for Indian children to have a similarly pacifying effect on Indian people's resistance. The Quaker Indian agent, John Miles, for example, wrote to Pratt, "There are so many points gained in placing Indian children in school. . . . 1st. The child being in school the parents are much easier managed; are loyal to the Government, to the Agent, and take an interest in the affairs of the Agency, and never dare, or desire, to commit a serious wrong."[48] Authorities made such policies explicit, as, for example, when the commissioner of Indian Affairs expressly ordered Pratt to obtain children from two reservations with hostile Indians, the Spotted Tail and Red Cloud agencies, "saying that the children, if brought east, would become hostages for tribal good behavior."[49]

In Australia, similar desires to control indigenous people influenced policy. Yet in this case, in contrast to the United States, the eugenics movement heavily influenced government officials; they were especially concerned with "miscegenation" between white men and Aboriginal women and the "half-caste menace" that resulted from such liaisons. In South Australia, officials began to remove a few "half-caste" children in the early 1900s under the provisions of the 1895 State Children's Act. The Protector of Aborigines defended his policies by arguing that all "half-caste" children should be regarded as neglected, yet he also divulged his belief that by removing "half-caste" children "it should not be forgotten that each succeeding generation will undoubtedly become whiter, as the children of half-castes are as a rule much lighter than their parents, and no doubt the process will continue until the blacks will altogether disappear."[50] In Western Australia and the Northern Territory, each of the Chief Protectors of Aborigines also recommended "breeding out the colour" of part-Aboriginal people by encouraging marriages and sexual liaisons between "half-caste" women and white men. Interestingly, though some white women's groups suggested that this "menace" could be eliminated simply by regulating white men's access to Aboriginal women, white male officials never seriously entertained such a proposition.[51] The control of white male sexuality seemed unthinkable to them; the regulation of Aboriginal women's sexuality and the taking of their children, however, seemed natural and desirable.

Thus it was officials' and reformers' desire to control indigenous populations that drove the policy of indigenous child removal. Although many authorities touted the policy as a means to absorb or assimilate indigenous people into the mainstream, we must look beyond stated justifications to ask what purpose assimilation served. By comparing the boarding school system with Australia's policy of removing children, we are forced to look deeper, to examine the underlying purpose of boarding school education and why assimilation appealed to government officials. Ultimately, assimilation and its requirement of indigenous child removal were designed to render indigenous people more dependent and compliant.

Furthermore, the means by which authorities removed indigenous children were intended to illustrate to indigenous people their powerlessness against the hegemony of the state. In Australia, state laws gave Aborigines Protection Boards and Chief Protectors broad powers to take Aboriginal children away without a court hearing to prove neglect or abuse (as was required for the state to remove white children from their families). In the United States, laws were more ambiguous. In 1891 Congress prevented "educational expulsion from the reservation without the consent of parents," though it did allow for compulsory attendance for boarding or day schools *on* the reservation.[52] Government authorities took advantage of this exception by literally forcing many Indian children to attend on-reservation boarding schools at gunpoint. Helen Sekaquaptewa, a Hopi woman, remembers that "very early one morning toward the end of October, 1906, we awoke to find our camp surrounded by troops who had come during the night from Keams Canyon. Superintendent Lemmon . . . told the men . . . that the government had reached the limit of its patience; that the children would have to go to school. . . . All children of school age were lined up to be registered and taken away to school. . . . We were taken to the schoolhouse in New Oraibi, with military escort." The next day government authorities along with a military escort loaded Helen and eighty-one other Hopi children onto wagons and took them to Keams Canyon Boarding School.[53]

Additionally, authorities found other ways to circumvent the law when Indian people resisted attempts to remove their children. The acting Indian agent at the reservation of the Mescalero Apaches in New Mexico described his experience: "The greatest opposition came from the objection of the men to having their hair cut, and from that of the women to having their children compelled to attend school. . . . The deprivation of supplies and the arrest of the old women soon worked a change. Willing or unwilling every child five years of age was forced into school."[54] Withholding annuity goods—including food—developed into a common method whereby government agents compelled Indian parents to send their children to school.[55] Such heavy-handed methods created great hardship and terror in indigenous communities and ironically fostered the very conditions—poverty, hunger, and disease—that authorities claimed as justification for removing indigenous children in the first place.

Over time, as many scholars have shown, some Indian communities in the United States began to willingly send their children to the schools, even to claim the schools as their own.[56] Such a process does not seem to have occurred as commonly in Australia, perhaps because the government intended separation to be permanent and because so few children returned to their communities from the schools. Although some Indian peoples grew to accept the schools, we should not lose sight of the initial motivation for the schools and the coercive ways in which the government forced many Indian children to attend them.

Through exploring the experience of indigenous children within institutions, we can also come to a greater understanding of how the removal and institutionalization of indigenous children dramatically altered indigenous lifeways. Upon arrival at their new institutions, indigenous children endured a hauntingly similar initiation ritual on both sides of the Pacific. First, authorities bathed them, then cut or shaved off their hair. At the Forrest River Mission in Western Australia, Connie Nungulla McDonald recalls how, when the children "first came in, they were introduced to a western-style bath, that had hot water, soap and towels instead of a fresh running stream, dried acacia blossoms and a warm sunny rock."[57] Jean Carter, taken as a child to Cootamundra Home in New South Wales, remembers being "whisked away really quickly" from her home. "Next thing I remember we were in this place, it was a shelter sort of thing, and this big bath, huge bath, in the middle of the room, and all the smell of disinfectant, getting me [sic] hair cut, and getting this really scalding hot bath."[58]

Zitkala-Sa, a Lakota woman, devoted an entire chapter of her memoirs to the trauma of having her long hair cut by boarding school officials on her first day at school. When she learned what was to be done, she hid under a bed.

> I remember being dragged out, though I resisted by kicking and scratching wildly. In spite of myself, I was carried downstairs and tied fast in a chair.
> I cried aloud, shaking my head all the while until I felt the cold blades of the scissors against my neck, and heard them gnaw off one of my thick braids. Then I lost my spirit. . . . Not a soul reasoned quietly with me, as my own mother used to do; for now I was only one of many little animals driven by a herder.[59]

Cutting hair represented a particular indignity to many Native American children. As Zitkala-Sa put it, "Our mother had taught us that only unskilled warriors who were captured had their hair shingled by the enemy. Among our people, short hair was worn by mourners, and shingled hair by cowards!"[60] Thus at Carlisle, when barbers cropped the hair of the first group of Indian boys, one boy woke Mrs. Pratt from sleep with "discordant wailing." He told her that "his people always wailed after cutting their hair, as it was an evidence of mourning, and he had come out on the parade ground to show his grief." Mrs. Pratt recalled that "his voice had awakened the girls, who joined with their shrill voices, then other boys joined and hence the commotion."[61] Mrs. Pratt understood the boy's actions as a quaint but superstitious act. We might better understand it as an act of mourning for being uprooted and being shorn of one's identity, both literally and figuratively.

Through changing the children's mode of dress, institutions also aimed to reshape them. In the United States, following Pratt's model, many schools issued military uniforms to Indian boys and simple uniforms to Indian girls.[62] At least one Native American leader balked at such a practice. According to Pratt, Spotted Tail (Lakota) "found fault with the school because we were using soldier uniforms for the boys. He said he did not like to have their boys drilled, because they did not want them to become soldiers."[63] Connie McDonald recalls that at Forrest River Mission in Western Australia the missionaries sought to replace their nakedness or minimal clothing with government-issued clothes. "Most of our everyday clothes were made from materials from government stores, mainly flour bags, dungaree, calico, and khaki material," McDonald writes. "To our great embarrassment dresses made out of flour bags always had the brand stamp right in the middle of our sit-me-downs."[64]

Institutional authorities also sought to strip indigenous children of their identity by forbidding their inmates (as they called them) from speaking their own languages. Simon Ortiz from Acoma Pueblo writes: "In my childhood, the language we all spoke was Acoma, and it was a struggle to maintain it against the outright threats of corporal punishment, ostracism, and the invocation that it would impede our progress towards Americanization. Children in school were punished and looked upon with disdain if they did not speak and learn English quickly and smoothly, and so I learned it."[65]

Officials also attempted to remake the identities of indigenous children by renaming them. Daklugie, a Chiricahua Apache taken to Carlisle, recalls, "They marched us into a room and our interpreter ordered us to line up with our backs to a wall. . . . Then a man went down it. Starting with me he began: 'Asa, Benjamin, Charles, Daniel, Eli, Frank.' . . . I became Asa Daklugie. We didn't know till later that they'd even imposed meaningless new names on us, ... I've always hated that name. It was forced on me as though I had been an animal."[66] Connie McDonald remarks that "although I had a name when I arrived at the [Forrest River] mission, I now became Constance."[67] Marjorie Woodrow, removed to Cootamundra Home in New South Wales as a young teen, remembered that the Aboriginal girls there were given and addressed by numbers, "like a prison camp."[68]

Schools, missions, and homes resembled prison camps in other ways as well. Lame Deer recalls that "in those days the Indian schools were like jails and run along military lines, with roll calls four times a day. We had to stand at attention, or march in step."[69] Connie McDonald had a similar experience: "Morning and evening, we were marched to church like soldiers. In fact, wherever we went, we marched in military style with the matron 'bringing up the rear.' [70] Such conditions led Doris Pilkington, who was removed to Moore River Settlement in Western Australia, to conclude that the conditions there were "more like a concentration camp than a residential school for Aboriginal children."[71]

To maintain order and inculcate discipline, nearly every institution enacted a strict regimen. At an Episcopal school for Indian girls on the Fort Hall reservation in Idaho, twenty-six girls between five and sixteen years of age were "kept busy at work or play from 6:30 in the morning until 7:30 in the evening for the smaller ones, and 8:30 for the larger girls."[72] At Moore River, Alice Nannup remembers, "They always had me working, never left me free."[73] With such a schedule "there was no time for play or recreation," as Connie McDonald puts it.[74]

As part of their effort to transform and control children, all the institutions emphasized Christian training. Many indigenous children found these teachings mystifying. Connie McDonald wrestled with the contradictions she saw within the teachings of Christian missionaries:

> *I could see that for the tribal people in the camp, nudity was a way of life. One day I asked one of the missionaries, "Did God say we have to wear clothes? When God made Adam and Eve they were naked so whose rule is it that we wear clothes?"*
>
> *I was told, "Everybody wears clothes. It is society's rule."*[75]

Officials intended such Christian teachings to replace the "heathen" beliefs of their inmates. In so doing, officials often frightened children with the idea that indigenous religions were demonic. Barbara Cummings from the Northern Territory writes that small children were "inculcated with a deep fear of the 'blackfella' through Christian indoctrination that equated blackness and darkness with sin and whiteness with purity and goodness."[76]

Despite government administrators' assertions that they were rescuing indigenous children from "camps" in which they suffered neglect, some institutions failed to satisfy the most basic needs of their inmates. Alicia Adams, while institutionalized at Bomaderry in New South Wales, attended the local public school. "We used to walk, with no shoes on you know, . . . barefoot, even in winter."[77] Many Aboriginal people remember insufficient or spoiled food at the institutions. "We used to have this weevily porridge that I couldn't eat," Daisy Ruddick recounts. "I just couldn't eat that sort of food. But I tell you what! After the third day I was into everything! In the end I had to eat."[78] Unfamiliar and insufficient food as well as what Zitkala-Sa called "eating by formula" dismayed many Indian children as well.[79] Yet conditions varied by institution in both countries. Joy Williams, at Lutanda Children's Home in New South Wales, remembered, "I think I was converted six million times—was saved. That entailed another piece of cake on Sunday! Had nice clothes, always had plenty of food."[80] Elsie Roughsey, institutionalized at a mission in Queensland, recalled, "We were well fed. . . . We'd have porridge with fresh milk. At noon we'd have a big meal of rice with meat and things from the garden: pumpkin, cabbage, carrots, beets, beans, shallots, tomatoes, pineapples, custard apples, lemons, papaws."[81]

Poor conditions as well as the harsh regimens and homesickness led some children to run away. To prevent them from running away, officials often locked them in dormitories overnight with inadequate sanitation facilities. Daisy Ruddick recalls that at Kahlin Compound in Darwin, "We were locked up at night. . . . We had to take the kerosene tin to use it as a toilet in the building. Just imagine! At summer time, somebody had diarrhoea or something—well you can imagine what the smell was like!"[82] Edmund Nequatewa, a Hopi taken to Keams Canyon Boarding School, wrote in his memoir that the dormitories were always locked at night, and "no toilet facilities were provided." If they had to urinate at night, the boys tried to go through holes in the floorboards. One night, several desperate boys taught officials a lesson; they "decided that they will just crap all over the floor."

This act of rebellion resulted not in unlocking the dormitories but in supplying the children with buckets.[83]

Teachers, superintendents, disciplinarians, and matrons also often used harsh disciplinary tactics against indigenous children who failed to comply with all the new rules. Omaha Indian Francis La Flesche witnessed and experienced firsthand many incidents of brutality on the part of his missionary schoolmaster. In one instance, his teacher, whom he referred to as "Gray-beard," took the hand of Francis's friend Joe and beat it with a board. "Gray-beard dealt blow after blow on the visibly swelling hand. The man seemed to lose all self-control, gritting his teeth and breathing heavily, while the child writhed with pain, turned blue, and lost his breath." Francis could not forget the savagery of Gray-beard: "The vengeful way in which he fell upon that innocent boy created in my heart a hatred that was hard to conquer." Francis remarked, "I tried to reconcile the act of Gray-beard with the teachings of the Missionaries, but I could not do so from any point of view."[84]

Punishment was equally harsh for Aboriginal children. Alice Nannup remembers that when a young couple ran away from Moore River, "they brought [the girl] Linda to the middle of the main street right in front of the office. They made her kneel, then they cut all her hair off. . . . Then they took [the boy] Norman down to the shed, stripped him and tarred and feathered him. The trackers brought him up to the compound and paraded him around to show everybody . . . . [W]hen they'd finished they took Norman away and locked him up in the boob [jail]."[85]

In addition to the sanctioned physical abuse of children in the guise of discipline, authorities also engaged in other unsanctioned forms of abuse, namely sexual abuse. Of the Aboriginal witnesses called before Australia's National Inquiry into the Separation of Aboriginal and Torres Strait Islander Children from Their Families, "almost one in ten boys and just over one in ten girls allege they were sexually abused in a children's institution." The report of the inquiry carefully noted that "witnesses were not asked whether they had had this experience," so they estimate that many more Aboriginal people may have been abused but chose not to disclose this.[86] American Indian children also experienced sexual abuse. Helen Sekaquaptewa described a male teacher, "who when the class came up to 'read,' always called one of the girls to stand by him at the desk and look on the book with him. . . . He would put his arms around and fondle this girl, sometimes taking her on his lap." When it was Helen's turn and this teacher rubbed her arm and "put his strong whiskers on my face," she screamed until he put her down.[87]

Abuse, neglect, and the strict and unfamiliar regimen of institutional life were hard enough for children. When disease struck the schools, as it did all too frequently, a baffling experience could be made fatal. Disease, particularly tuberculosis, killed off large numbers of indigenous children in institutions in both areas of the world. Parents especially suffered when their children were struck by diseases within the schools. Rose Mitchell experienced the devastation of an illness among her children at boarding school, when school officials from Chinle Boarding School came to inform her that her daughter had died there:

> We had heard there was a sickness over at that school. . . . But because we had gotten no word, we thought our daughter, Pauline, wasn't one of the ones affected by that. Here, these men had come to tell us this sickness had already killed her and some of the other children. We didn't even know she was sick since they didn't let the children come home on weekends. . . . The officials had never notified us about any of it. The same was true with the other parents whose children passed away at that time; they weren't notified, either. So, lots of people got angry. . . . The officials said they had already buried the children who had passed away. That, too, upset us. We should have been asked about it, to see if we wanted to do it according to our own ways. But it was too late. . . . That made both of us very sad, and also angry at the schools and the way they treated parents of the children who were enrolled there.[88]

Rose's pain at the loss of her child was compounded by the callous manner in which officials dealt with her daughter's life. Her experience reveals that indigenous parents had little recourse against the apparatus of the state, even when it was truly neglecting and abusing their children.

Rose's experience makes clear that officials worked hard to ensure as little contact as possible between children and their families and communities. Such policies dealt a devastating blow to indigenous parents and communities, as is evidenced in the desperate letters from distraught parents that can be found in archives in the United States and Australia. In 1912, for example, an Aboriginal woman wrote to officials in Victoria:

> *Dear Sir,*
>
> *Please I wont [sic] you to do me a favour if you could help me to get*
> *my two girls out of the Homes as they were sent there as neglected*
> *children. . . . When they were sent away it was said by the Police*
> *Magistrate that they were to be sent to the Homes till we were ready*
> *to go on to a Mission Station. They were to be transferred . . . as it*
> *was no place of ours to be roaming about with so many children.*
> *. . . I then come out to Coranderrk Mission Station with a broken*
> *heart not seeing my own flesh and blood which God has given to*
> *me as a comfort & I would like them to live with me till death does*
> *part us. . . . Trusting in your help and in the Grace of God help [sic]*
> *I may be able to see my too [sic] dear girls again.*[89]

In 1914 this woman wrote again to the Aborigines Protection Board in
Victoria: "I wish to ask if I could have my two girls who were sent to the
Homes. Now that I have a home on Coranderrk where I am well able to look
after them . . . they were promised to me as soon as I got a home." The archives also reveal that Australian officials rarely granted such requests. On
this woman's plea they scribbled, "I consider the girls are much better off
where they are," "No promise has been made to return them and it is better they should learn to earn their living outside," and "It is not advisable
to remove the girls."[90]

When they could not get their children returned, many parents sought
to at least visit them. Australian archives are also replete with letters like
the following:

> *Sir,*
>
> *I wish to ask the Board's Permission for a pass to see my two daugh-*
> *ters which are in Melbourne. I have not seen them for a long time.*
> *Sir I would be very pleased if the Board could grant my request.*
> *. . . It hurts my feelings very much to know that they are so far away*
> *from me. A mother feels for her children."*[91]

In this case and in many others, Australian officials denied this mother the
opportunity to see her children.

In the United States we find similar pleas from traumatized parents. After their daughter Alice died at Carlisle, Omaha parents James and Lena
Springer wrote an anguished letter to Pratt:

We feel very sorry that we did not hear about the sickness of our daughter, in time to have her come home. . . . We feel that those who profess to have the management here of our children, feel but little interest in their welfare. . . . We would like the body of our daughter Alice sent to us. . . . We also want [our other children] Elsie and Willie sent home, as we have good schools here on the reserve. . . . We are anxious to have our children educated, but do not see the necessity of sending them so far away to be educated, when we have good schools at home, where we can see them when we wish, and attend to them when sick. Please send them as soon as possible, so as to get them home before cold weather. . . . Please do not deny our request, if you have any regard to a Father's and Mother's feelings.[92]

At first Pratt refused to send the other Springer children home, but after many more exchanges he finally agreed as long as the parents themselves paid for the expense of transporting their children home. Such letters reveal that policies of indigenous child removal not only transformed the experience of childhood for thousands of indigenous children but also exacted a heavy toll on indigenous communities.

By segregating indigenous children so thoroughly from their parents and communities, government officials effectively undermined the authority of indigenous parents. This was more pronounced in Australia than in the United States because officials sought to permanently separate children from their parents and therefore told children that they had been removed because their parents did not want them or had hurt them. For example, Pauline McLeod "was told that they'd [her parents] abused me, and that because of that abuse I was taken away, and that if they really cared or really loved [me], they would have contacted [me]." Later, when McLeod was able to obtain her file, she learned that "I had been taken away because we had no fixed place of abode. Totally contradicting . . . what I'd been told and believed all these years."[93] Even after reuniting with her mother after decades apart, Joy Williams says frankly, "Part of me still believes what the Home says that she didn't want me."[94]

While institutions sought to replace parental with government authority, they proved to be unsuccessful in this endeavor; instead, indigenous children came to rely on each other for socialization, and a new indigenous peer culture evolved. This had devastating consequences for the cohesion of indigenous communities, as older ways of transmitting cultural values and knowledge through elders were eroded and some cultural knowledge was lost. Within the institutions, however, these new peer cultures could provide solace and comfort to children who were separated from their loved ones. In *The Middle Five*, Francis La Flesche describes the close camaraderie that developed between himself and four other Omaha schoolboys when they attended a mission school in Nebraska.[95] Ruth Elizabeth Hegarty, taken with her family to Cherbourg in Queensland (but then separated from her mother and other family members), recalls that in the dormitory, "I grew up with all these girls. The thing is, I think, whilst it was the government's policy to institute us, we became one family. We became a family of all of us in there. We still take care of each other." Hegarty found it frightening to have to leave the dormitory and mission and her new family at the age of fourteen when she was sent out to work. "It might have been an institution," she says, "but at least it provided me with some comfort, when you knew that there were people around you that supported you."[96]

Yet the peer cultures of the institutional dormitories also could be cruel and ruthless. Daisy Ruddick remembers that the big girls "were nearly as bad as the Matron. They used to call us their little maid. 'Get the water, wash me this, go and get me that.' If you didn't do it, you'd get a hiding."[97] Helen Sekaquaptewa recalled how the Navajos and the older Hopi children at Keams Canyon Boarding School always got more food than the younger children. "It seemed . . . the Navajos would have their plates heaping full, while little Hopi girls just got a teaspoonful of everything. I was always hungry and wanted to cry because I didn't get enough food." Helen further recalled that "sometimes the big boys would even take bread away from the little ones." In the girls' dormitory, too, older girls were "detailed to come and braid the hair of the little girls." While this could be a pleasant bonding experience for some of the girls, in Helen's case the older girl demanded that she give her some of her food or she would pull Helen's hair as she combed it.[98] The peer culture of the boarding schools thus could be both an empowering and an oppressive component in indigenous children's lives. Whatever its impact on children, however, the replacement of indigenous systems of education with colonial institutionalization and the substitution of white officials for indigenous elders contributed to a breakdown of indigenous ways of transmitting knowledge.

In the name of "civilizing" and "assimilating" indigenous people in the late nineteenth and early twentieth centuries, governments in both the United States and Australia carried out a drastic scheme of removing indigenous children from their families and communities for a number of crucial years in their development. In the United States, some scholars have been too willing to excuse this policy as a misguided but well-meaning attempt to move away from the more violent policies that preceded it. The most recent focus in the scholarship on the unintended positive consequences of the boarding schools has also contributed to a benign view of the U.S. government's assimilation policy. A comparative study, however, between U.S. and Australian policies and practices leads us to a more sobering view of Indian boarding schools. Assimilation and absorption emerge not as the true aims of these policies but rather as their justification. Instead, through a deeper analysis of government practices, it becomes clear that colonial control of indigenous peoples provided the primary motivation for removing indigenous children. Through taking indigenous children hostage, government officials sought to compel indigenous parents to cooperate more fully with government wishes and to render their children more "useful" to colonial aims.

Notes

The epigraph is from an interview with Marjorie Woodrow by Colleen Hattersley, September 29, 1999, TRC 5000/43, p. 13, Bringing Them Home Oral History Project, National Library of Australia, Canberra. The author wishes to thank Doreen Mellor and the Bringing Them Home Oral History Project for permission to quote from Woodrow's interview.

1. Rose Mitchell, *Tall Woman: The Life Story of Rose Mitchell, a Navajo Woman, c. 1874–1977*, ed. Charlotte Frisbie (Albuquerque: University of New Mexico Press, 2001), 61–62.
2. Iris Yumadoo Kochallalya Burgoyne, *The Mirning We Are the Whales* (Broome, Western Australia: Magabala Books, 2000), 65–66.
3. Burgoyne, *The Mirning*, 66.
4. Canada also practiced indigenous child removal in the late nineteenth and twentieth centuries, but a comparison with Canada is beyond the scope of this essay.

For more on Canada's policy toward indigenous children see J. R. Miller, *Shingwauk's Vision: A History of Native Residential Schools* (Toronto: University of Toronto Press, 1996).

5. See, e.g., Richard Henry Pratt, *Battlefield and Classroom: Four Decades with the American Indian, 1867–1904*, ed. Robert Utley (New Haven: Yale University Press, 1964); Frederick E. Hoxie, *A Final Promise: The Campaign to Assimilate the Indians* (Lincoln: University of Nebraska Press, 1984); Francis Paul Prucha, *The Great Father: The United States Government and the American Indians*, 2 vols. (Lincoln: University of Nebraska Press, 1984).

6. David Wallace Adams, *Education for Extinction: American Indians and the Boarding School Experience, 1875–1928* (Lawrence: University Press of Kansas, 1995); Robert A. Trennert Jr., *The Phoenix Indian School: Forced Assimilation in Arizona, 1891–1935* (Norman: University of Oklahoma Press, 1988). More general histories of Indian education that include material on the boarding schools include Margaret Connell Szasz, *Education and the American Indian: The Road to Self-Determination, 1928–1973* (Albuquerque: University of New Mexico Press, 1974); David H. DeJong, *Promises of the Past: A History of Indian Education in the United States* (Golden CO: Fulcrum, 1993).

7. See, e.g., Brenda Child, *Boarding School Seasons* (Lincoln: University of Nebraska Press, 1998); Tsianina Lomawaima, *They Called It Prairie Light: The Story of the Chilocco Indian School* (Lincoln: University of Nebraska Press, 1994); Clyde Ellis, *To Change Them Forever: Indian Education at the Rainy Mountain Boarding School, 1893–1920* (Norman: University of Oklahoma Press, 1996); Scott Riney, *The Rapid City Indian School, 1898–1933* (Norman: University of Oklahoma Press, 1999); Michael Coleman, *American Indian Children at School, 1850–1930* (Jackson: University Press of Mississippi, 1993); Hazel Hertzberg, *The Search for an American Indian Identity: Modern Pan-Indian Movements* (Syracuse NY: Syracuse University Press, 1971). For a beautifully produced and moving book that represents all these approaches see Margaret Archuleta, Brenda Child, and Tsianina Lomawaima, eds., *Away from Home: American Indian Boarding School Experiences, 1879–2000* (Phoenix: Heard Museum, 2000).

8. Mitchell, *Tall Woman*.

9. See, e.g., Francis La Flesche, *The Middle Five: Indian Schoolboys of the Omaha Tribe*, foreword by David Baerreis (1900; reprint, Lincoln: University of Nebraska Press, 1978); Helen Sekaquaptewa, *Me and Mine: The Life Story of Helen Sekaquaptewa*, as told to Louise Udall (Tucson: University of Arizona Press, 1969); Polingaysi Qoyawayma (Elizabeth Q. White), *No Turning Back: A Hopi Indian Woman's Struggle to Live in Two Worlds*, as told to Vada Carlson (Albuquerque: University of New Mexico Press, 1964).

10. See, e.g., Russell McGregor, *Imagined Destinies: Aboriginal Australians and the Doomed Race Theory, 1880–1939* (Melbourne [Victoria, Australia]: Melbourne University Press, 1997).

11. For more on White Australia policy and its concern with people of mixed European and Aboriginal descent, see Anna Haebich, *Broken Circles: Fragmenting Indig-*

enous Families, 1800–2000 (Fremantle, Western Australia: Fremantle Arts Centre Press, 2000), 132–37, 156–58.

12. Within the Australian historiography, scholars capitalize Homes and Missions to distinguish them from individual homes, but for the purposes of this volume the words appear in lowercase. The literature on the Stolen Generations is vast. A sampling includes Human Rights and Equal Opportunity Commission, *Bringing Them Home: A Report of the National Inquiry into the Separation of Aboriginal and Torres Strait Islander Children from Their Families* (Sydney: Human Rights and Equal Opportunity Commission, 1997); Peter Read, *A Rape of the Soul So Profound: The Return of the Stolen Generations* (St. Leonards, New South Wales, Australia: Allen and Unwin, 1999): Haebich, *Broken Circles*; Anna Haebich, *For Their Own Good: Aborigines and Government in the Southwest of Western Australia, 1900–1940* (Nedlands, Western Australia: University of Western Australia Press, 1988); Link-Up and Tikka Jan Wilson, *In the Best Interest of the Child? Stolen Children: Aboriginal Pain/White Shame* (Canberra, Australia: Link-Up New South Wales and Aboriginal History, 1997); Rowena MacDonald and Australian Archives, *Between Two Worlds: The Commonwealth Government and the Removal of Aboriginal Children of Part Descent in the Northern Territory* (Alice Springs, Northern Territory, Australia: IAD Press, 1995). To date, although some state officials have expressed regret for Aboriginal child removal policies and many white Australians have participated in "Sorry Days," the Commonwealth government has refused to issue an apology.

13. Pratt, *Battlefield and Classroom*.

14. Adams, *Education for Extinction*, 57–58.

15. See, e.g., Marc Mannes, "Factors and Events Leading to the Passage of the Indian Child Welfare Act," *Child Welfare* 74, no. 1 (1995): 39; Joan Heifetz Hollinger, "Beyond the Best Interests of the Tribe: The Indian Child Welfare Act and the Adoption of Indian Children," *University of Detroit Law Review* 66 (1989): 451–501.

16. For an example of an Australian official's general reference to policy in other countries, see Testimony of A. O. Neville, November 18, 1927, in Parliament of the Commonwealth of Australia, Report of the Royal Commission on the Constitution (Canberra: Government of the Commonwealth of Australia, 1929), 488.

17. Quoted in Victoria Haskins, "The Apprenticing of Aboriginal Girls to Domestic Service in New South Wales between the Wars: Eugenic Preoccupations and the Feminist Response," *2000 History and Sociology of Eugenics Conference Abstracts* (University of Newcastle, New South Wales, Australia, April 27–28, 2000), 191. Haskins notes a "shift from philanthropic discourse to an obsession with eliminating an allegedly unhealthy and morally contaminating sector of society" among white Australian officials.

18. T. J. Morgan, "Indian Contract Schools," *Baptist Home Mission Monthly* 18, no. 2 (1896): 392.

19. Harry C. James, *Pages from Hopi History* (Tucson: University of Arizona Press, 1974), 166; Leo Crane, *Indians of the Enchanted Desert* (Boston: Little, Brown, 1925), 157–80; quotes from 173.

20. Jan McKinley Wilson, " 'You Took Our Children': Aboriginal Autobiographical

Narratives of Separation in New South Wales, 1977–1997" (Ph.D. diss., Australian National University, 2001), 70.

21. Quoted in Carol Devens, "'If We Get the Girls, We Get the Race': Missionary Education of Native American Girls," in *American Nations: Encounters in Indian Country, 1850 to the Present*, ed. Frederick E. Hoxie, Peter C. Mancall, and James H. Merrell (New York: Routledge, 2001), 158.

22. "Donna's Story," in *The Stolen Children: Their Stories*, ed. Carmel Bird (Sydney: Random House, 1998), 100.

23. Quoted in Pratt, *Battlefield and Classroom*, 162.

24. Ella Cara Deloria, *Waterlily* (Lincoln: University of Nebraska Press, 1988), 20.

25. Lame Deer and Richard Erdoes, *Lame Deer: Seeker of Visions* (New York: Washington Square Press, 1972), 13.

26. Deloria, *Waterlily*, 34.

27. H. E. Thonemann, ed., *Tell the White Man: The Life Story of an Aboriginal Lubra* (Sydney: Collins, 1949), 34. "Lubra" is a derogatory term for an Aboriginal woman, akin to "squaw."

28. Sub-Protector of Aborigines Besley, 1892, quoted in Andrew Hall, *A Brief History of the Laws, Policies, and Practices in South Australia Which Led to the Removal of Many Aboriginal Children: A Contribution to Reconciliation*, 2nd ed. (Adelaide, South Australia: Department of Human Services, 1998), 7. Wilson also notes in her dissertation the ubiquity of the term "usefulness." Wilson, " 'You Took Our Children,' " 68.

29. Heather Goodall, " 'Saving the Children': Gender and the Colonization of Aboriginal Children in New South Wales, 1788 to 1990," *Aboriginal Law Bulletin* 2, no. 44 (1990): 6–9; Inara Walden, " 'To Send Her to Service': Aboriginal Domestic Servants," *Aboriginal Law Bulletin* 3, no. 76 (1995): 12–14; Walden, " 'That Was Slavery Days': Aboriginal Domestic Servants in New South Wales in the Twentieth Century," in *Labour History: Aboriginal Workers*, no. 69, ed. Ann McGrath and Kay Saunders (Sydney: Australian Society for the Study of Labour History, 1995), 196–207; Victoria Haskins, "My One Bright Spot: A Personal Insight into Relationships between White Women and Aboriginal Women under the New South Wales Aborigines Protection Board Apprenticeship Policy, 1920–1942" (Ph.D. thesis, University of Sydney, 1998); Raymond Evans and Joanne Scutt, " 'Fallen among Thieves': Aboriginal Labour and State Control in Inter-War Queensland," in McGrath and Saunders, *Labour History: Aboriginal Workers*, 115–31; Loretta de Plevitz, "Working for the Man: Wages Lost to Queensland Workers 'Under the Act,' " *Aboriginal Law Bulletin* 3, no. 81 (1996): 4–8; Rosalind Kidd, *The Way We Civilise: Aboriginal Affairs—The Untold Story* (St. Lucia: University of Queensland Press, 1997).

30. Pratt, *Battlefield and Classroom*; Lomawaima, *They Called It Prairie Light*; Archuleta, Child, and Lomawaima, *Away from Home*.

31. "Central Australia, Sir Baldwin Spencer's Visit," *Melbourne Age*, July 14, 1923, Commonwealth Record Series A1 1930/1542, Australian Archives, Australian Capital Territory, Canberra.

32. "The Indians of Idaho," *Woman's Auxiliary* 76, no. 6 (1914): 470–71, in Box 64, Archives of the Episcopal Diocese of Idaho, MSS 91, Special Collections, Boise State University, Idaho.

33. Richard Henry Pratt, "The Outing System," from an address at the Annual Lake Mohonk Conference, reprinted in *Indian's Friend* (the journal of the Women's National Indian Association) 4, no. 4 (1891): 18; "Sketch of a Prominent Indian Educational Institution," *Indian Craftsman* (Carlisle Indian School's journal, which later became *The Red Man*) 1, no. 2 (1909): 36–37; see also Jason Betzinez with Wilbur Sturtevant Nye, *I Fought with Geronimo* (Lincoln: University of Nebraska Press, 1959), 156–59; Adams, *Education for Extinction*, 54.

34. Thomas C. Battey, *The Life and Adventures of a Quaker among the Indians* (Boston: Less and Shepard, 1875), 60.

35. *Indian's Friend* 2, no. 5 (1890): 2.

36. *Indian's Friend* 9, no. 8 (1897): 10.

37. *Indian's Friend* 3, no. 10 (1891): 4.

38. *Indian's Friend* 3, no. 11 (1891): 2.

39. *Indian's Friend* 3, no. 4 (1890): 4; Morgan quoted in *Indian's Friend* 4, no. 5 (1892): 1.

40. Woodward B. Skinner, *The Apache Rock Crumbles: The Captivity of Geronimo's People* (Pensacola FL: Skinner Publications, 1987), 52, 56, 73, 75–77, 105; Betzinez, *I Fought with Geronimo*, 140–42. The U.S. government made no distinction between so-called hostile and friendly Indians. Even those Apaches who had opposed Geronimo's military resistance or who had even helped to track him down in the Sierra Madre of Mexico were sent into exile.

41. Henrietta Stockel, *Survival of the Spirit: Chiricahua Apaches in Captivity* (Reno: University of Nevada Press, 1993), 113.

42. Quoted in Eve Ball, with Nora Henn and Lynda A. Sánchez, *Indeh: An Apache Odyssey* (Norman: University of Oklahoma Press, 1988), 130.

43. Skinner, *The Apache Rock Crumbles*, 137–38; Stockel, *Survival of the Spirit*, 114–17.

44. Quoted in Skinner, *The Apache Rock Crumbles*, 138.

45. Betzinez, *I Fought with Geronimo*, 149.

46. Skinner, *The Apache Rock Crumbles*, 161–92, 208–20. Later in 1887, Geronimo and his followers who were imprisoned at Fort Pickens were reunited with the rest of their tribe at Mount Vernon.

47. Quoted in Pratt, *Battlefield and Classroom*, 163.

48. Quoted in Pratt, *Battlefield and Classroom*, 244.

49. Pratt, *Battlefield and Classroom*, 202; also see 220 and 227.

50. Quoted in Peggy Brock, "Aboriginal Families and the Law in the Era of Segregation and Assimilation, 1890s–1950s," in *Sex Power and Justice: Historical Perspectives of Law in Australia*, ed. Diane Kirkby (Melbourne: Oxford University Press, 1995), 137; see also Hall, *A Brief History of the Laws*, 7.

51. See, e.g., the endeavors of Olive Pink, as detailed in McGregor, *Imagined Destinies*, 242–43.

52. *Indian's Friend* 3, no. 10 (1891): 2; Quinton quoted in *Indian's Friend* 3, no. 11 (1891): 2.

53. Sekaquaptewa, *Me and Mine*, 91–92.

54. *Indian's Friend* 10, no. 1 (1897): 10. See also Ball, *Indeh*, 219. Ball notes that at Mescalero, after building a boarding school on the reservation in 1884, agents took

children forcibly to school and "incarcerated" them there. "To prevent their escape the windows were nailed shut" (219).

55. See, e.g., Crane, *Indians of the Enchanted Desert*; Henrietta Mann, *Cheyenne-Arapaho Education, 1871–1982* (Niwot CO: University Press of Colorado, 1997).

56. See, e.g., Child, *Boarding School Seasons*; Lomawaima, *They Called It Prairie Light*; Ellis, *To Change Them Forever*; Riney, *Rapid City Indian School*.

57. Connie Nungulla McDonald with Jill Finnane, *When You Grow Up* (Broome, Western Australia: Magabala Books, 1996), 26.

58. Jean Carter, interview in Coral Edwards and Peter Read, *The Lost Children: Thirteen Australians Taken from Their Aboriginal Families Tell of the Struggle to Find Their Natural Parents* (Sydney: Doubleday, 1989), 5.

59. Zitkala-Sa, *American Indian Stories*, foreword by Dexter Fisher (1921; reprint, Lincoln: University of Nebraska Press, 1985), 55–56.

60. Zitkala-Sa, *American Indian Stories*, 54.

61. Pratt, *Battlefield and Classroom*, 232.

62. See, e.g., Pratt, *Battlefield and Classroom*, 233; Trennert, *The Phoenix Indian School*, 115.

63. Pratt, *Battlefield and Classroom*, 237.

64. McDonald, *When You Grow Up*, 27.

65. Simon Ortiz, "The Language We Know," in *Growing Up Native American*, ed. Patricia Riley (New York: Avon Books, 1993), 30.

66. Quoted in Ball, *Indeh*, 144.

67. McDonald, *When You Grow Up*, 4.

68. Marjorie Woodrow, interview, p. 11.

69. Lame Deer, *Seeker of Visions*, 23.

70. McDonald, *When You Grow Up*, 25.

71. Quoted in Human Rights and Equal Opportunity Commission, *Bringing Them Home*, 159.

72. Alice M. Larery, "My Indian Children," *Woman's Auxiliary* 87 (October 1922): 655, in Box 64, Archives of the Episcopal Diocese of Idaho.

73. Alice Nannup, Lauren Marsh, and Stephen Kinnane, *When the Pelican Laughed* (Fremantle, Western Australia: Fremantle Arts Centre Press, 1992), 71.

74. McDonald, *When You Grow Up*, 15.

75. McDonald, *When You Grow Up*, 27.

76. Barbara Cummings, *Take This Child . . . From Kahlin Compound to the Retta Dixon Children's Home* (Canberra, Australia: Aboriginal Studies Press, 1990), 84.

77. Alicia Adams, interview in Edwards and Read, *The Lost Children*, 44.

78. Daisy Ruddick as told to Kathy Mills and Tony Austin, " 'Talking about Cruel Things': Girls' Life in the Kahlin Compound," *Hecate* 15, no. 1 (1989): 16. See also Marjorie Woodrow, interview, p. 9, and Ruth Elizabeth Hegarty, interview by Helen Curzon-Siggers, December 14, 1999, TRC-5000/79, Bringing Them Home Oral History Project, for two more examples. Many other interviewees in this project as well as many Aboriginal autobiographers mention the inadequate food.

79. Zitkala-Sa, *American Indian Stories*, 54.

80. Joy Williams, interview in Edwards and Read, *The Lost Children*, 50.

81. Quoted in Virginia Huffer, *The Sweetness of the Fig: Aboriginal Women in Transition* (Sydney: New South Wales University Press, 1980), 36–37.

82. Ruddick, " 'Talking about Cruel Things,' " 15.

83. David Seaman, ed., *Born a Chief: The Nineteenth Century Hopi Boyhood of Edmund Nequatewa*, as told to Alfred Whiting (Tucson: University of Arizona Press, 1993), 91–92.

84. La Flesche, *The Middle Five*, 138.

85. Nannup, Marsh, and Kinnane, *When the Pelican Laughed*, 75.

86. Human Rights and Equal Opportunity Commission, *Bringing Them Home*, 163, 162.

87. Sekaquaptewa, *Me and Mine*, 106.

88. Mitchell, *Tall Woman*, 178–79.

89. K.M. to Secretary of the Board of Protection of Aborigines, July 1, 1912, Victorian Public Record Series [VPRS] 1694, Unit 5, Public Record Office of Victoria [PROV], Melbourne, Australia.

90. K.M. to Secretary of the Board of Protection of Aborigines, March 10, 1914, VPRS 1694, Unit 5, PROV.

91. R.F. to "Sir," June 20, 1918, VPRS 1694, Unit 6, PROV.

92. James Springer and Lena [signed Lenora] Springer to Pratt, November 20, 1883, Box 1, MS 4558, Alice Cunningham Fletcher and Francis La Flesche Papers, National Anthropological Archives, Smithsonian Institution, Washington DC.

93. Pauline McCleod, interview in Edwards and Read, *The Lost Children*, 16, 21.

94. Joy Williams, interview in Edwards and Read, *The Lost Children*, 55.

95. La Flesche, *The Middle Five*.

96. Ruth Elizabeth Hegarty, interview, 15, 22. The author wishes to thank Doreen Mellor and the Bringing Them Home Oral History Project for permission to quote from Hegarty's interview.

97. Ruddick, " 'Talking about Cruel Things,' " 19, 21.

98. Sekaquaptewa, *Me and Mine*, 94, 103–4.

10. The Place of American Indian Boarding Schools in Contemporary Society

Patricia Dixon and Clifford E. Trafzer

Patricia Dixon and Clifford E. Trafzer teach Native American history, culture, and education. Dixon is a professor at Palomar College, and Trafzer teaches at the University of California, Riverside. In this essay they focus primarily on Sherman Indian High School, in Riverside, California, drawing on written statements by contemporary Indian students who explain their reasons for attending and remaining at an off-reservation boarding school. In light of the history and perception of Indian boarding schools, the fact that some Indian children prefer to attend the schools may seem paradoxical.

The authors believe that Indian boarding schools occupy a unique and positive place in contemporary American Indian society. Students at Sherman argue that the schools are now controlled by Indians and often offer courses on Indian history, culture, and language. Today, Indians have a say in the operation and direction of the schools. The schools have produced many committed leaders in Indian country, people who learned from other Indian students and established a network of former students. Contemporary students sometimes attend boarding schools to escape abuse, drugs, alcohol, and poor learning environments, but others attend to benefit from the school's academic programs, sport opportunities, and music programs. Students also enjoy being with friends and relatives who attend the schools. They find new horizons at the schools, and this is significant to understanding the place of Indian boarding schools among Native Americans today.

Growing up on my reservation, the Pauma-Yima Indian Reservation, I frequently listened to my grandfather speak Indian to my great-aunt, his sister. Once a month she spent the day with her brother, and they softly laughed, spoke quietly in guttural clicking tones, and frequently talked about their days at Sherman Institute for Indians in Riverside, California. Both of them were

forced to attend and both of them ran away several times. My grandfather had
run away so often that he was declared incorrigible, unable to learn. The au-
thorities stopped hunting for him. He was nine years old. My great-aunt stayed
at school, became close to a white family that had her come over on holidays and
summers for her "outing" experiences. She made Sherman sound exciting.

I wanted to attend Sherman, but by the early 1960s, if you were a Califor-
nia Indian you had to be incorrigible before the government would let you at-
tend the school. I was not. Instead, my parents sent me to an all-girls Catholic
high school where I boarded for two and a half years. My experience, in many
ways, corresponds with the emotional experiences of some of the Sherman In-
dian High School students that are quoted here: the intense feeling of loyalty,
strong emotional ties with classmates, individual responsibility and account-
ability, and learning about other cultures. What I did not have was the compan-
ionship of other tribal people, and it was lonely. Given the history of boarding
schools, the reader may ask, why did I want to attend an off-reservation board-
ing school, and why do these Indian students, for the most part, speak highly of
their off-reservation boarding school experiences?

Patricia Dixon, Luiseño

The American Indian boarding schools that emerged in the United States
in 1869 developed out of the mission schools established by religious orders
during the colonial era. Mission schools and off-reservation government
boarding schools for Indian students significantly changed Native American cultures, sometimes for the benefit of the tribes, but often to the detriment of students, families, and communities. In the past, boarding schools
sought to destroy American Indian languages, cultures, and religions. Giv-
en the history of off-reservation boarding schools, it might seem paradoxical for some Native Americans to promote and support American Indian
boarding schools today, but American Indian schools off the reservations
have a positive place in contemporary American Indian societies, in spite
of problems that continue to exist at some of the schools. Like those at other contemporary off-reservation boarding schools, students at Sherman Indian High School are diverse in their backgrounds, perspectives, and views.
Some chose to attend Sherman, but others attended the schools as a site of
last resort.

High schools on or near reservations or Indian communities sometimes refuse to enroll some students, particularly if they have a history of problems. Schools expel Indian students who have repeat offenses caused by truancy, drugs, alcohol, fighting, or theft or for other social and legal reasons. Parents and authorities sometimes send Indian students away to boarding schools, including Sherman. The schools become the site for difficult students, a "dumping ground" for juvenile offenders who have proved to be delinquent before arriving in an off-reservation boarding school. For a few students at Sherman, the school has become their last hope for social and educational redemption. Some of them suffer medical problems, while others are bright and engaging people who lack the will or interest to channel their innate intelligence into schoolwork. Some fail as a result, but others succeed, finding a space at the school that encourages Indian students through sports, clubs, cultural activities, and academics. Not all Indian people would agree, but for some students the Indian boarding schools provide a place in contemporary society for Native children and thus have a role to play in contemporary Indian society.[1]

Certainly some American Indian students—past and present—believe the schools have a place in contemporary Native society. And a few students at Sherman recently voiced their approval of their off-reservation boarding school. In response to a question posed to a few Sherman students in 2002 during an English class, students explained whether or not they believed American Indian boarding schools had a place in modern Indian society. Of course, such a sample is not scientific and may not represent the views of most students, but the assignment proved enlightening and instructive. The students who responded to the assignment clearly articulated their belief that the boarding schools have a role to play in Indian country today. Nearly all of the students who participated in the writing assignment explained from the outset that non-Natives have a biased view of contemporary boarding schools based on historical presentations about the schools, not from firsthand experience in dealing with an Indian school today.[2]

Students at Sherman pointed out that many white people believe that Indian boarding schools "are bad."[3] But non-Indians often "think that way because all that they know about boarding schools is what they read in the history books about how the [government] stole . . . Native American children and converted them to the white settlers ways." When some contemporary

Indian students from Sherman hear this, they "explain to them that boarding schools are different. These days boarding schools are in a lot of ways trying to give back to the Native American communities." In fact, Indian boarding schools today "understand that you can't erase the past and that we can only move [on] and work to better boarding schools and use them to unite all the Native American tribes so that we can Stand tall . . . fight for everything that we have lost throughout history."[4] Since the nineteenth century, when the United States began the boarding school system, some families and tribes have sent their children to the schools to acquire the skills to understand the non-Indian people and the American government. This calculated risk by Native Americans evolved into a family or tribal tradition. Alumni sometimes enjoyed elements of their educational experiences, including meeting diverse Indian people, playing sports, or learning music in the school band. They sometimes reported to friends and relatives that they enjoyed such extracurricular activities. For many years now, American Indian students have attended certain schools, and over time their families have developed a loyalty to Sherman, Haskell, Chemawa, Riverside, Bacone, Hampton, and other schools.

Today many public, government, or mission schools on or near the reservations generate strong school spirit and community loyalty, but sometimes they lack the structure, curriculum, or philosophy desired by particular Native students or their families. As a result, these students seek to attend an off-reservation boarding school where the educational experience will be more in line with their objectives. A particular boarding school may provide access to a college, university, or trade school that could not be as easily obtained if they remained at home. Thus, contemporary American Indian students are attracted to boarding schools for a variety of reasons, not the least of which is future employment opportunities.

Some boarding school students wish to escape problems on the reservation or at their reservation schools. Others wish to escape a home life that is not conducive to furthering their educations. Some students grow up in families where drug abuse, alcoholism, and violence are common. Gang violence has increased dramatically on some reservations, making it dangerous for serious students to remain at school or at home.[5] At other times, students grow up in dysfunctional families with divorce, unemployment, and abusive or absent parents. Sometimes Indian children are raised with only one parent, while the other is serving a sentence in prison, or they grow up in the homes of grandparents, aunts, and other relatives. For some students, off-reservation boarding schools offer sanctuary from family violence. In some cases they provide neutral ground, a place where students can escape and rethink the direction of their lives. American Indian boarding schools provide some students with a sphere where they can be with other Indian students their age and work out a plan for the present and future. For some students, the schools help Indian students negotiate the larger, dominant world while allowing them to maintain and nurture their Indianness. The schools also offer students a fairly safe haven and degree of relief from personal problems, although some problems exist at all of the schools. And for other students, off-reservation boarding schools provide a "last chance" to follow a new path away from crime and violence that might have brought them into the juvenile court system on or off their reservations.[6]

Regardless of what factors bring students to Indian boarding schools, several students leave the campuses with positive outcomes. Through the schools, students join a new community of Native Americans, students— and sometimes faculty—who care about each other and about the preservation of Indian cultural traditions. Native American students can acquire a new or renewed respect for Indian cultures, and they often learn about the diverse tribes within Indian America. Students learn from each other and in turn teach others about Native cultural diversity. Often the cultural interactions of contemporary students enhance the general education of Indian students. Leroy Miranda, a former Sherman student and currently vice-chair of the Pala band of Mission Indians, explained that he learned the importance of "being Indian" as a result of attending the boarding school. This young man also met his future wife at school, a woman from another tribe. Together they have forged a successful marriage and partnership that has led to a new leadership family and many cultural-renewal projects on the Pala Indian Reservation of southern California.[7]

In a very real sense, off-reservation boarding schools have created a network of former students that has benefited many Indian people from diverse communities—urban and rural. And as in the example above, boarding schools have fostered many love stories and marriages that tie people and their communities together. The grandparents of Patricia Dixon met at Sherman. In the latter half of the twentieth century, tribal leaders who

had once attended boarding schools broadened their educations and en-
riched their understanding of Native culture, history, music, philosophy,
sport, and art.

The political activism of the late 1960s and 1970s brought reservation and
urban Indians together, and these people often formed bonds and alliance
to seek remedies for the poverty, deprivation, and lack of education that
plagued Native American youth. Tribal communities visited Indian boarding schools and demanded changes. Tribal members rose in the ranks of the
Bureau of Indian Affairs, and they created and implemented new policies.
The school also provided Indian students with detailed knowledge of Native
policies and sovereignty issues that resonate within Indian country today.
American Indian boarding schools have become Native American institutions. This is not what the founders of the boarding school system intended
in the nineteenth century, but it is what emerged in the late twentieth century. American Indian agency and activism resulted in "turning the power" and making a bad situation one that could be positive for some Indian
children. Contemporary off-reservation boarding schools are a product of a
power change, one that is intended to be of positive value to American Indian students. Not all students or Native people today would agree, but some
students share this opinion, and their thoughts about schools today are instructive and illuminating.

Several Indian children presently enrolled at off-reservation boarding
schools chose to go to a particular school because their parents, grandparents, cousins, siblings, or friends attended that school. One student attending Sherman reported, "My sister went here and said nothing but good
about this school."[8] Another stated, "My cousin . . . came to Sherman Indian High School. She told me wondrous things about Sherman and it seemed
as though the perfect chance to go some where and really accomplish my
goals."[9] Another student remembers that her sister came back after her first
year at Sherman "saying it was a really good school." The first student encouraged her sister to attend Sherman because she "would like it." Furthermore, the sister pointed out that Sherman "had a good basketball team."
The reports from this student's sisters about Sherman Indian High School
proved so attractive that the young woman enrolled as a sophomore the next
year, excelling in sports and academics.[10] Sports, academics, music, clubs,
and other opportunities found at the Indian boarding schools attracted po-

tential students. Students heard stories about glorious football teams, talented track stars, organized music programs, and outstanding instruction in certain areas of study. Sometimes students heard stories about how their parents or grandparents had met and fallen in love at a particular boarding school. Some of these former students had ultimately married and started their own families, sharing their life experiences, including their schools days, with their family and friends.[11]

The role of parents, grandparents, and other relatives in popularizing Indian boarding schools cannot be overstated. Not only did these individuals offer positive reports about Indian boarding schools, but they also actively recruited young people to attend. Of course this was not true in every case, because not all former students enjoyed their boarding school days. Still, some contemporary students at Sherman reported that they came because of encouragement from their mothers and grandmothers. "The reason why I came to Sherman Indian high school is because my mom wanted me to get away," wrote one student whose mother encouraged her to seek opportunities at Sherman.[12] Another student reported: "My mother wanted me to live up to my best potential." Still another asserted that her grandmother urged her to attend a boarding school. "The reason I came to Sherman Indian High School," she wrote, "was due to my grandmother," who had "found out about this school and wanted my cousin and I to attend." Her grandmother "wanted us to continue school so we could live a good life and have something positive for our younger siblings to look up to."[13] So, rather than viewing contemporary boarding schools as a place of confinement and conformity to non-Native values, some parents and grandparents see off-reservation boarding schools as sites where children might find opportunities.

Indian children today attend off-reservation boarding schools in large part because of the opportunities they believe the schools offer. One of these opportunities is to leave home and attend a school located far from their homes on the reservation. Some students find such places exciting if not exotic. American Indian boarding schools appear alluring to some students who wish to escape the "boredom" of the reservation. Furthermore, some students seek to escape poverty, abuse, and other social problems on the reservation. One student stated that she "wanted to get off the reservation" because she had "seen the other youth that live on my reservation," and "most of them were exposed to drugs and alcohol." Since this "wasn't the life for me," she decided to attend Sherman.[14] For some students, the boarding schools provided a sanctuary rather than "a dead end" that some perceived on their reservation or within the "bad environments" surrounding their homes.[15] Thus, in the larger sense, boarding schools offered students an opportunity to leave the reservation and begin a new life that might lead to other challenges that they could face better as a result of their education at a boarding school.

One contemporary student remarked that her educational experience at Sherman "has only made me stronger and more" self-reliant. Her days at Sherman "opened . . . [many] opportunities for me," and she looked forward to taking "advantage of all of them."[16] Another student remarked that the decision to attend an off-reservation boarding school "expanded my horizons" and changed her views of the world. She felt that her time at Sherman had made her "more responsible, generous, and wise." In sum, she said that her decision to attend an off-reservation boarding school had been "the best decision I could have made for myself."[17] Such sentiment is mirrored by another student who announced plainly that "Sherman Indian High School has been a life changing experience that I will carry with me forever." When the student "heard about the opportunity to change my surroundings and actually be around other Native Americans . . . I knew that Sherman was the place." Like other students, she felt that attending boarding school provided an opportunity to be independent. "For the first time in my life," she wrote, "I felt like I was on my own" and "there was nothing that would stop me." She reported that the main reason she chose to attend Sherman was "to learn" things in general and specifically "to learn more about what it means to be Native Americans."[18] Another student commented that she hoped "to make something of myself or just keep going to school learning more new things."[19]

Students at Indian boarding schools had always learned from each other, and some attended the schools to be with other Native American students interested in learning about the diverse cultures, languages, and histories found within Indian America. From her first days at Sherman, one student "was amazed with all the various representation" of tribes on campus, and she offered that when she graduates from Sherman she will "leave knowing it's not so much what you can learn through a book but what those around you can teach you."[20] She learned cultural and social values that she believed she would treasure throughout her life, and she believed this was a sentiment shared by many students at Sherman. Indeed, several students commented that their time at Sherman had brought about new friendships and a network of relationships that "will be with me to guide, mentor, and assist me throughout my life."[21]

Students attending contemporary off-reservation American Indian boarding schools do not have uniform experiences or outcomes resulting from their boarding school days. Some students failed school, and administrators expelled others for truancy, drugs, alcohol, fighting, or the lack of academic performance. Not all contemporary students at Sherman remember their schools days fondly, but others believe that their time there changed their lives forever, sometimes in a positive manner. Some students who attended Indian boarding schools during the last twenty years forged lifelong friendships and associations that benefit themselves and their tribes. But this is only one of the positive aspects of the current boarding school experience. Boarding schools create new Native communities by bringing diverse Indian people together to learn from one another. This association serves many Indian people over lengthy time periods, forming new circles of friends who work together through alumni associations, the National Museum of the American Indian, the National Congress of American Indians, the National Indian Gaming Association, and a host of other Native American organizations.

While students attend boarding schools, they are relatively safe from violence, drug and alcohol abuse, and environments unsupportive of formal education. Contemporary Indian students understand the unfortunate truths about their schools historically, but they also know that their institutions became "Indian" in some ways during the late twentieth century. More than ever before, off-reservation boarding schools today respond to the needs and objectives of Indian people. In spite of the sordid past filled with forced assimilation, physical and psychological abuse, homesickness, and exploitation, American Indian boarding schools have become a part of contemporary Indian society. The few Sherman students who participated in the writing assignment had not forgotten that boarding schools had once torn Indian students from their families and communities and had actively sought to destroy elements of Native American cultures and languages.[22] They knew that some communities had rejected some Indian students when they returned home because some community members considered boarding school students to be tainted by white culture and Christianity. But these Sherman students also pointed out the benefits of formal education, the friendships formed there, and the joy of attending school with other Indians.

The future of off-reservation boarding schools is uncertain. It will be contingent on American Indian decisions as well as directives of Congress and the Department of the Interior. The place of off-reservation boarding schools will be negotiated by both Indians and non-Indians, and former students of the boarding school system will have a voice in future decisions. Their perspectives are important today, and they will be more important in the future when they share their positive and negatives experiences, their memories of their own boarding school seasons.[23]

Notes

1. Student 1, Writing Assignment, Sherman Indian High School, fall 2002, Sherman Indian School Museum Archive [SISMA].
2. Comments by students are derived from a writing assignment, not a formal survey. Patricia Dixon asked the students to write an essay about the place of American Indian boarding schools and of Sherman Indian High School. She asked students to explain why they attended Sherman. The essays are on file at the Sherman Indian School Museum, Riverside, California.
3. Student 1, Writing Assignment, SISMA.
4. Student 1, Writing Assignment, SISMA.
5. Eric Henderson, Stephen J. Kunitz, and Jerrold E. Levy, "The Origins of Navajo Youth Gangs," in *Medicine Ways: Disease, Health, and Survival among Native Americans*, ed. Clifford E. Trafzer and Diane Weiner (Walnut Creek CA: Alta Mira Press, 2001), 222–33.
6. Students 1, 2, 5, Writing Assignment, SISMA.
7. Leroy Miranda, oral presentation, Sherman Indian High School, "Boarding School Blues" symposium, November 2002, Riverside, California; Leroy Miranda, interview, Sherman Indian High School, January 17, 2004.
8. Student 1, Writing Assignment, SISMA.
9. Student 3, Writing Assignment, SISMA.
10. Student 3, Writing Assignment, SISMA.
11. Margaret L. Archuleta, Brenda J. Child, and K. Tsianina Lomawaima, eds., *Away from Home: American Indian Boarding School Experiences* (Phoenix: Heard Museum, 2000), 98–114.
12. Student 2, Writing Assignment, SISMA.

13. Student 5, Writing Assignment, SISMA.

14. Student 1, Writing Assignment, SISMA.

15. Students 3, 5, Writing Assignment, SISMA.

16. Student 1, Writing Assignment, SISMA.

17. Student 3, Writing Assignment, SISMA.

18. Student 4, Writing Assignment, SISMA.

19. Student 2, Writing Assignment, SISMA.

20. Student 4, Writing Assignment, SISMA.

21. Student 4, Writing Assignment, SISMA.

22. Diana Meyers Bahr, *Viola Martinez: California Paiute* (Norman: University of Oklahoma Press, 2003), 58–60, 83–87.

23. The phrase "boarding school seasons" is taken from the title of Brenda Child's book *Boarding School Seasons* (Lincoln: University of Nebraska Press, 1999).

About the Editors

Clifford E. Trafzer is Professor of History, Director of Graduate Studies, and Director of Public History at the University of California, Riverside. He has published *Death Stalks the Yakama: Epidemiological Transitions and Mortality on the Yakama Indian Reservation, The People of San Manuel*, and *As Long as the Grass Shall Grow and Rivers Flow*. In 2004 he coedited, with Cree scholar Gerald McMaster, *Native Universe: Voices of Indian America*, the inaugural book of the National Museum of the American Indian and winner of an award presented by the American Association of Museums.

Jean A. Keller teaches American Indian History and Public History at Palomar College and the University of California, Riverside. She serves on the board of Sherman Indian Museum and is the author of *Empty Beds: Indian Student Health at Sherman Institute, 1902–1922*. Trained as an archaeologist and historian, Keller also works as a cultural resources consultant in southern California, where she lives with her family not far from the beach.

Lorene Sisquoc has been the Curator of Sherman Indian Museum since 1991. She is a descendent of Mountain Cahuilla and a member of the Fort Sill Apache tribe of Oklahoma. She is co-founder of Mother Earth Clan and of Nex'wetem organizations, through which she teaches about Native American cultures. Sisquoc is a well-known basket maker, and she serves on the board of directors of the California Indian Basketweavers Association and the Malki Museum. In 1997 the city of Riverside, California, honored her with the Dr. Martin Luther King Jr. Visionary Award for community cultural awareness.

Index

CPSIA information can be obtained
at www.ICGtesting.com
Printed in the USA
LVHW040016180120
644023LV00015B/399